COBRA
G.I. JOE

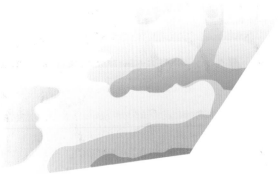

Written by **Chuck Dixon** and **Mike Costa** (Cobra #9)

Art by **Alex Cal**

Colors by **J. Brown**

Lettering by **Shawn Lee** and **Neil Uyetake**

Series Edits by **John Barber** and **Carlos Guzman**

Cover by **Dave Wilkins**

Collection Edits by **Justin Eisinger** and **Alonzo Simon**

Collection Design by **Shawn Lee**

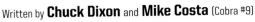

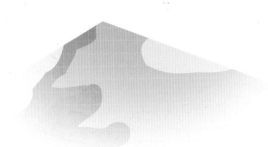

Special thanks to Hasbro's Aaron Archer, Andy Schmidt, Derryl DePriest, Joe Del Regno, Ed Lane, Joe Furfaro, Jos Huxley, and Michael Kelly for their invaluable assistance.

IDW founded by Ted Adams, Alex Garner, Kris Oprisko, and Robbie Robbins | International Rights Representative, Christine Meyer: christine@gfloystudio.com

ISBN: 978-1-61377-221-8

15 14 13 12 1 2 3 4

Licensed By:

Ted Adams, CEO & Publisher
Greg Goldstein, President & COO
Robbie Robbins, EVP/Sr. Graphic Artist
Chris Ryall, Chief Creative Officer/Editor-in-Chief
Matthew Ruzicka, CPA, Chief Financial Officer
Alan Payne, VP of Sales

Become our fan on Facebook **facebook.com/idwpublishing**
Follow us on Twitter **@idwpublishing**
Check us out on YouTube **youtube.com/idwpublishing**
www.IDWPUBLISHING.com

Originally published as G.I. JOE SEASON 2 #9, SNAKE EYES #9, G.I. JOE COBRA: VOL. 2 #9, and G.I. JOE SEASON 2 #10.

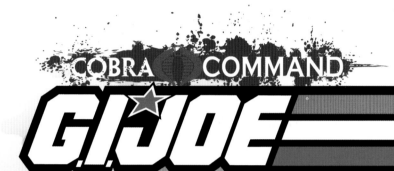

COBRA COMMAND
G.I. JOE

When Cobra Commander was killed by an undercover G.I. JOE agent, the Cobra council began a contest to find a new Commander. The rules were simple: whichever member of Cobra High Command caused the most damage to G.I. JOE would be elected the new leader of Cobra. At the end of the contest, it was Krake who had amassed the most destruction, and he ascended to the role of Cobra Commander.

Meanwhile, G.I. JOE has been hit hard: they lost the Pit and had to find a new base of operations, their Washington, D.C. installation was infiltrated by a Cobra double-agent, and Duke was almost eliminated by a deadly virus developed by a member of Cobra High Command. Now, Hawk must answer to his superiors in Washington in order to justify the catastrophic losses... but Cobra isn't done yet.

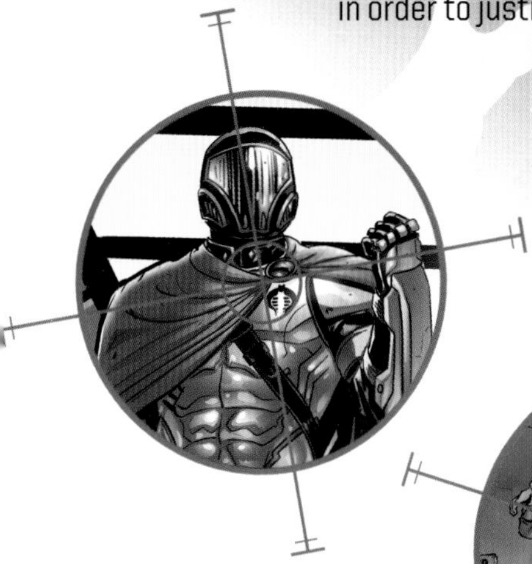

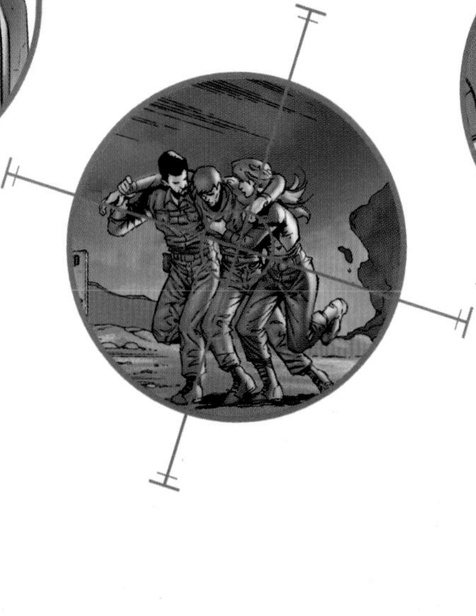

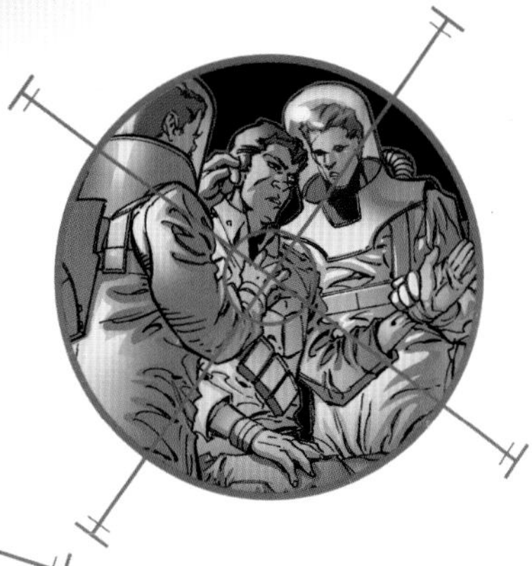

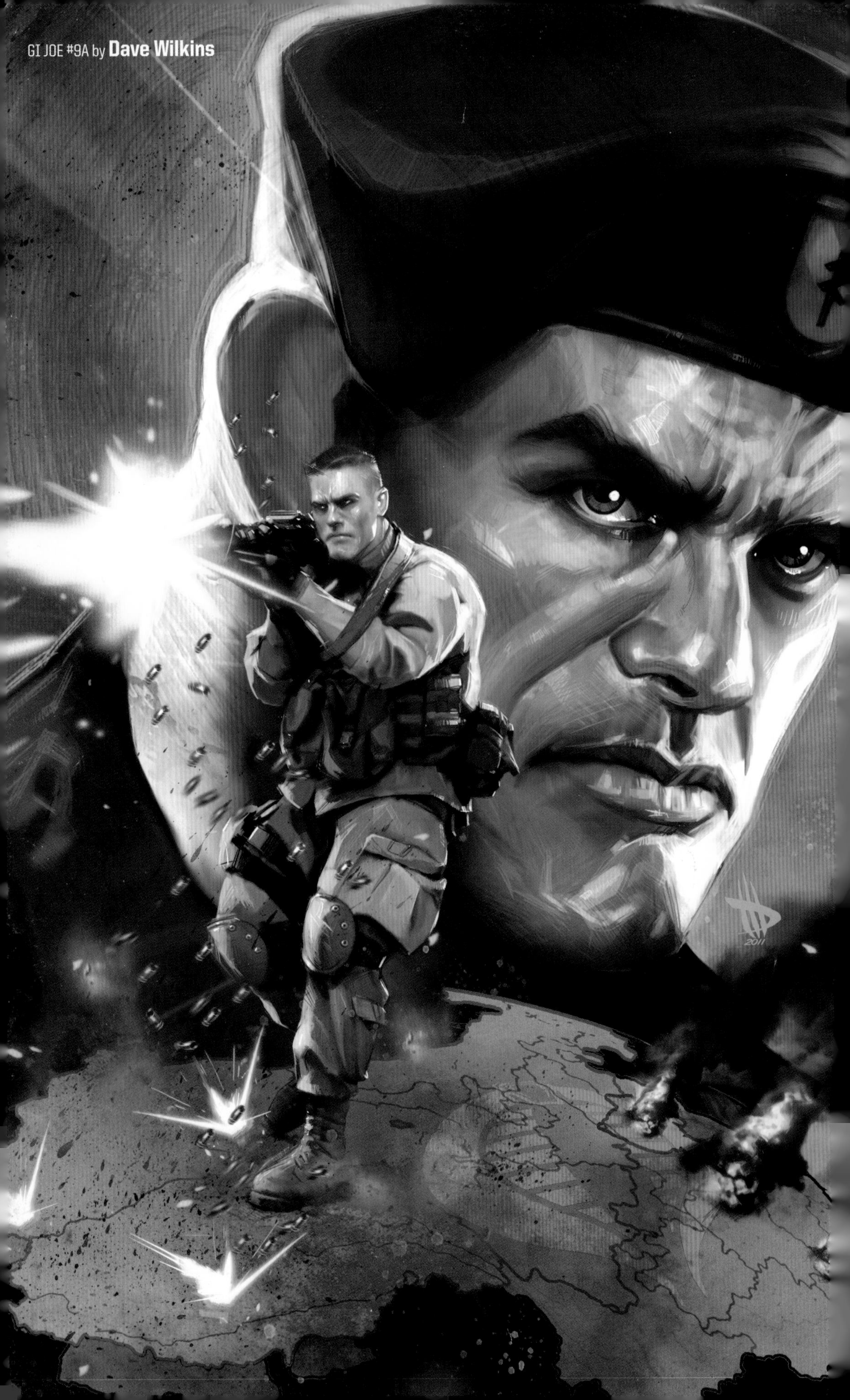

GI JOE #9A by **Dave Wilkins**

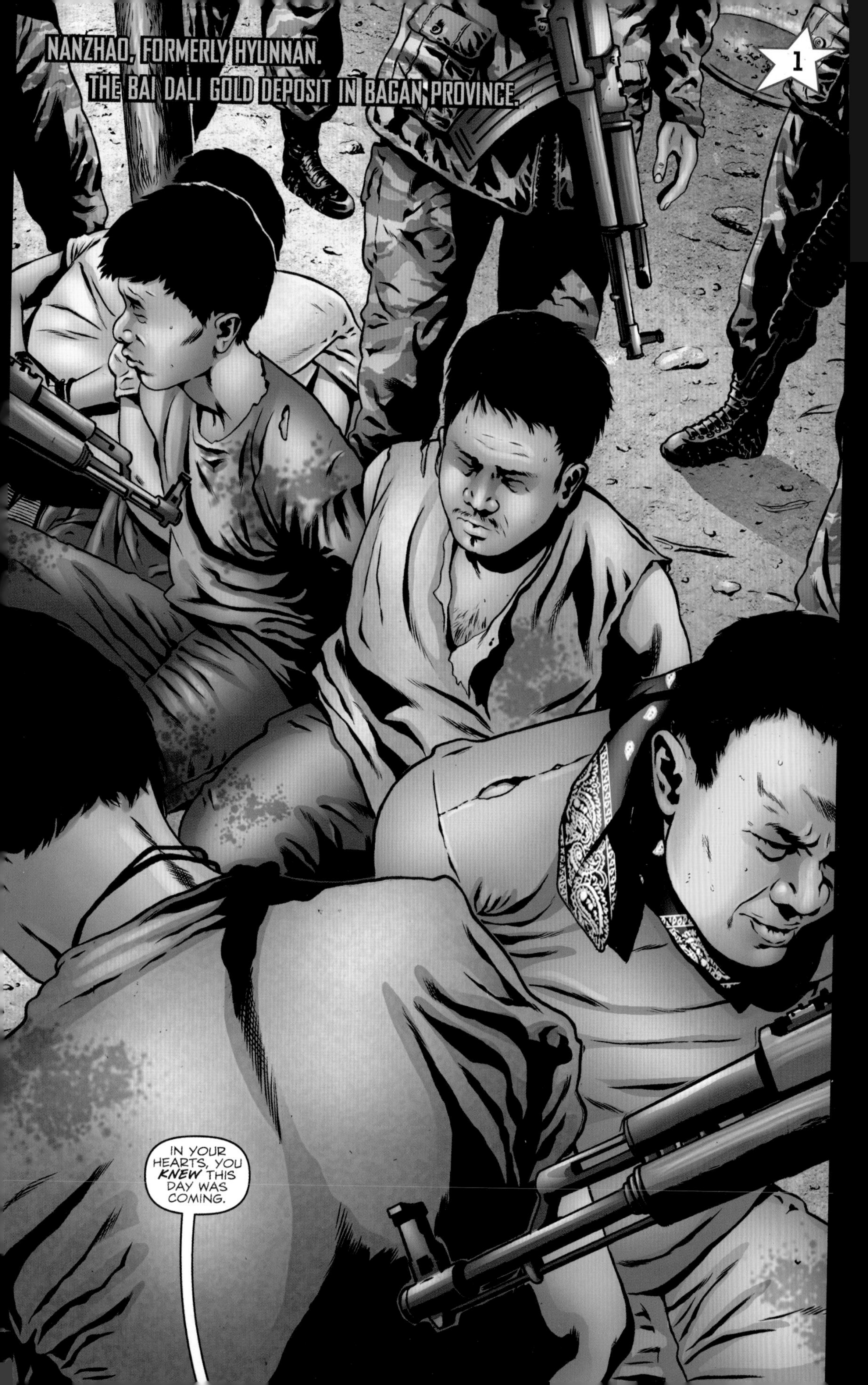
NANZHAO, FORMERLY HYUNNAN.
THE BAI DALI GOLD DEPOSIT IN BAGAN PROVINCE.
1
IN YOUR HEARTS, YOU KNEW THIS DAY WAS COMING.

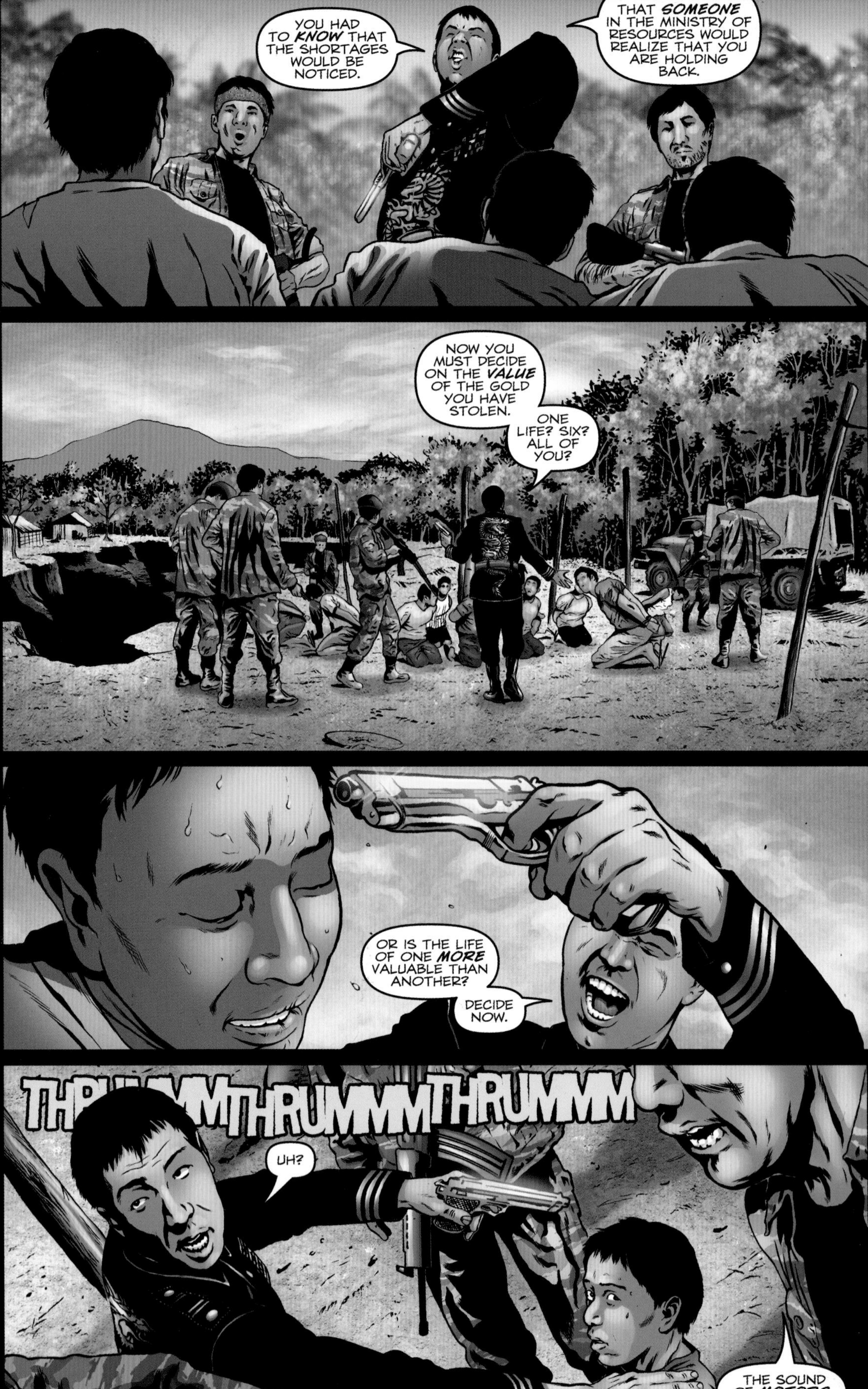
YOU HAD TO KNOW THAT THE SHORTAGES WOULD BE NOTICED.
THAT SOMEONE IN THE MINISTRY OF RESOURCES WOULD REALIZE THAT YOU ARE HOLDING BACK.
NOW YOU MUST DECIDE ON THE VALUE OF THE GOLD YOU HAVE STOLEN.
ONE LIFE? SIX? ALL OF YOU?
OR IS THE LIFE OF ONE MORE VALUABLE THAN ANOTHER?
DECIDE NOW.
THRUMMMTHRUMMM
UH?
THE SOUND OF MOTORS APPROACHING.

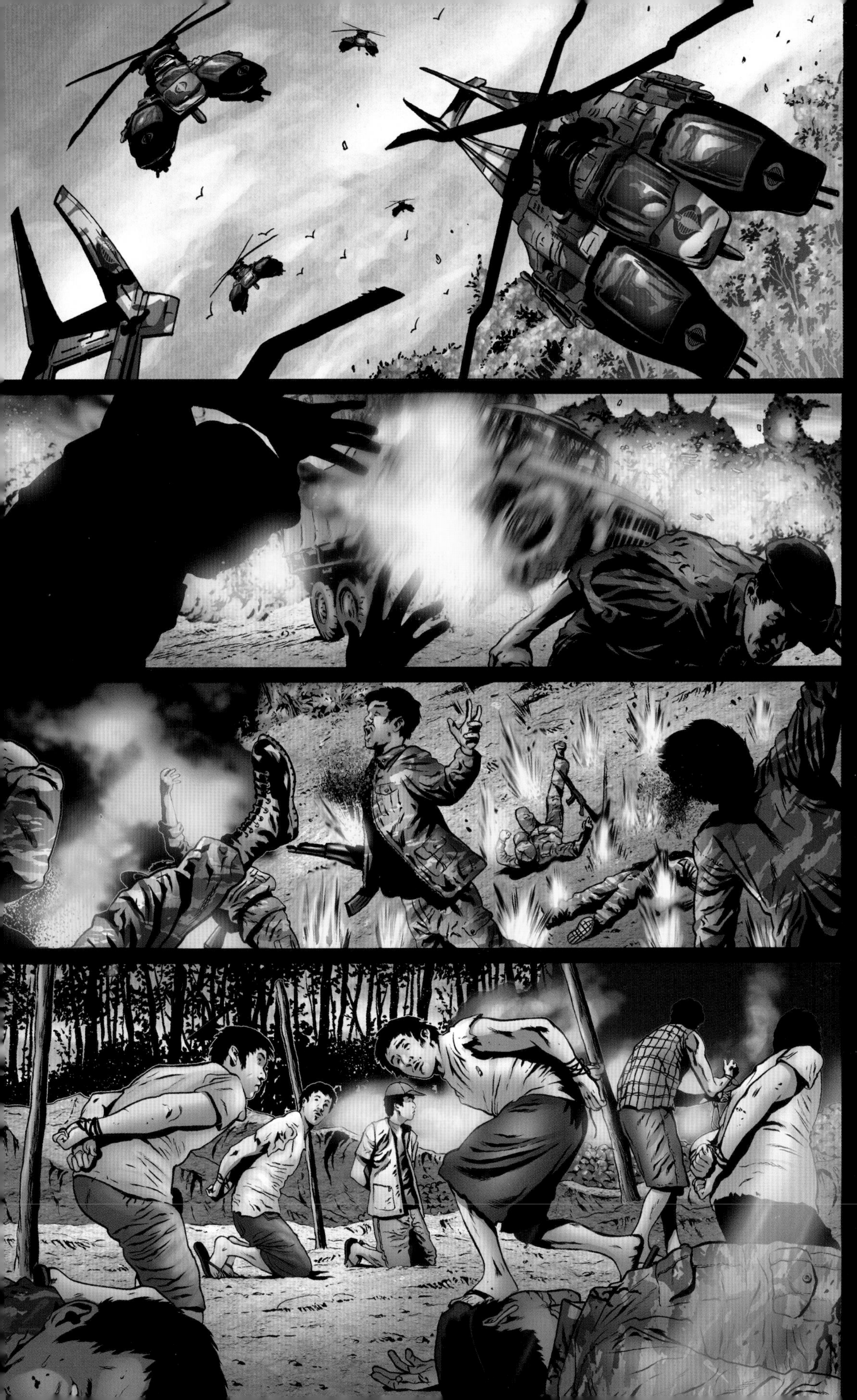

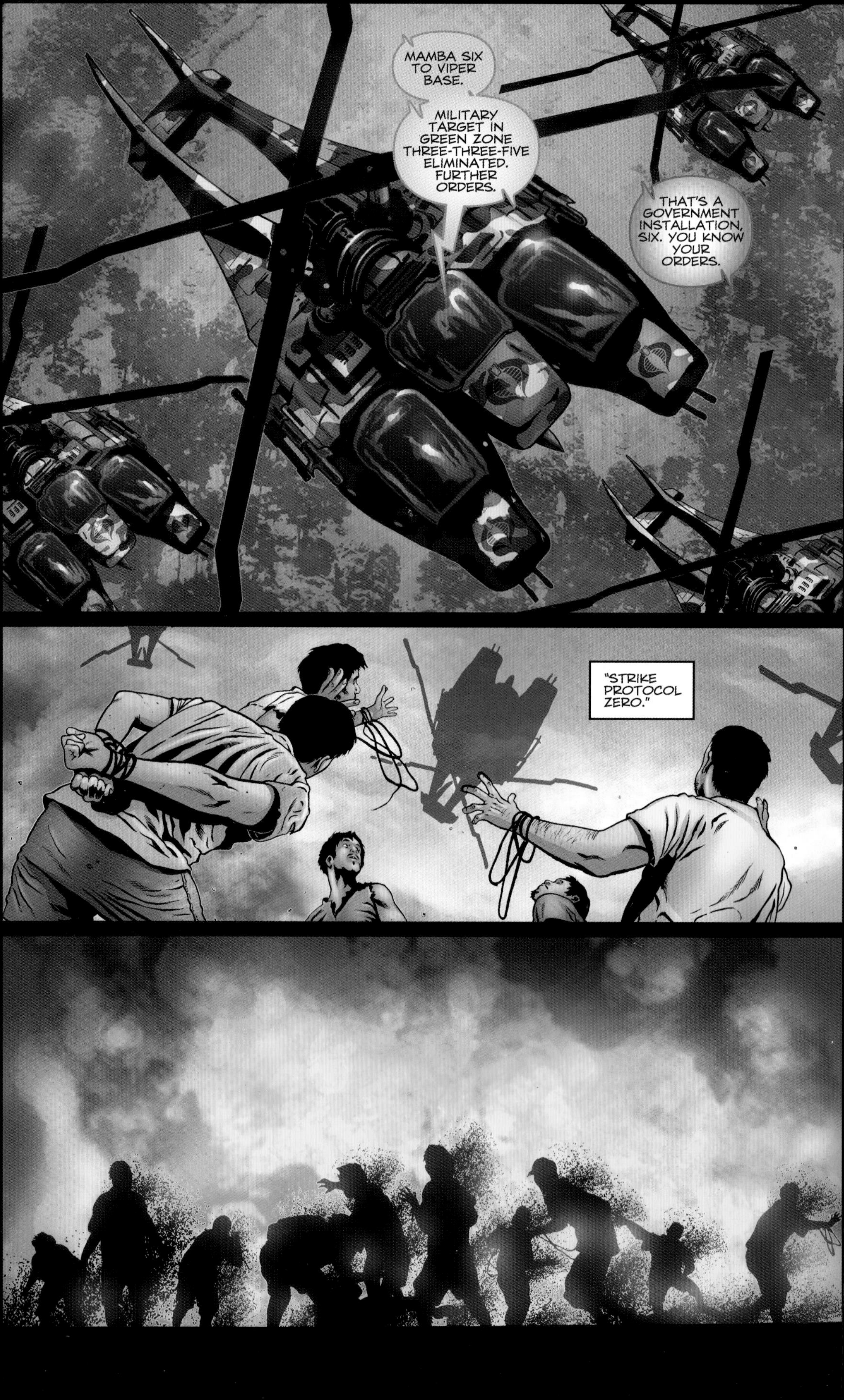
MAMBA SIX TO VIPER BASE.
MILITARY TARGET IN GREEN ZONE THREE-THREE-FIVE ELIMINATED. FURTHER ORDERS.
THAT'S A GOVERNMENT INSTALLATION, SIX. YOU KNOW YOUR ORDERS.
"STRIKE PROTOCOL ZERO."

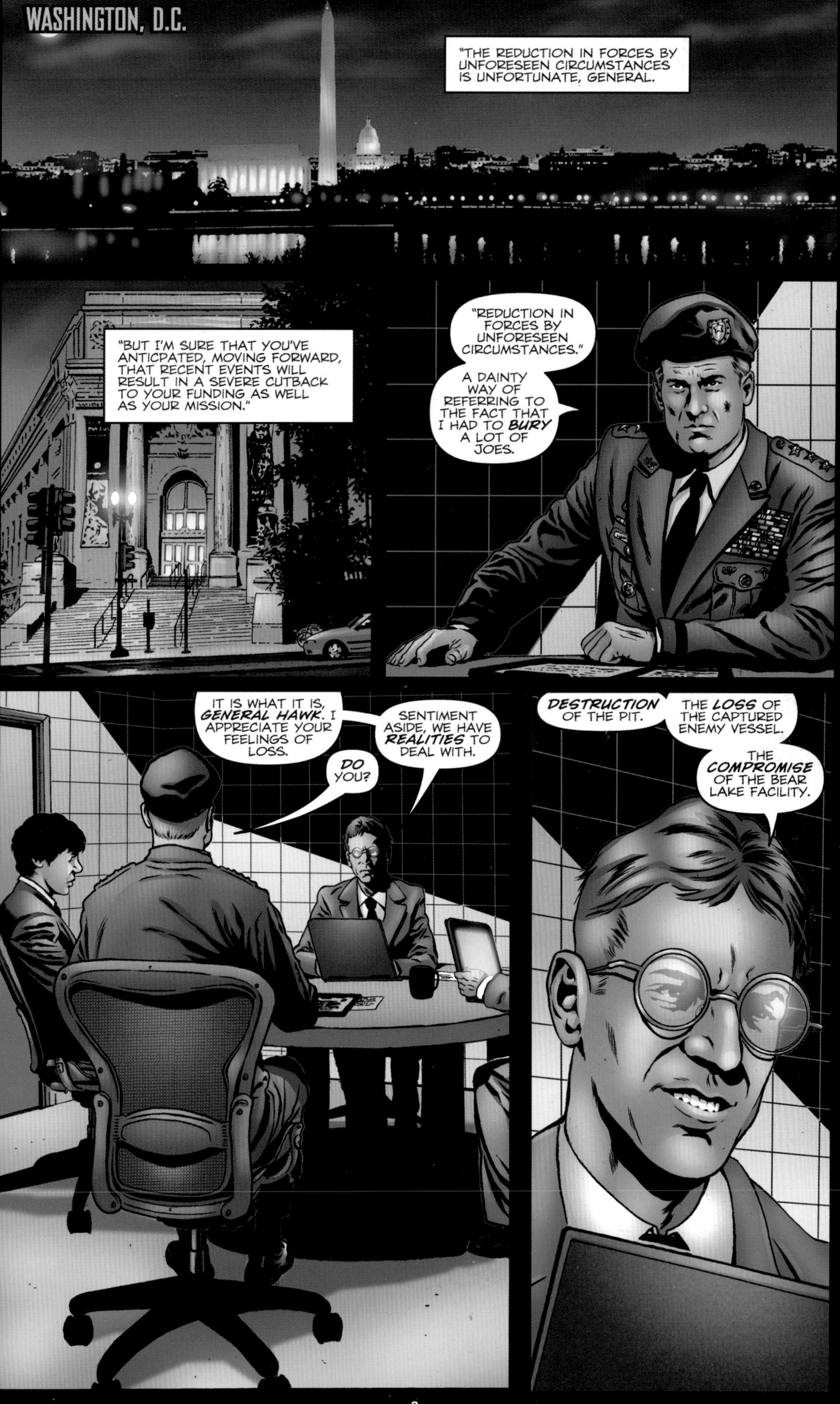
WASHINGTON, D.C.
"THE REDUCTION IN FORCES BY UNFORESEEN CIRCUMSTANCES IS UNFORTUNATE, GENERAL.
"BUT I'M SURE THAT YOU'VE ANTICPATED, MOVING FORWARD, THAT RECENT EVENTS WILL RESULT IN A SEVERE CUTBACK TO YOUR FUNDING AS WELL AS YOUR MISSION."
"REDUCTION IN FORCES BY UNFORESEEN CIRCUMSTANCES."
A DAINTY WAY OF REFERRING TO THE FACT THAT I HAD TO BURY A LOT OF JOES.
IT IS WHAT IT IS, GENERAL HAWK. I APPRECIATE YOUR FEELINGS OF LOSS.
DO YOU?
SENTIMENT ASIDE, WE HAVE REALITIES TO DEAL WITH.
DESTRUCTION OF THE PIT.
THE LOSS OF THE CAPTURED ENEMY VESSEL.
THE COMPROMISE OF THE BEAR LAKE FACILITY.

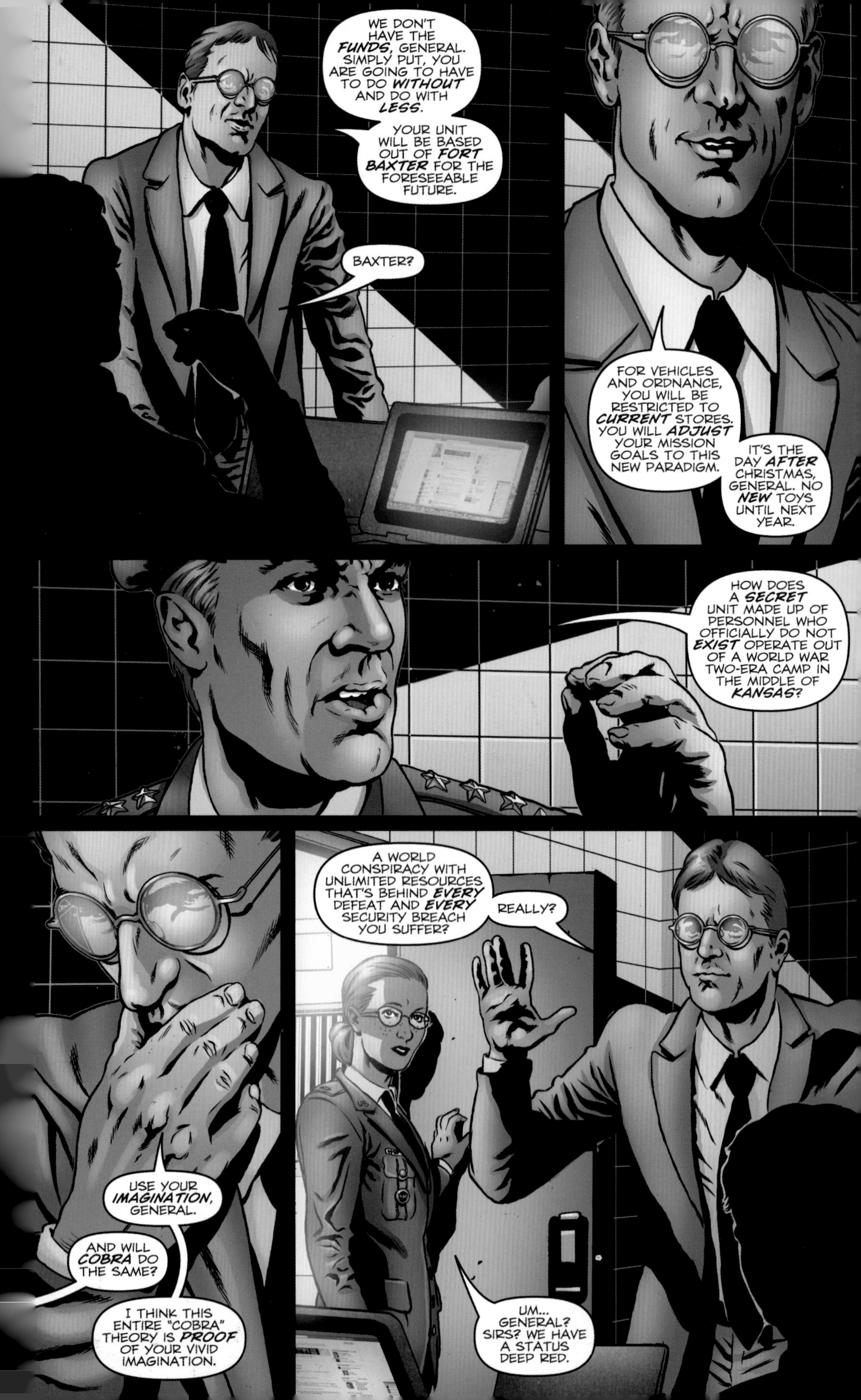

WE DON'T HAVE THE FUNDS, GENERAL. SIMPLY PUT, YOU ARE GOING TO HAVE TO DO WITHOUT AND DO WITH LESS.
YOUR UNIT WILL BE BASED OUT OF FORT BAXTER FOR THE FORESEEABLE FUTURE.
BAXTER?
FOR VEHICLES AND ORDNANCE, YOU WILL BE RESTRICTED TO CURRENT STORES. YOU WILL ADJUST YOUR MISSION GOALS TO THIS NEW PARADIGM.
IT'S THE DAY AFTER CHRISTMAS, GENERAL. NO NEW TOYS UNTIL NEXT YEAR.
HOW DOES A SECRET UNIT MADE UP OF PERSONNEL WHO OFFICIALLY DO NOT EXIST OPERATE OUT OF A WORLD WAR TWO-ERA CAMP IN THE MIDDLE OF KANSAS?
USE YOUR IMAGINATION, GENERAL.
AND WILL COBRA DO THE SAME?
I THINK THIS ENTIRE "COBRA" THEORY IS PROOF OF YOUR VIVID IMAGINATION.
A WORLD CONSPIRACY WITH UNLIMITED RESOURCES THAT'S BEHIND EVERY DEFEAT AND EVERY SECURITY BREACH YOU SUFFER?
REALLY?
UM... GENERAL? SIRS? WE HAVE A STATUS DEEP RED.

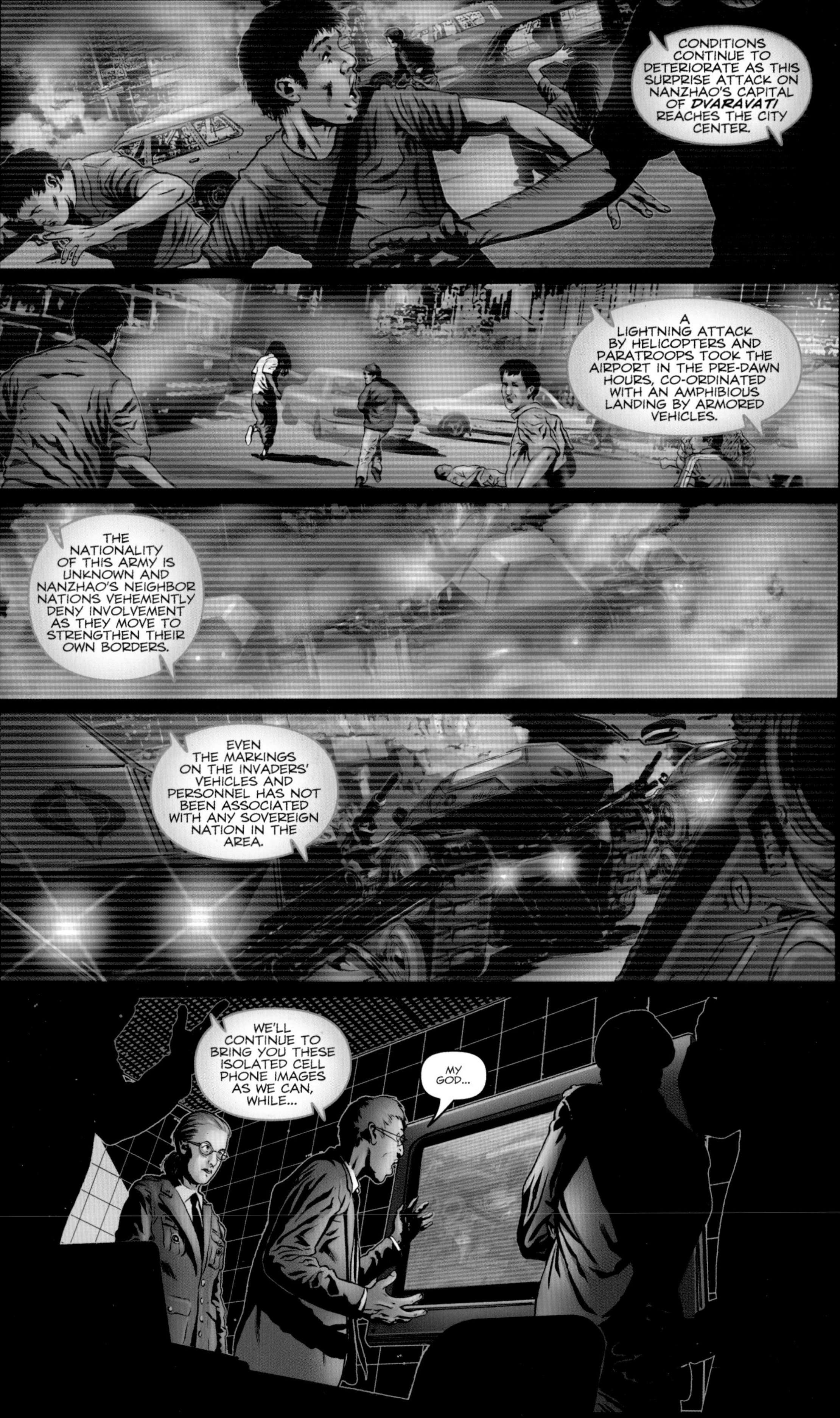
CONDITIONS CONTINUE TO DETERIORATE AS THIS SURPRISE ATTACK ON NANZHAO'S CAPITAL OF DVARAVATI REACHES THE CITY CENTER.
A LIGHTNING ATTACK BY HELICOPTERS AND PARATROOPS TOOK THE AIRPORT IN THE PRE-DAWN HOURS, CO-ORDINATED WITH AN AMPHIBIOUS LANDING BY ARMORED VEHICLES.
THE NATIONALITY OF THIS ARMY IS UNKNOWN AND NANZHAO'S NEIGHBOR NATIONS VEHEMENTLY DENY INVOLVEMENT AS THEY MOVE TO STRENGTHEN THEIR OWN BORDERS.
EVEN THE MARKINGS ON THE INVADERS' VEHICLES AND PERSONNEL HAS NOT BEEN ASSOCIATED WITH ANY SOVEREIGN NATION IN THE AREA.
WE'LL CONTINUE TO BRING YOU THESE ISOLATED CELL PHONE IMAGES AS WE CAN, WHILE...
MY GOD...

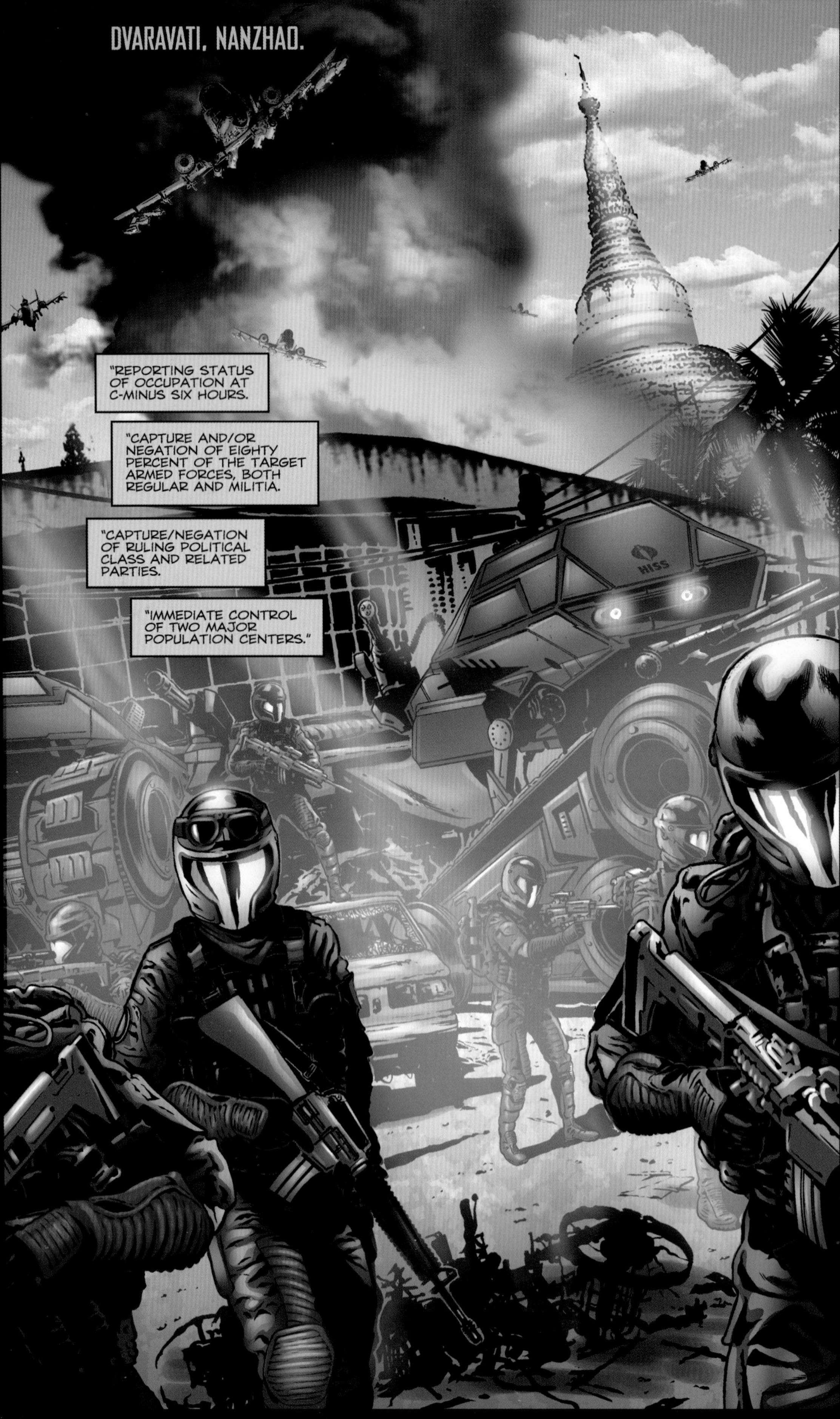

DVARAVATI, NANZHAO.
"REPORTING STATUS OF OCCUPATION AT C-MINUS SIX HOURS.
"CAPTURE AND/OR NEGATION OF EIGHTY PERCENT OF THE TARGET ARMED FORCES, BOTH REGULAR AND MILITIA.
"CAPTURE/NEGATION OF RULING POLITICAL CLASS AND RELATED PARTIES.
"IMMEDIATE CONTROL OF TWO MAJOR POPULATION CENTERS."
HISS

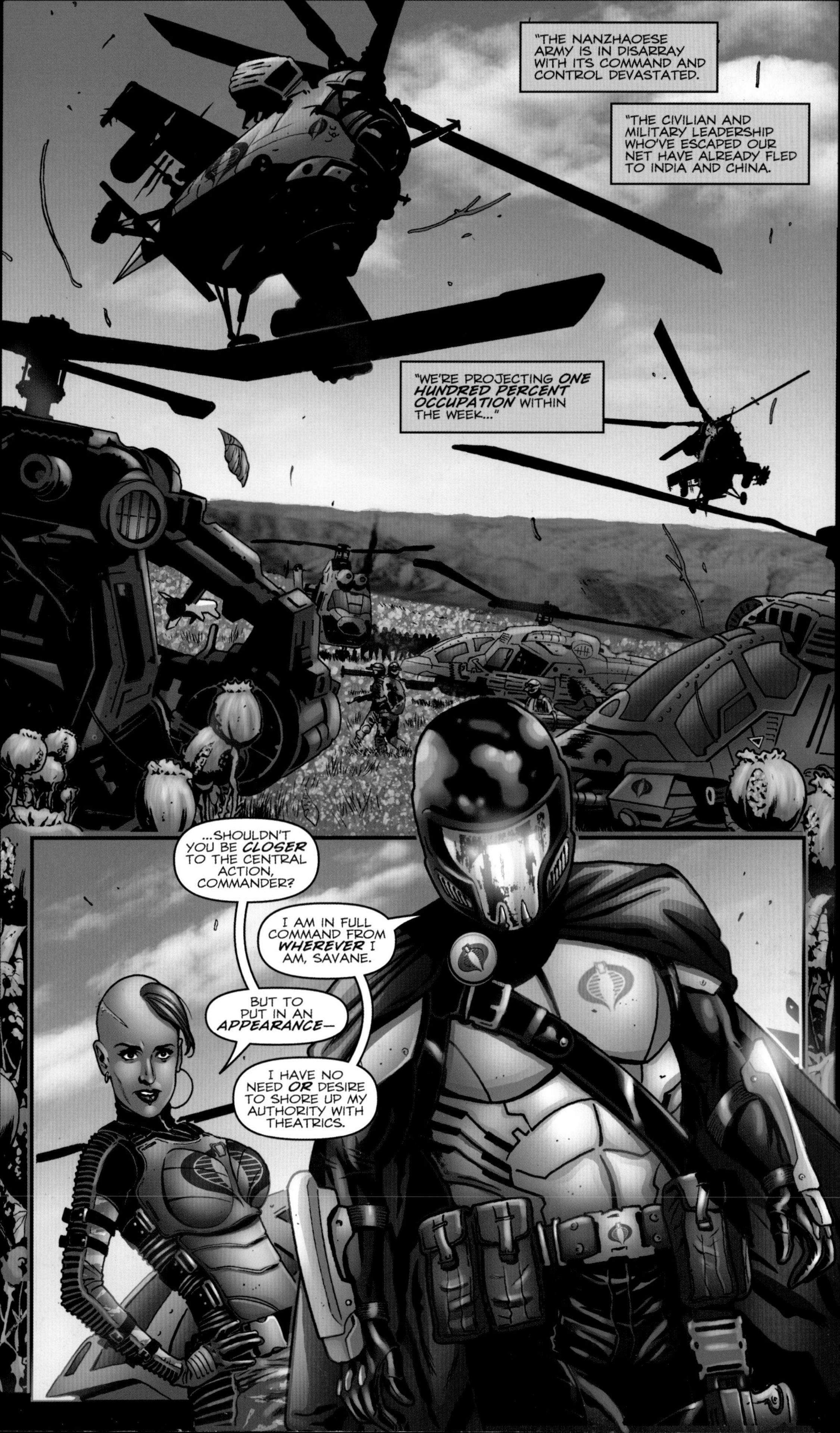
"THE NANZHAOESE ARMY IS IN DISARRAY WITH ITS COMMAND AND CONTROL DEVASTATED.
"THE CIVILIAN AND MILITARY LEADERSHIP WHO'VE ESCAPED OUR NET HAVE ALREADY FLED TO INDIA AND CHINA.
"WE'RE PROJECTING ONE HUNDRED PERCENT OCCUPATION WITHIN THE WEEK..."
...SHOULDN'T YOU BE CLOSER TO THE CENTRAL ACTION, COMMANDER?
I AM IN FULL COMMAND FROM WHEREVER I AM, SAVANE.
BUT TO PUT IN AN APPEARANCE—
I HAVE NO NEED OR DESIRE TO SHORE UP MY AUTHORITY WITH THEATRICS.

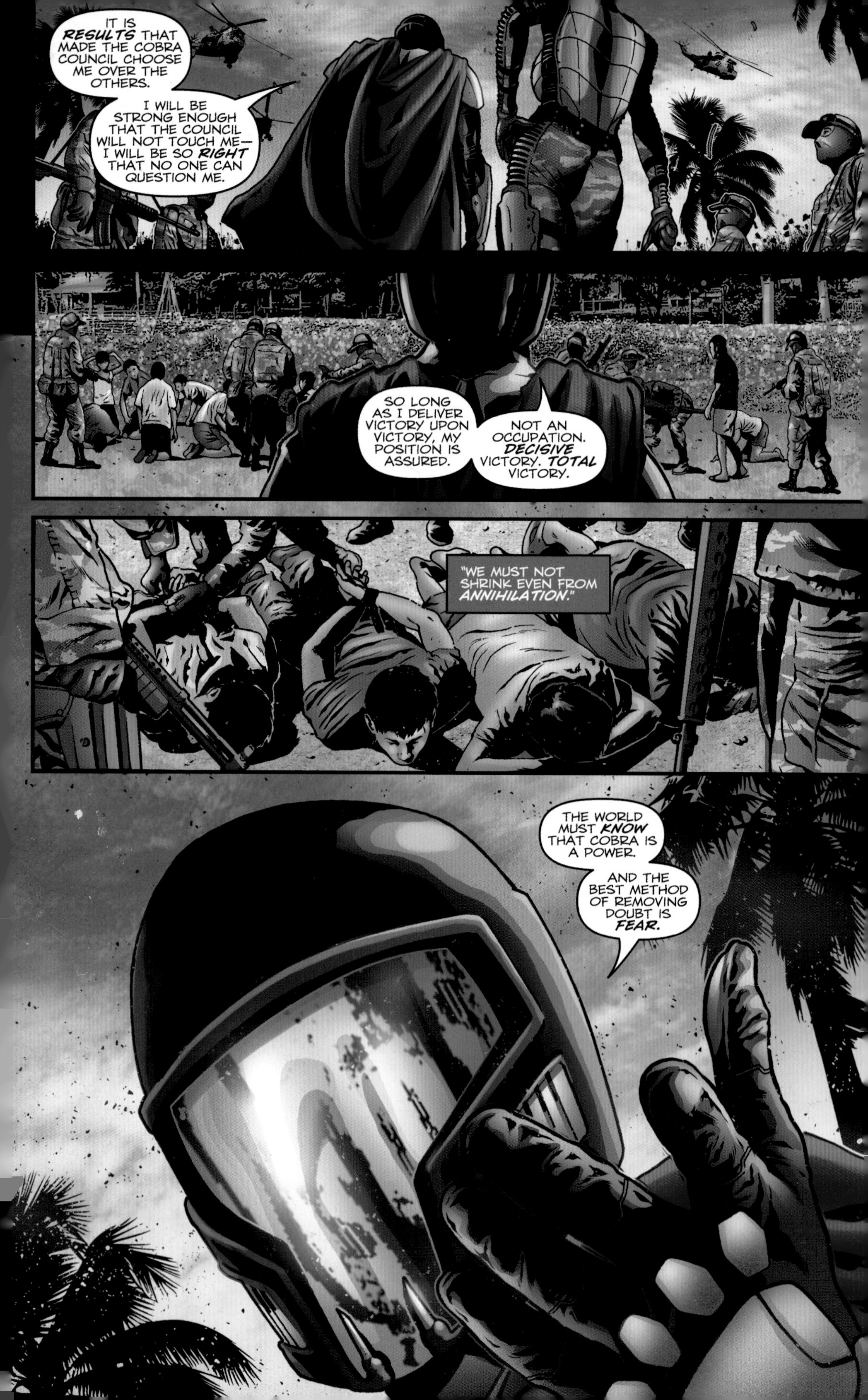
IT IS RESULTS THAT MADE THE COBRA COUNCIL CHOOSE ME OVER THE OTHERS.
I WILL BE STRONG ENOUGH THAT THE COUNCIL WILL NOT TOUCH ME— I WILL BE SO RIGHT THAT NO ONE CAN QUESTION ME.
SO LONG AS I DELIVER VICTORY UPON VICTORY, MY POSITION IS ASSURED.
NOT AN OCCUPATION. DECISIVE VICTORY. TOTAL VICTORY.
"WE MUST NOT SHRINK EVEN FROM ANNIHILATION."
THE WORLD MUST KNOW THAT COBRA IS A POWER.
AND THE BEST METHOD OF REMOVING DOUBT IS FEAR.

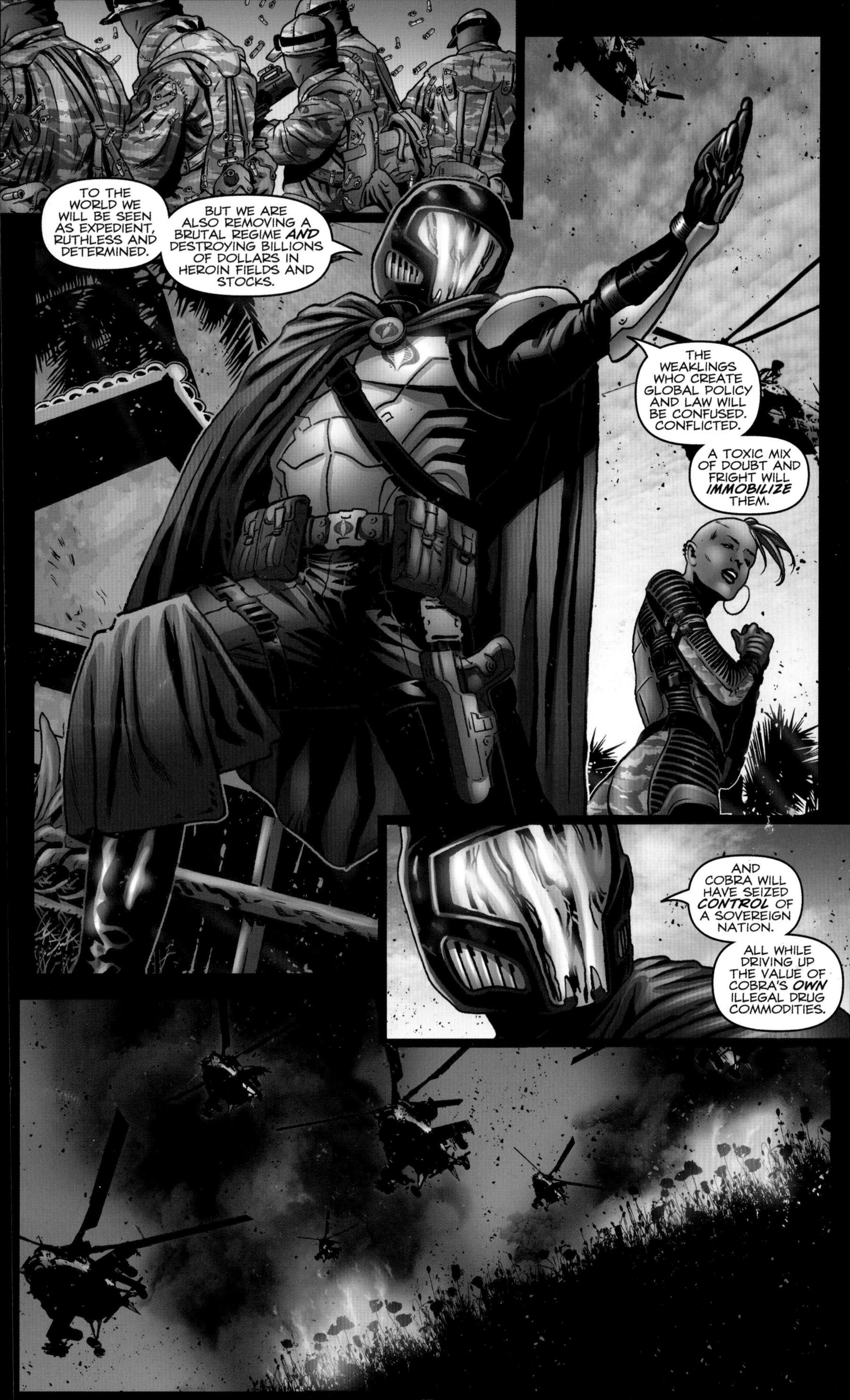
TO THE WORLD WE WILL BE SEEN AS EXPEDIENT, RUTHLESS AND DETERMINED.
BUT WE ARE ALSO REMOVING A BRUTAL REGIME AND DESTROYING BILLIONS OF DOLLARS IN HEROIN FIELDS AND STOCKS.
THE WEAKLINGS WHO CREATE GLOBAL POLICY AND LAW WILL BE CONFUSED. CONFLICTED.
A TOXIC MIX OF DOUBT AND FRIGHT WILL IMMOBILIZE THEM.
AND COBRA WILL HAVE SEIZED CONTROL OF A SOVEREIGN NATION.
ALL WHILE DRIVING UP THE VALUE OF COBRA'S OWN ILLEGAL DRUG COMMODITIES.

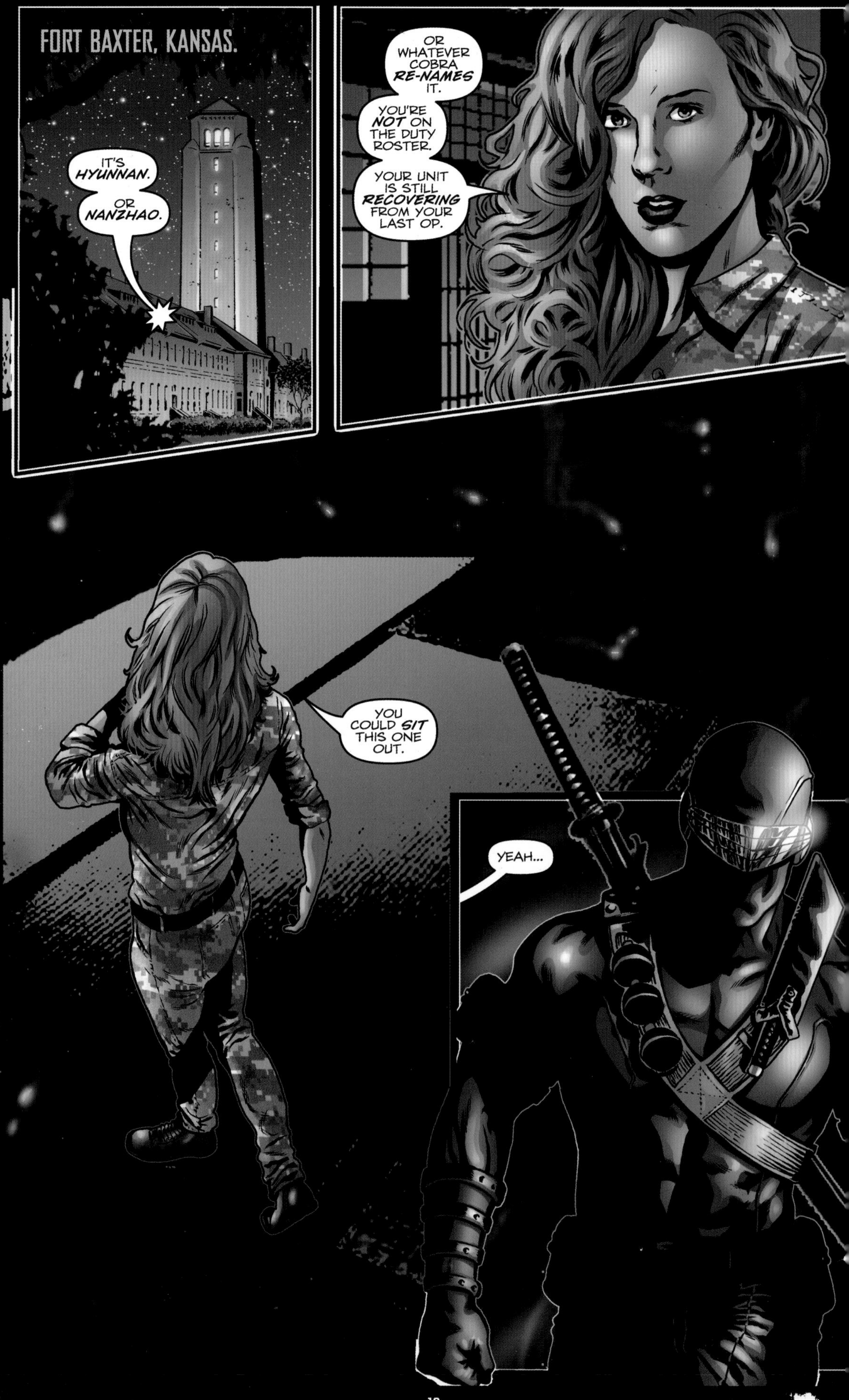
FORT BAXTER, KANSAS.
IT'S HYUNNAN.
OR NANZHAO.
OR WHATEVER COBRA RE-NAMES IT.
YOU'RE NOT ON THE DUTY ROSTER.
YOUR UNIT IS STILL RECOVERING FROM YOUR LAST OP.
YOU COULD SIT THIS ONE OUT.
YEAH...

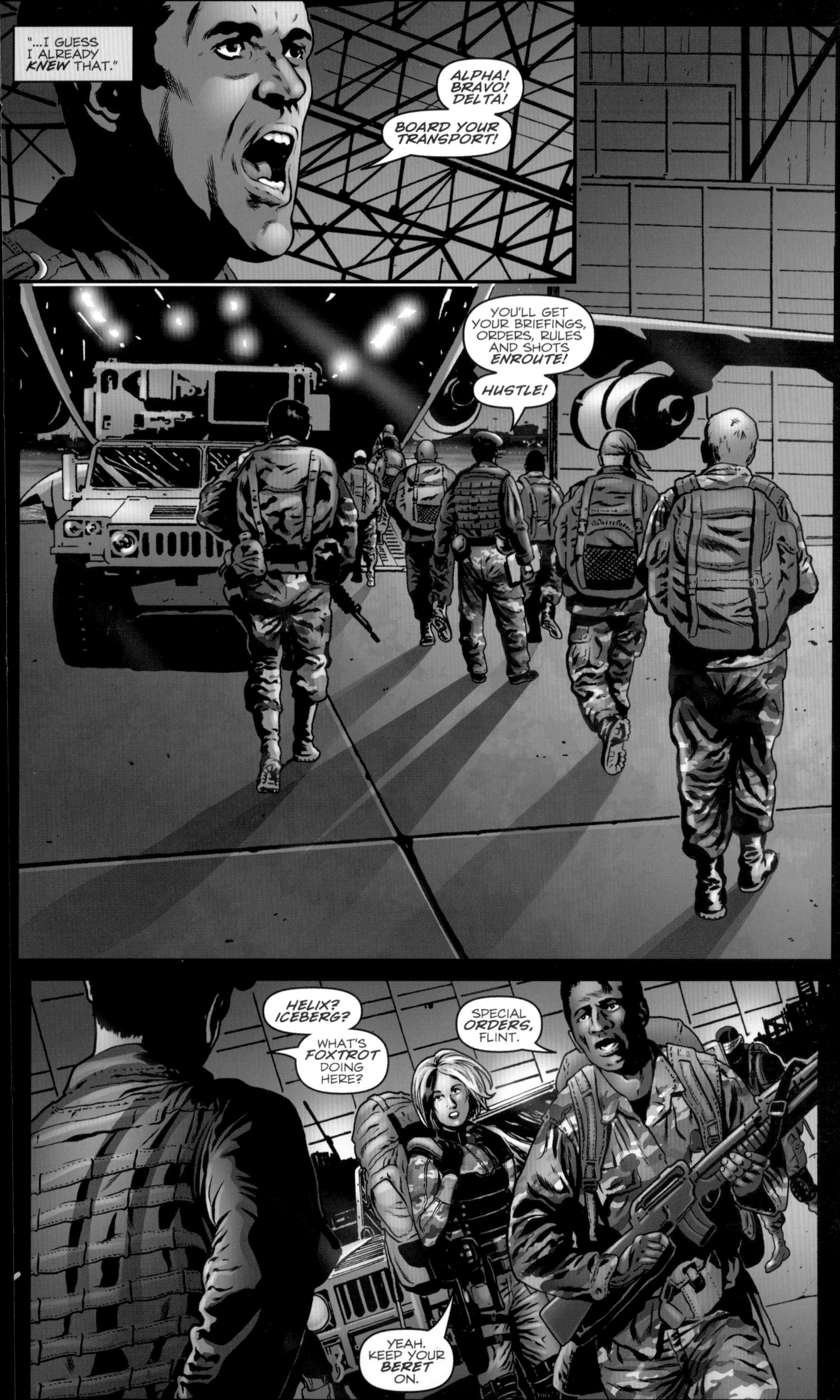
"...I GUESS I ALREADY *KNEW* THAT."
ALPHA! BRAVO! DELTA!
BOARD YOUR TRANSPORT!
YOU'LL GET YOUR BRIEFINGS, ORDERS, RULES AND SHOTS *ENROUTE!*
HUSTLE!
HELIX? ICEBERG?
WHAT'S *FOXTROT* DOING HERE?
SPECIAL *ORDERS,* FLINT.
YEAH. KEEP YOUR *BERET* ON.

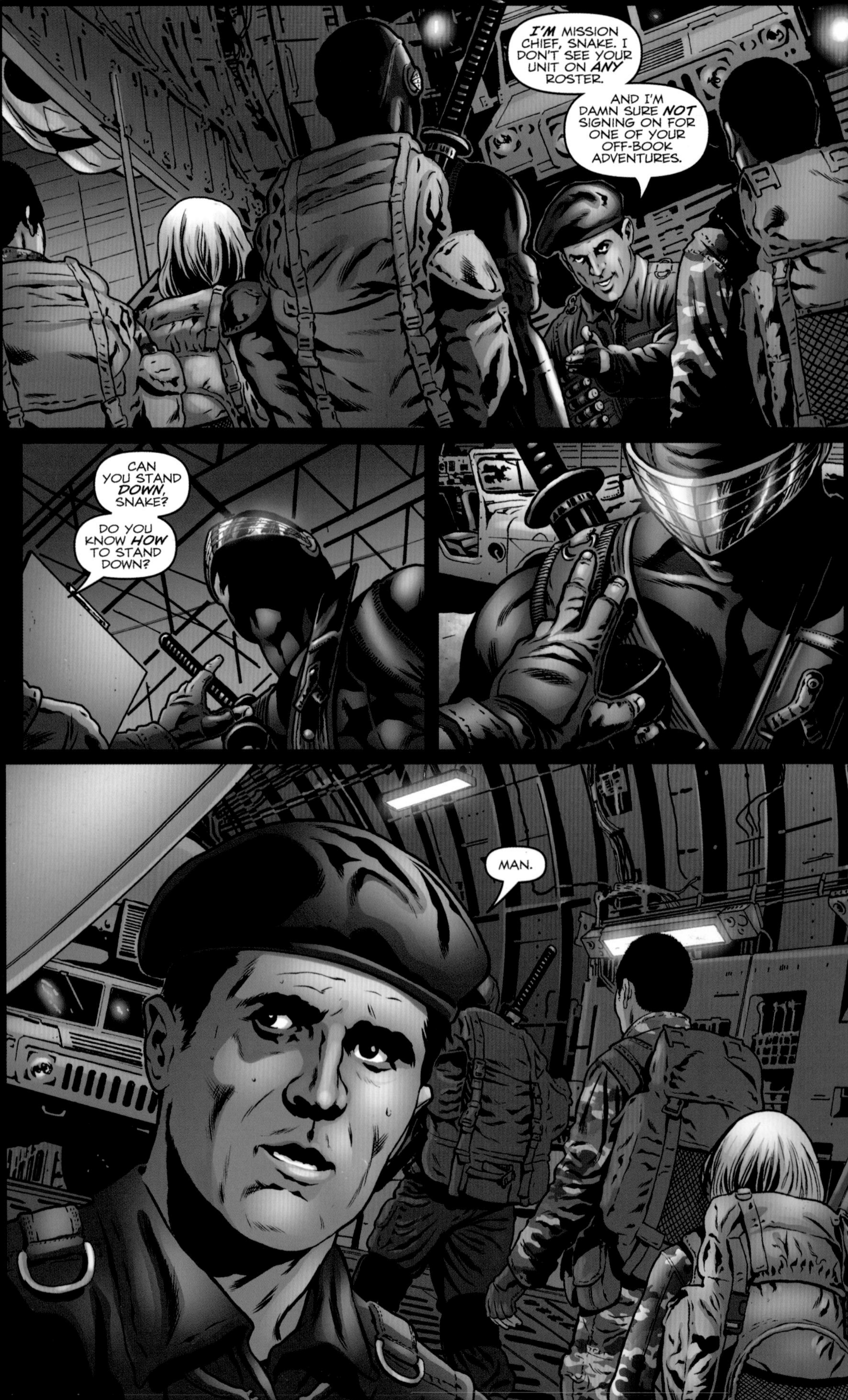
I'M MISSION CHIEF, SNAKE. I DON'T SEE YOUR UNIT ON ANY ROSTER.
AND I'M DAMN SURE NOT SIGNING ON FOR ONE OF YOUR OFF-BOOK ADVENTURES.
CAN YOU STAND DOWN, SNAKE?
DO YOU KNOW HOW TO STAND DOWN?
MAN.

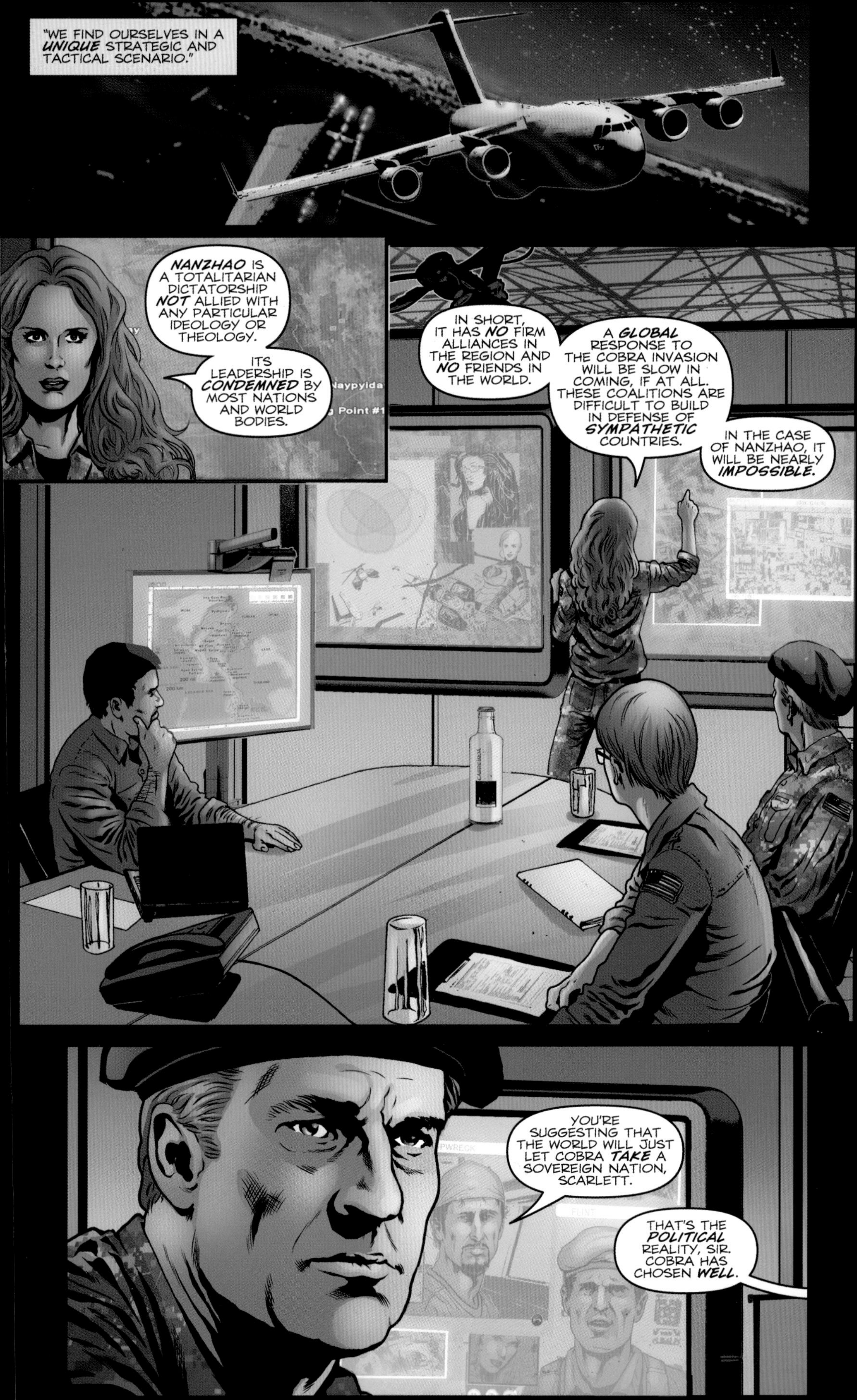
"WE FIND OURSELVES IN A UNIQUE STRATEGIC AND TACTICAL SCENARIO."
NANZHAO IS A TOTALITARIAN DICTATORSHIP NOT ALLIED WITH ANY PARTICULAR IDEOLOGY OR THEOLOGY.
ITS LEADERSHIP IS CONDEMNED BY MOST NATIONS AND WORLD BODIES.
Naypyidaw
IN SHORT, IT HAS NO FIRM ALLIANCES IN THE REGION AND NO FRIENDS IN THE WORLD.
A GLOBAL RESPONSE TO THE COBRA INVASION WILL BE SLOW IN COMING, IF AT ALL. THESE COALITIONS ARE DIFFICULT TO BUILD IN DEFENSE OF SYMPATHETIC COUNTRIES.
IN THE CASE OF NANZHAO, IT WILL BE NEARLY IMPOSSIBLE.
YOU'RE SUGGESTING THAT THE WORLD WILL JUST LET COBRA TAKE A SOVEREIGN NATION, SCARLETT.
THAT'S THE POLITICAL REALITY, SIR. COBRA HAS CHOSEN WELL.

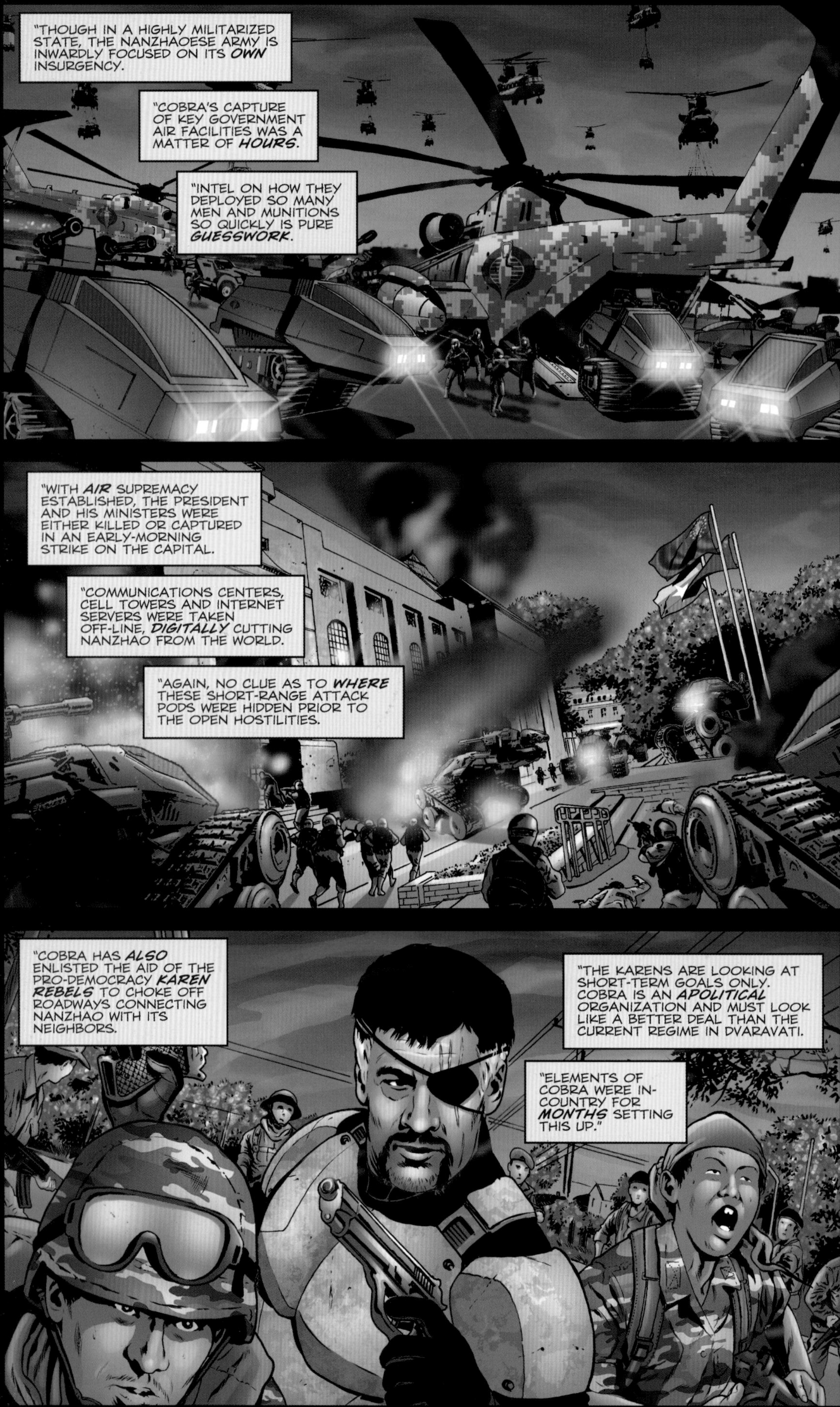
"THOUGH IN A HIGHLY MILITARIZED STATE, THE NANZHAOESE ARMY IS INWARDLY FOCUSED ON ITS OWN INSURGENCY.
"COBRA'S CAPTURE OF KEY GOVERNMENT AIR FACILITIES WAS A MATTER OF HOURS.
"INTEL ON HOW THEY DEPLOYED SO MANY MEN AND MUNITIONS SO QUICKLY IS PURE GUESSWORK.
"WITH AIR SUPREMACY ESTABLISHED, THE PRESIDENT AND HIS MINISTERS WERE EITHER KILLED OR CAPTURED IN AN EARLY-MORNING STRIKE ON THE CAPITAL.
"COMMUNICATIONS CENTERS, CELL TOWERS AND INTERNET SERVERS WERE TAKEN OFF-LINE, DIGITALLY CUTTING NANZHAO FROM THE WORLD.
"AGAIN, NO CLUE AS TO WHERE THESE SHORT-RANGE ATTACK PODS WERE HIDDEN PRIOR TO THE OPEN HOSTILITIES.
"COBRA HAS ALSO ENLISTED THE AID OF THE PRO-DEMOCRACY KAREN REBELS TO CHOKE OFF ROADWAYS CONNECTING NANZHAO WITH ITS NEIGHBORS.
"THE KARENS ARE LOOKING AT SHORT-TERM GOALS ONLY. COBRA IS AN APOLITICAL ORGANIZATION AND MUST LOOK LIKE A BETTER DEAL THAN THE CURRENT REGIME IN DVARAVATI.
"ELEMENTS OF COBRA WERE IN-COUNTRY FOR MONTHS SETTING THIS UP."

THE FIRST QUARTER GOES TO *COBRA* AND THEY'VE RACKED UP A BIG SCORE. A WIN SEEMS *INEVITABLE* IN THE NEXT FEW WEEKS.

WE'LL HAVE TO WAIT TO SEE WHAT THEY MEAN TO *DO* WITH THIS PRIZE. *THAT'S* THE SITUATION.

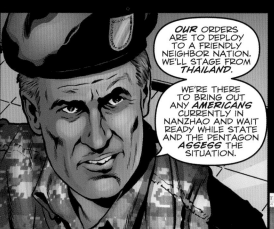

OUR ORDERS ARE TO DEPLOY TO A FRIENDLY NEIGHBOR NATION. WE'LL STAGE FROM *THAILAND.*

WE'RE THERE TO BRING OUT ANY *AMERICANS* CURRENTLY IN NANZHAO AND WAIT READY WHILE STATE AND THE PENTAGON *ASSESS* THE SITUATION.

I'LL WORK UP MODELS OF WHAT MIGHT COME *NEXT* BASED ON COBRA'S HISTORY.

SHIPWRECK

WE'RE MAKING SPEED FOR THE ANDAMAN SEA TO FORWARD-DEPLOY AND KEEP AN EYE ON OCEAN-GOING *TRAFFIC.*

FLINT

ALPHA, BRAVO AND DELTA ARE EN ROUTE. SHORT STOP AT DIEGO GARCIA AND WE'LL BE *IN* THEATER.

OH, AND A SMALL ELEMENT OF FOXTROT HAS STOWED AWAY.

I *AUTHORIZED* TEAM FOXTROT, FLINT.

SNAKE EYES HAS BEEN ON THE *GROUND* IN THE AREA.

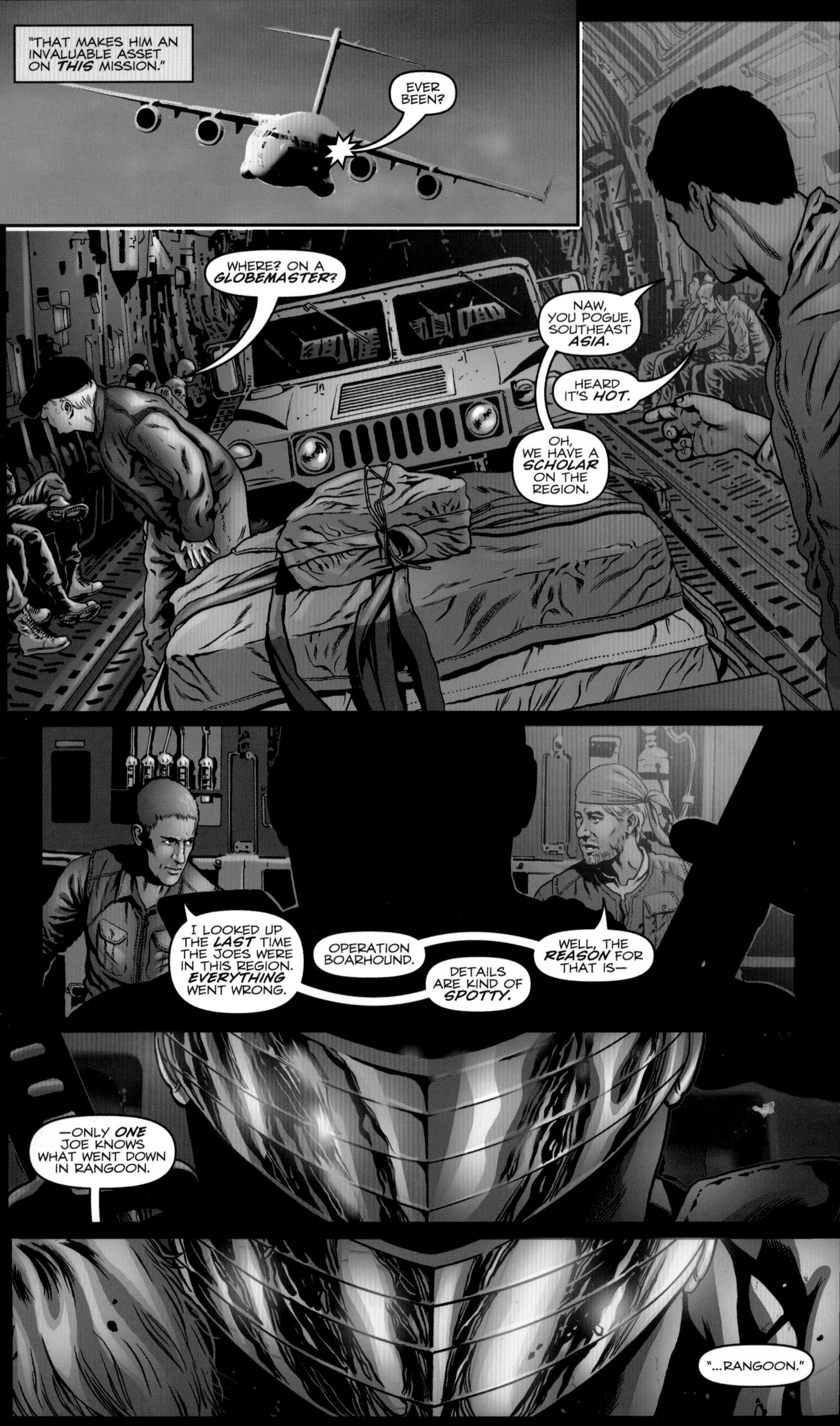
"THAT MAKES HIM AN INVALUABLE ASSET ON *THIS* MISSION."
EVER BEEN?
WHERE? ON A *GLOBEMASTER?*
NAW, YOU POGUE. SOUTHEAST *ASIA.*
HEARD IT'S *HOT*.
OH, WE HAVE A *SCHOLAR* ON THE REGION.
I LOOKED UP THE *LAST* TIME THE JOES WERE IN THIS REGION. *EVERYTHING* WENT WRONG.
OPERATION BOARHOUND.
DETAILS ARE KIND OF *SPOTTY.*
WELL, THE *REASON* FOR THAT IS—
—ONLY *ONE* JOE KNOWS WHAT WENT DOWN IN RANGOON.
"...RANGOON."

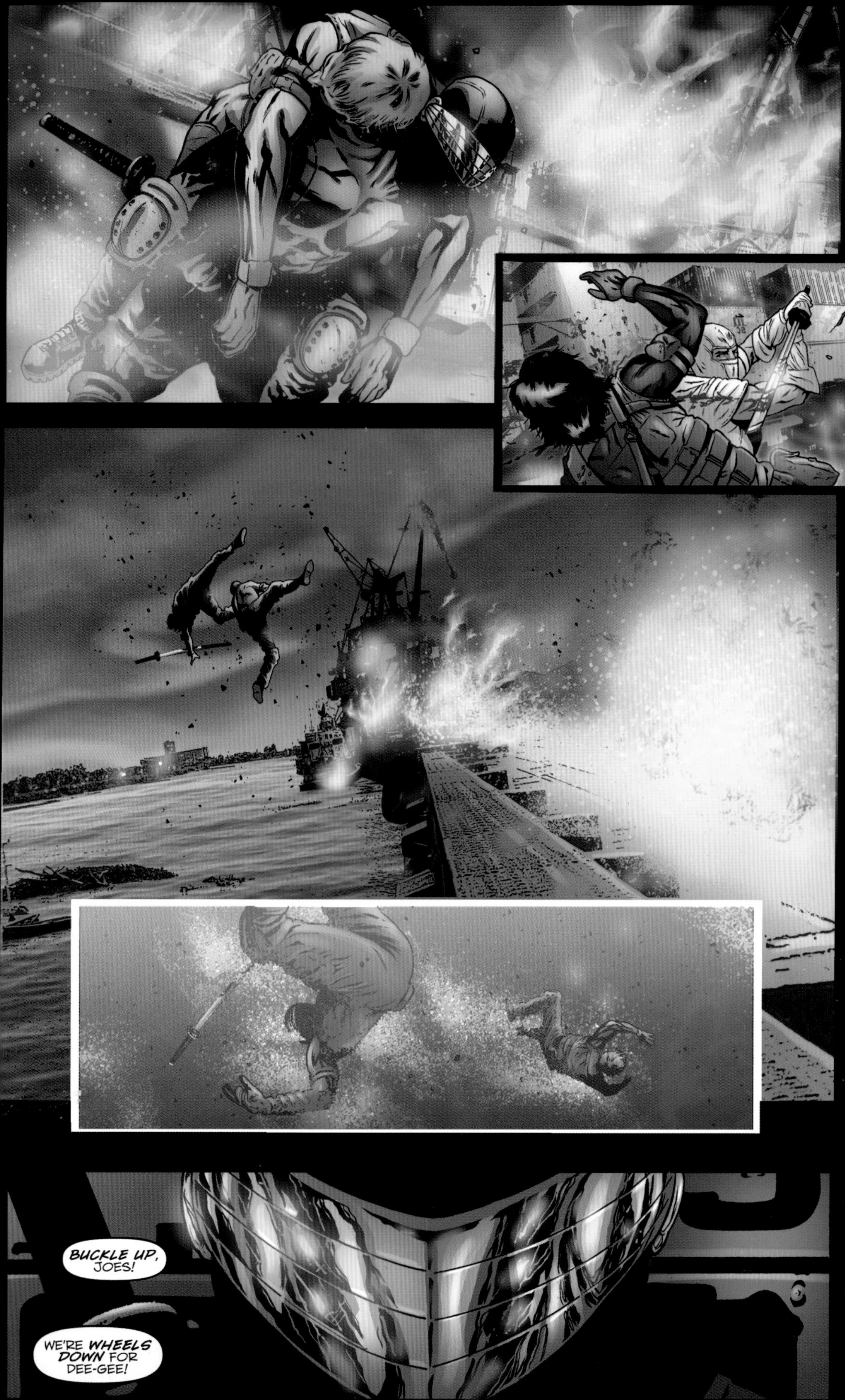
BUCKLE UP, JOES!
WE'RE WHEELS DOWN FOR DEE-GEE!

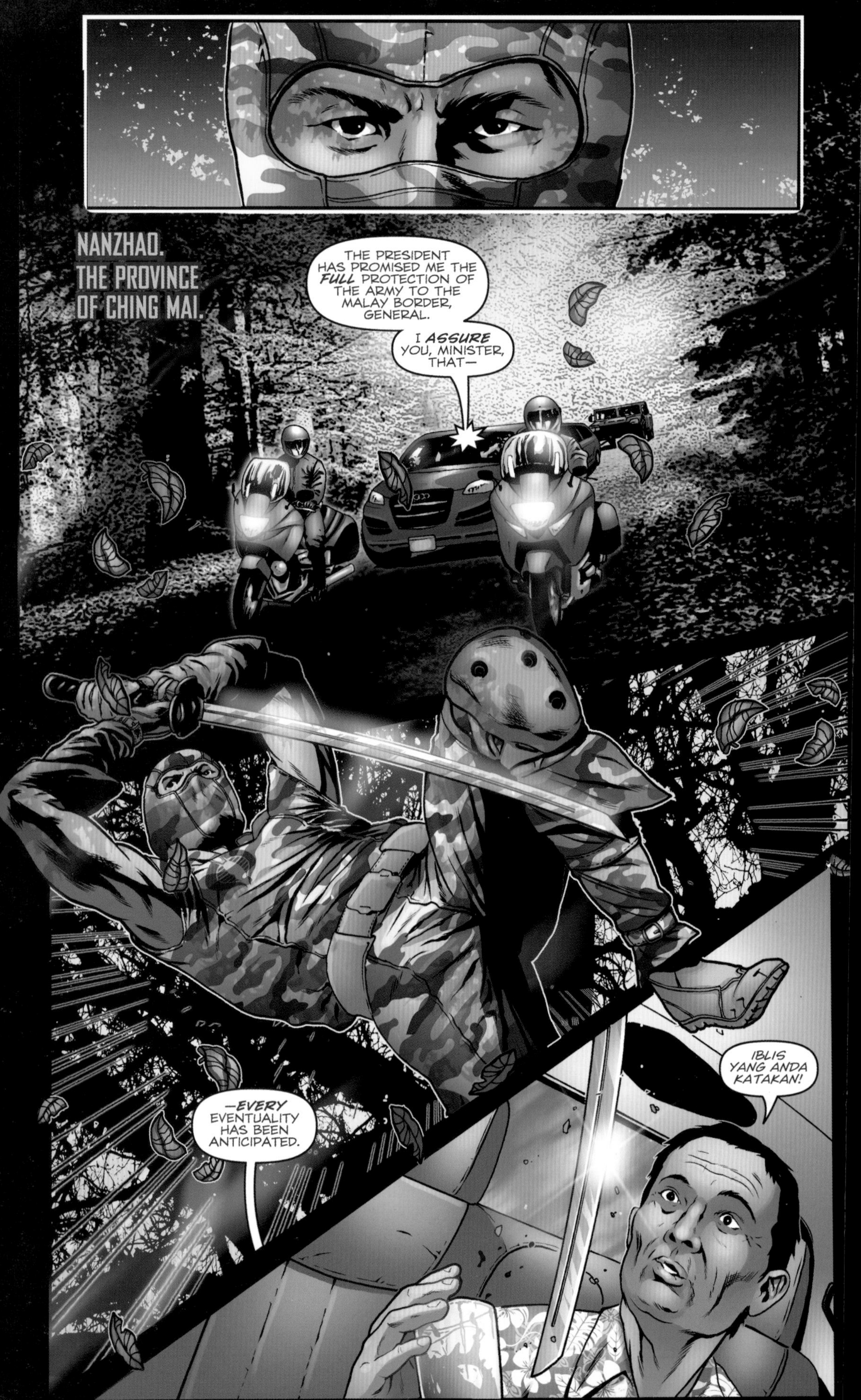
NANZHAO. THE PROVINCE OF CHING MAI.
THE PRESIDENT HAS PROMISED ME THE FULL PROTECTION OF THE ARMY TO THE MALAY BORDER, GENERAL.
I ASSURE YOU, MINISTER, THAT—
—EVERY EVENTUALITY HAS BEEN ANTICIPATED.
IBLIS YANG ANDA KATAKAN!

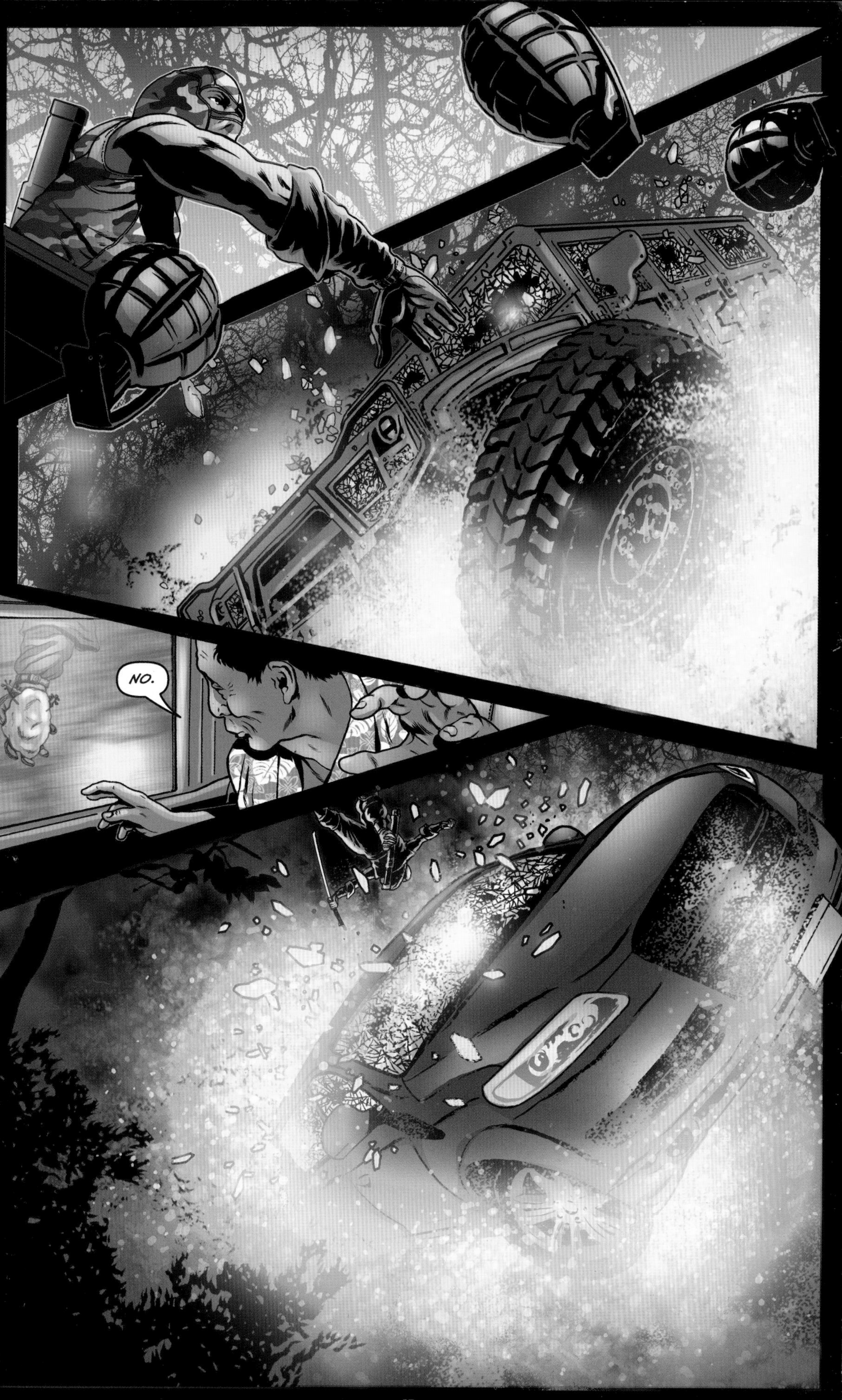
NO.

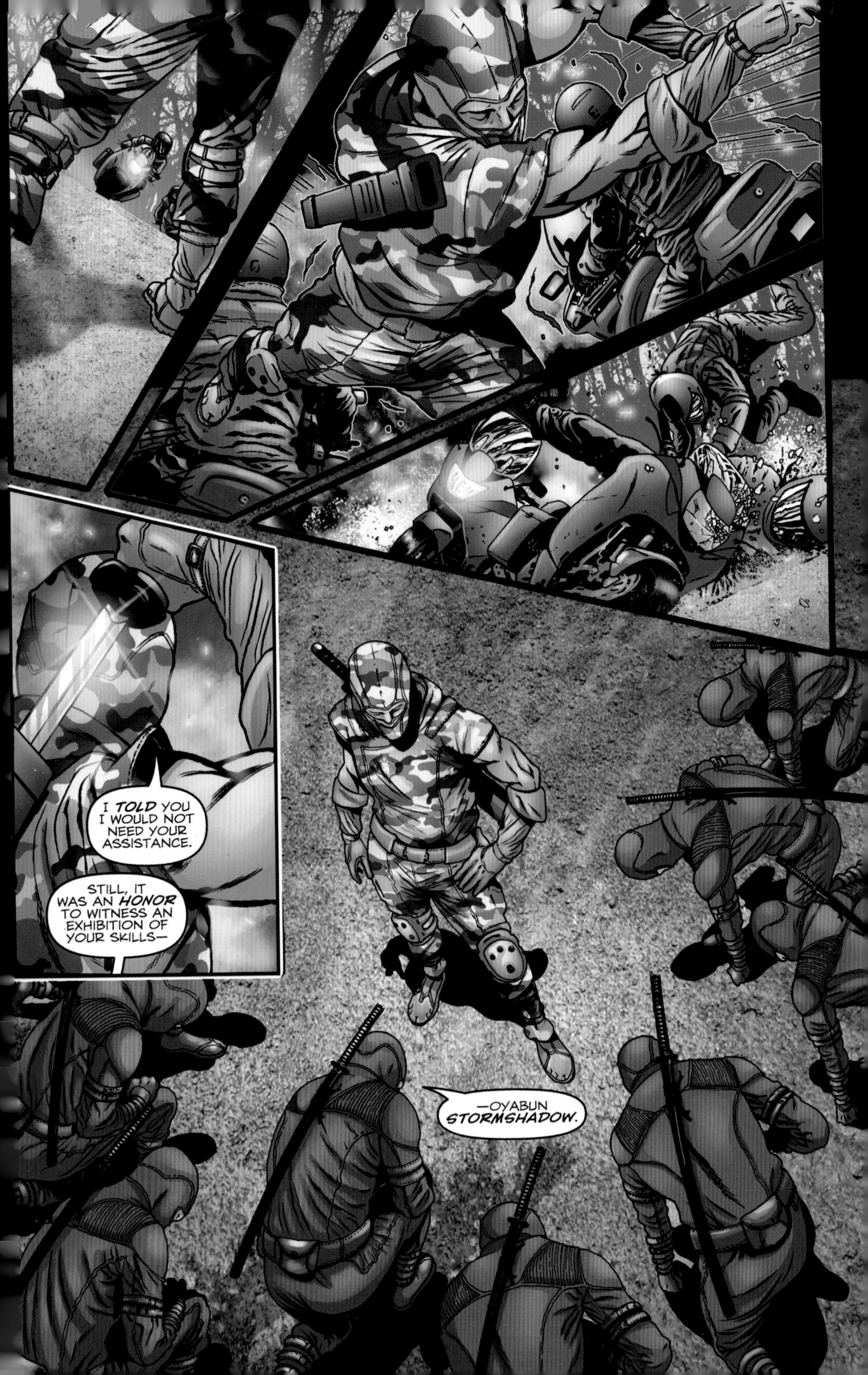
I TOLD YOU I WOULD NOT NEED YOUR ASSISTANCE.
STILL, IT WAS AN HONOR TO WITNESS AN EXHIBITION OF YOUR SKILLS—
—OYABUN STORMSHADOW.

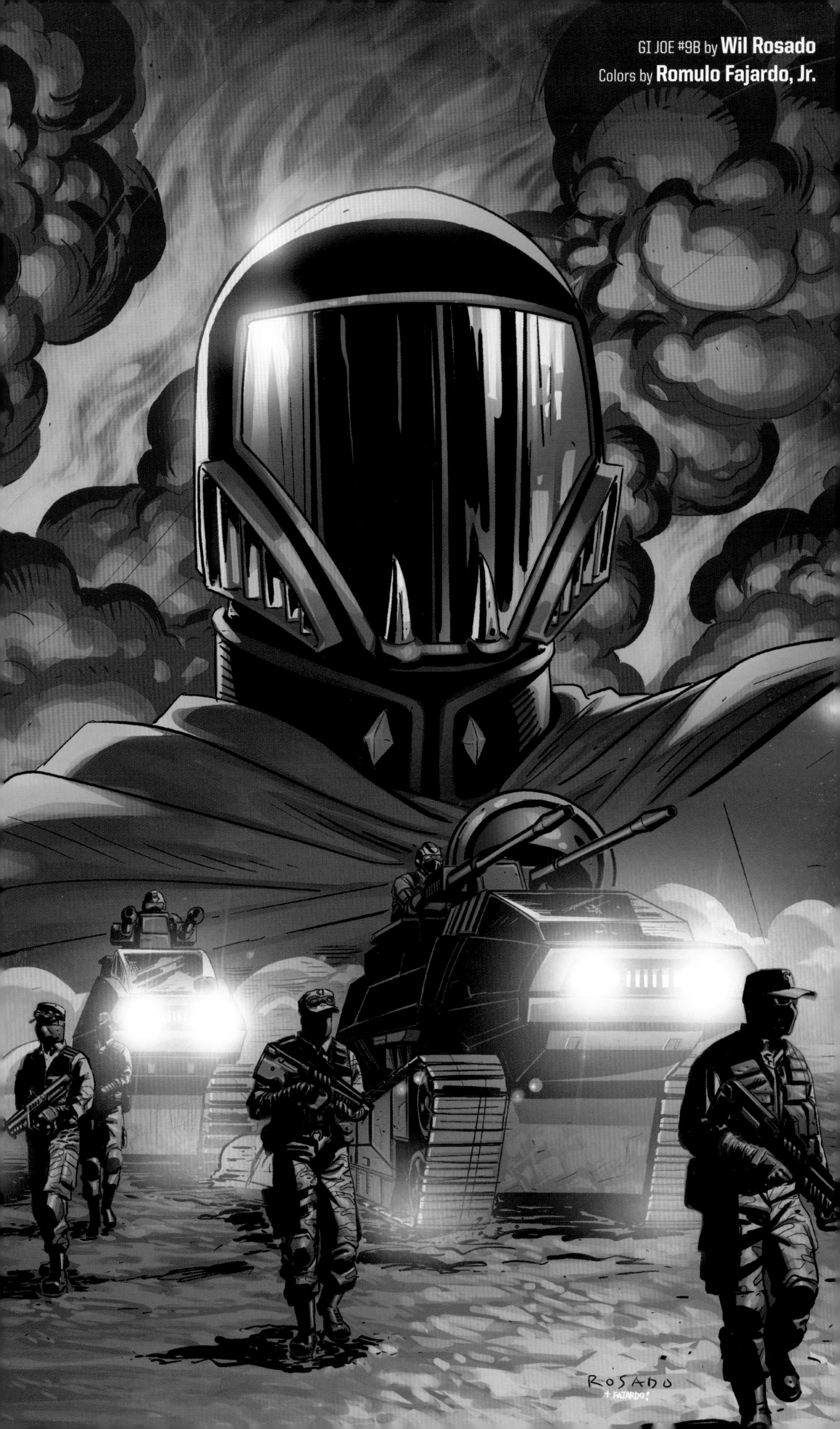
ROSADO
+ FAJARDO!

GI JOE #9B by **Wil Rosado**
Colors by **Romulo Fajardo, Jr.**

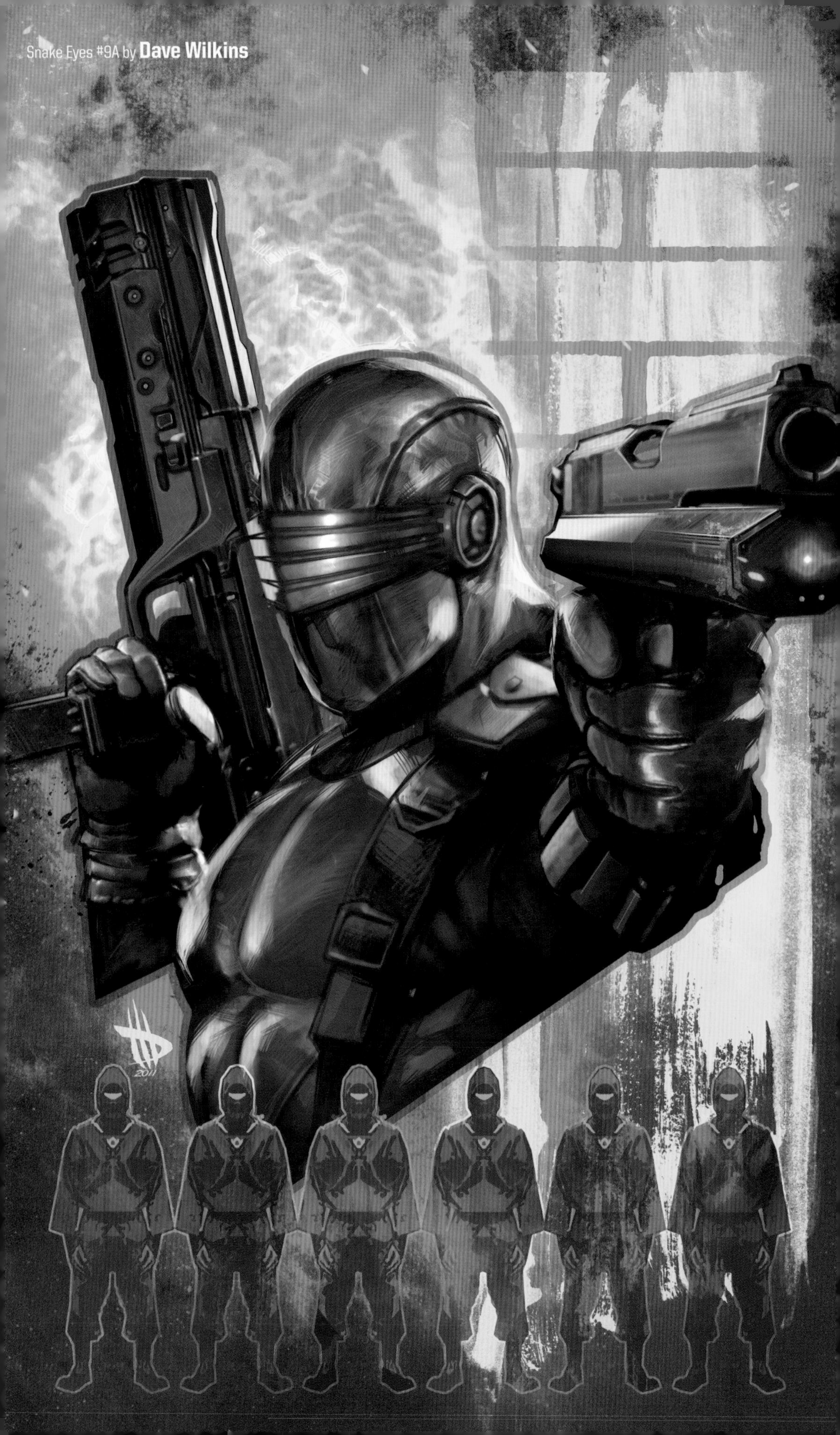

Snake Eyes #9A by **Dave Wilkins**

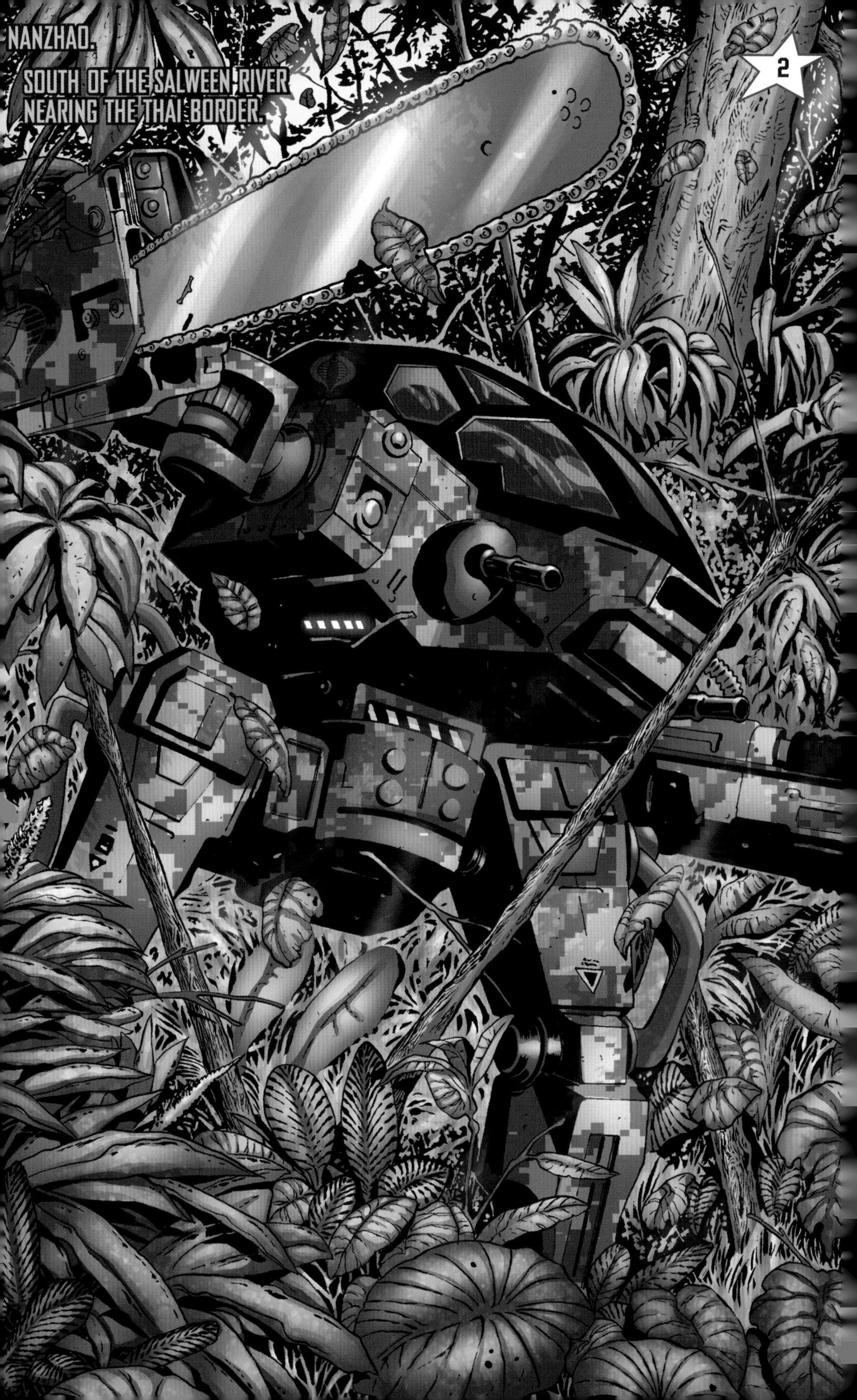
NANZHAO.
SOUTH OF THE SALWEEN RIVER NEARING THE THAI BORDER.
2

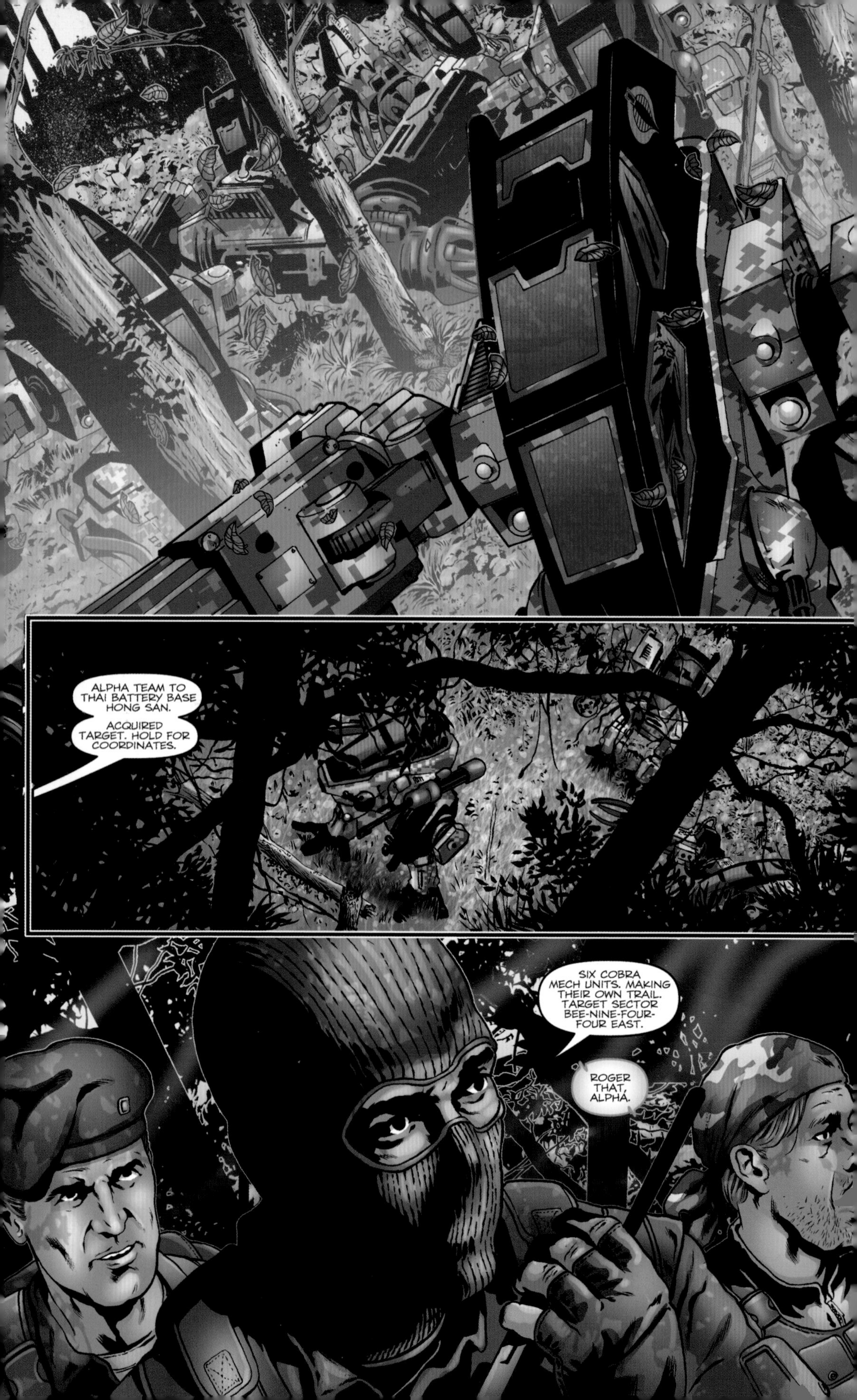
ALPHA TEAM TO THAI BATTERY BASE HONG SAN.
ACQUIRED TARGET. HOLD FOR COORDINATES.
SIX COBRA MECH UNITS. MAKING THEIR OWN TRAIL. TARGET SECTOR BEE-NINE-FOUR-FOUR EAST.
ROGER THAT, ALPHA.

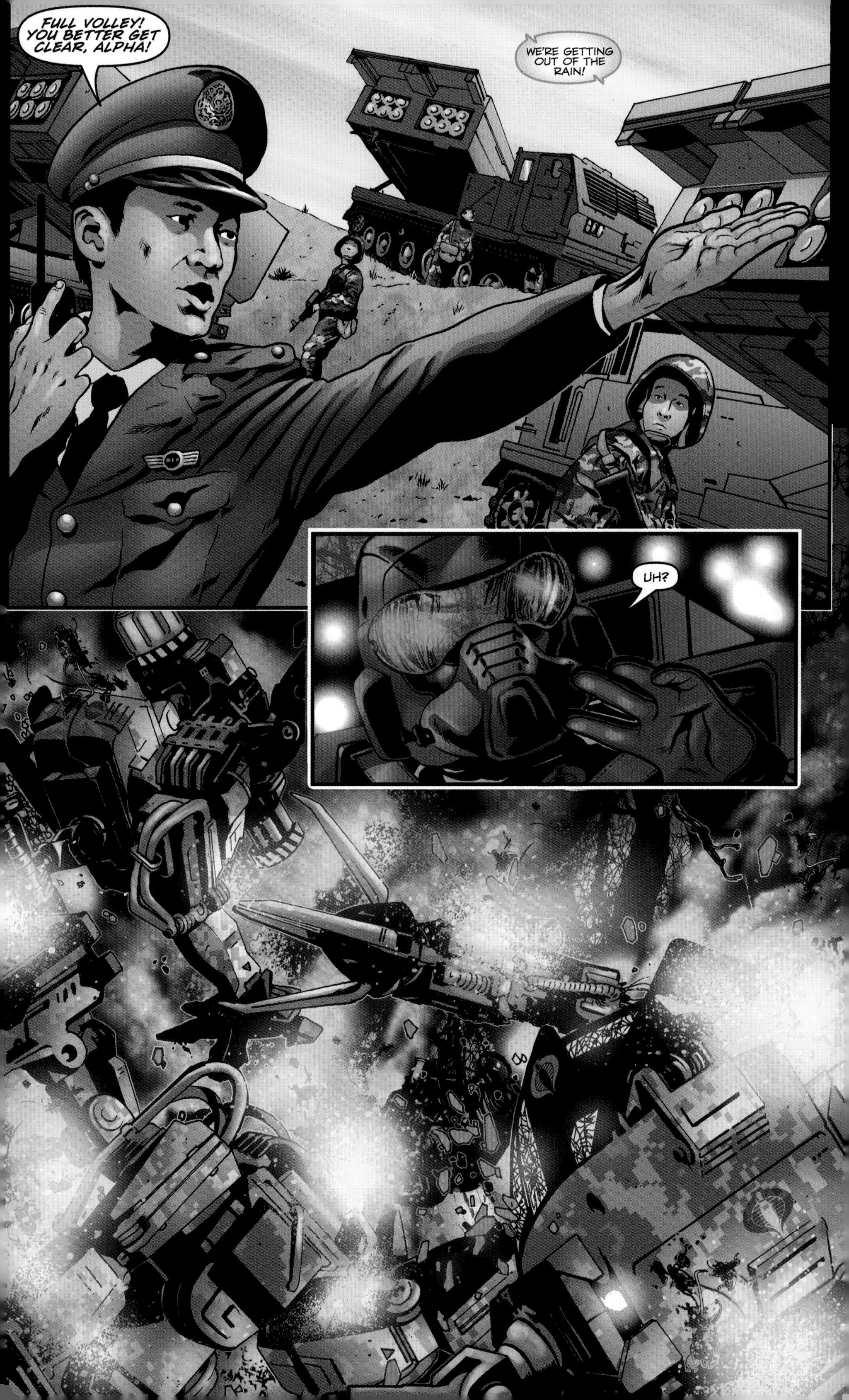
FULL VOLLEY! YOU BETTER GET CLEAR, ALPHA!
WE'RE GETTING OUT OF THE RAIN!
UH?

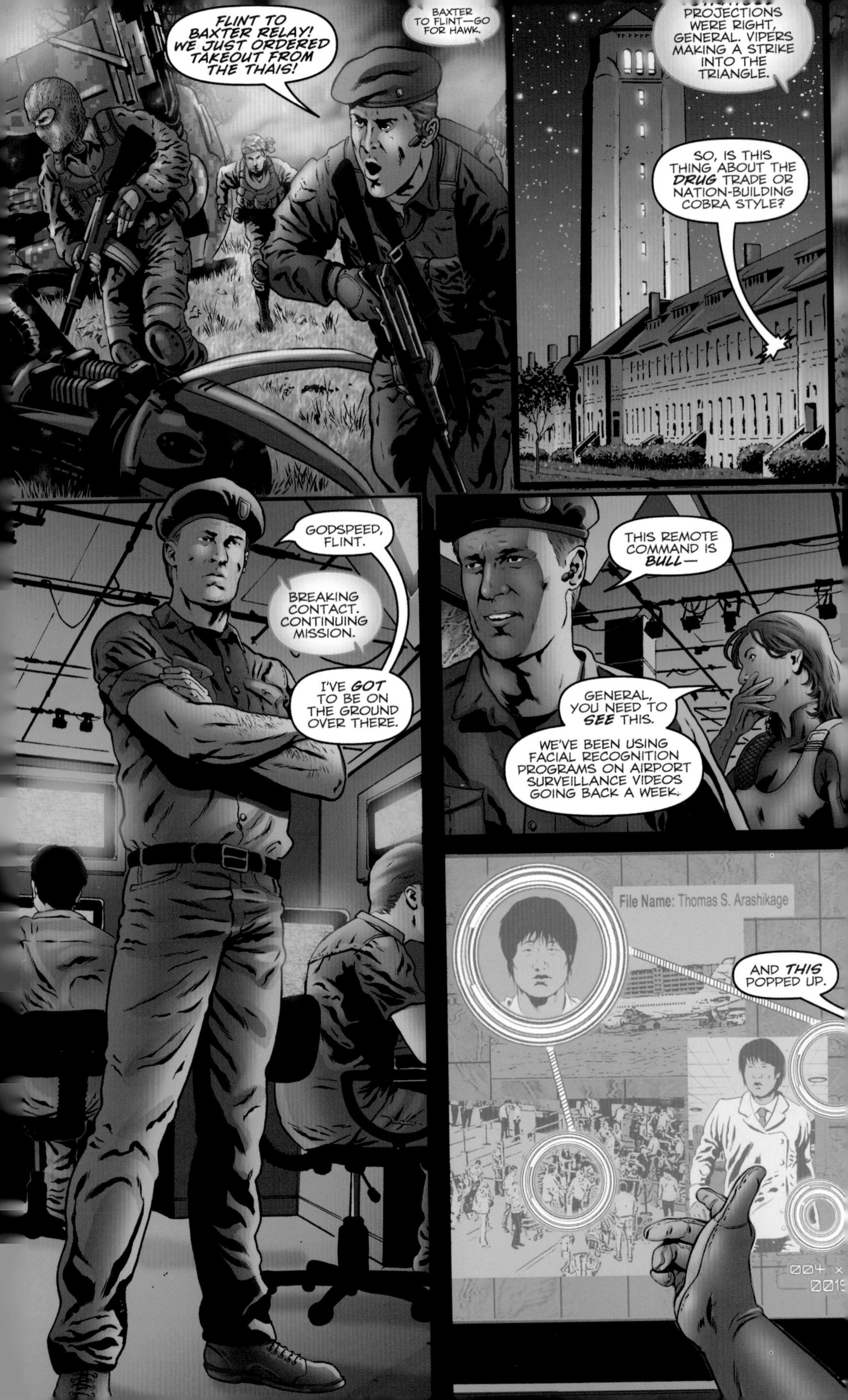
FLINT TO BAXTER RELAY! WE JUST ORDERED TAKEOUT FROM THE THAIS!
BAXTER TO FLINT—GO FOR HAWK.
PROJECTIONS WERE RIGHT, GENERAL. VIPERS MAKING A STRIKE INTO THE TRIANGLE.
SO, IS THIS THING ABOUT THE DRUG TRADE OR NATION-BUILDING COBRA STYLE?
GODSPEED, FLINT.
BREAKING CONTACT. CONTINUING MISSION.
I'VE GOT TO BE ON THE GROUND OVER THERE.
THIS REMOTE COMMAND IS BULL—
GENERAL, YOU NEED TO SEE THIS.
WE'VE BEEN USING FACIAL RECOGNITION PROGRAMS ON AIRPORT SURVEILLANCE VIDEOS GOING BACK A WEEK.
File Name: Thomas S. Arashikage
AND THIS POPPED UP.

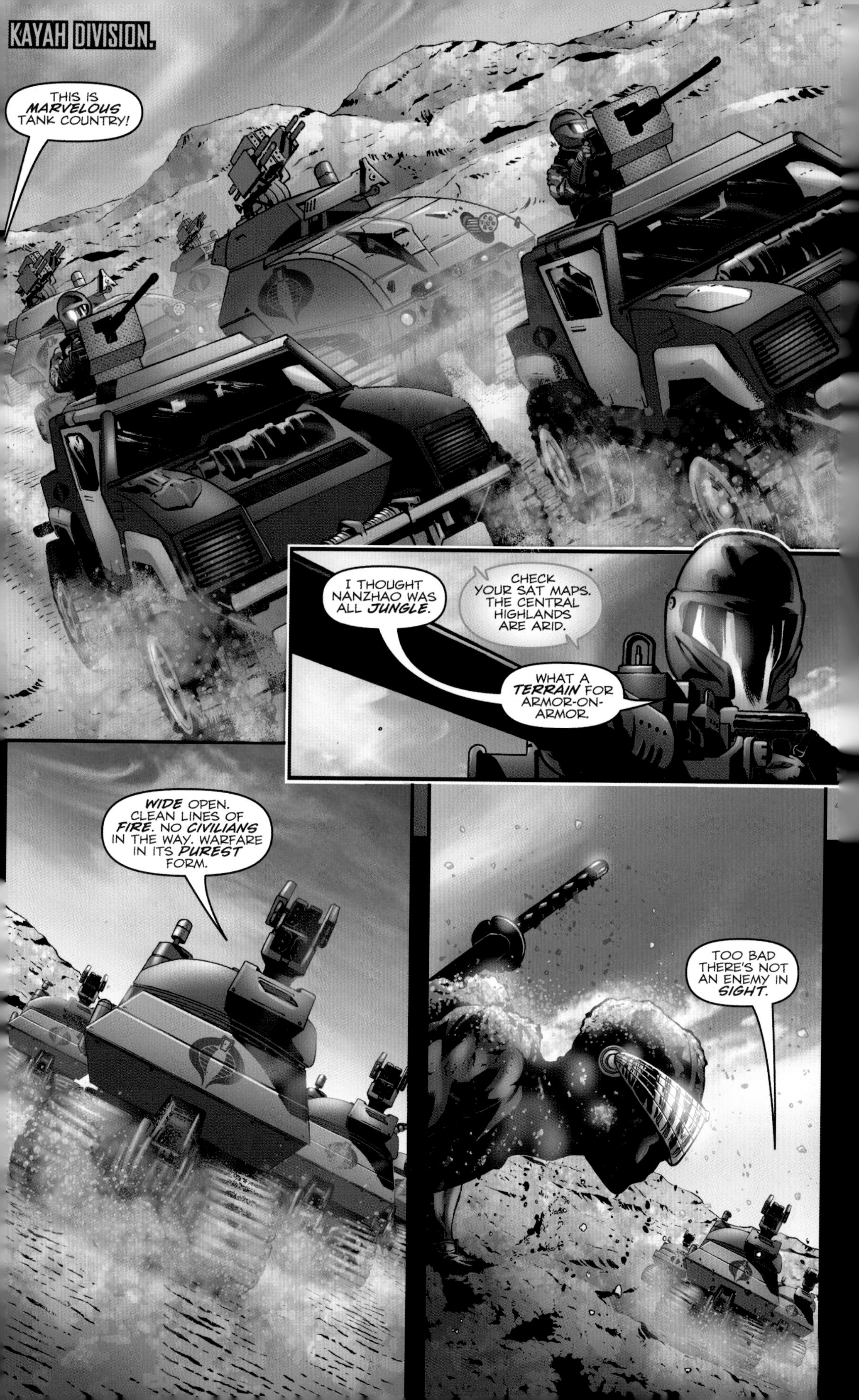
KAYAH DIVISION.
THIS IS MARVELOUS TANK COUNTRY!
I THOUGHT NANZHAO WAS ALL JUNGLE.
CHECK YOUR SAT MAPS. THE CENTRAL HIGHLANDS ARE ARID.
WHAT A TERRAIN FOR ARMOR-ON-ARMOR.
WIDE OPEN. CLEAN LINES OF FIRE. NO CIVILIANS IN THE WAY. WARFARE IN ITS PUREST FORM.
TOO BAD THERE'S NOT AN ENEMY IN SIGHT.

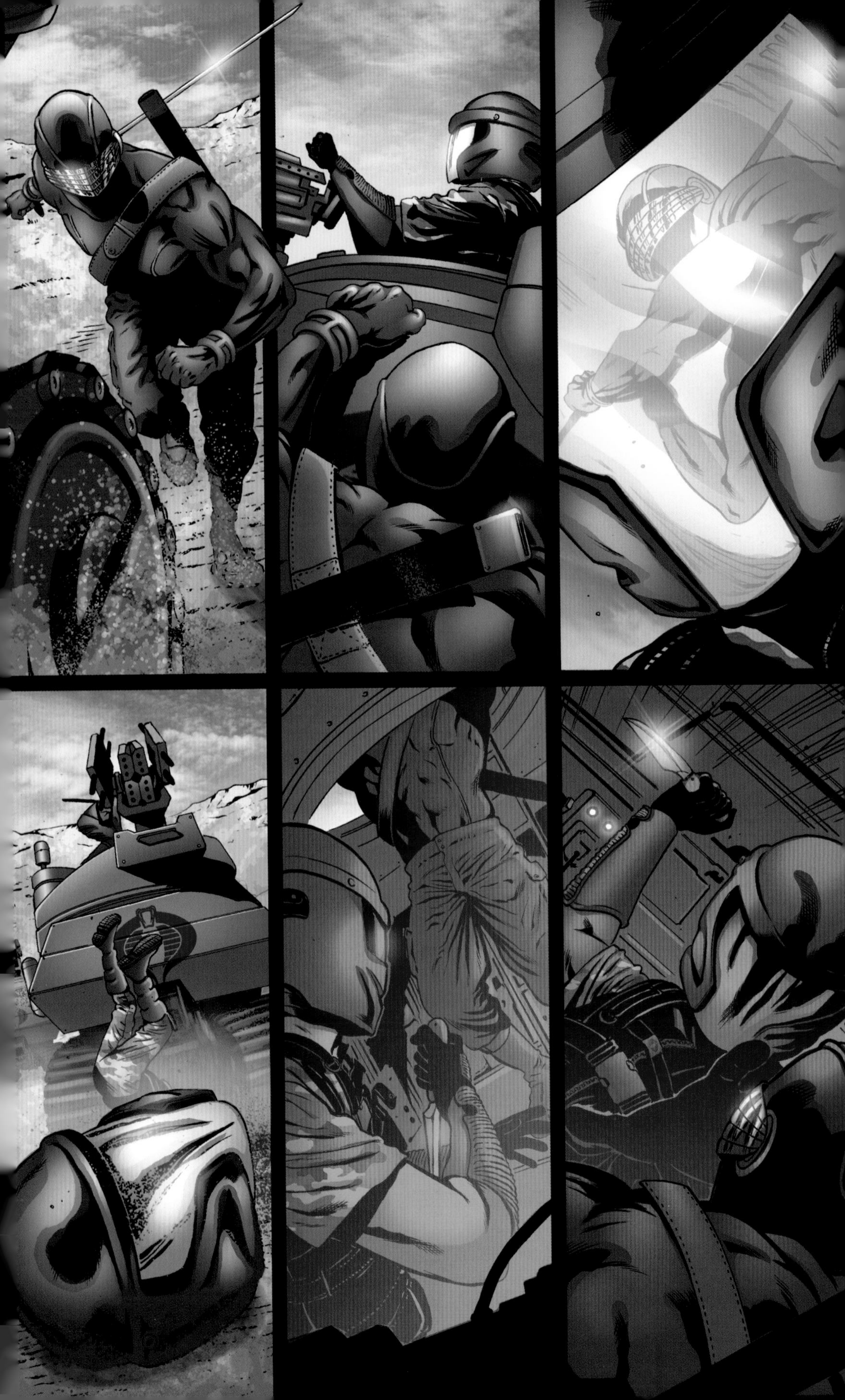

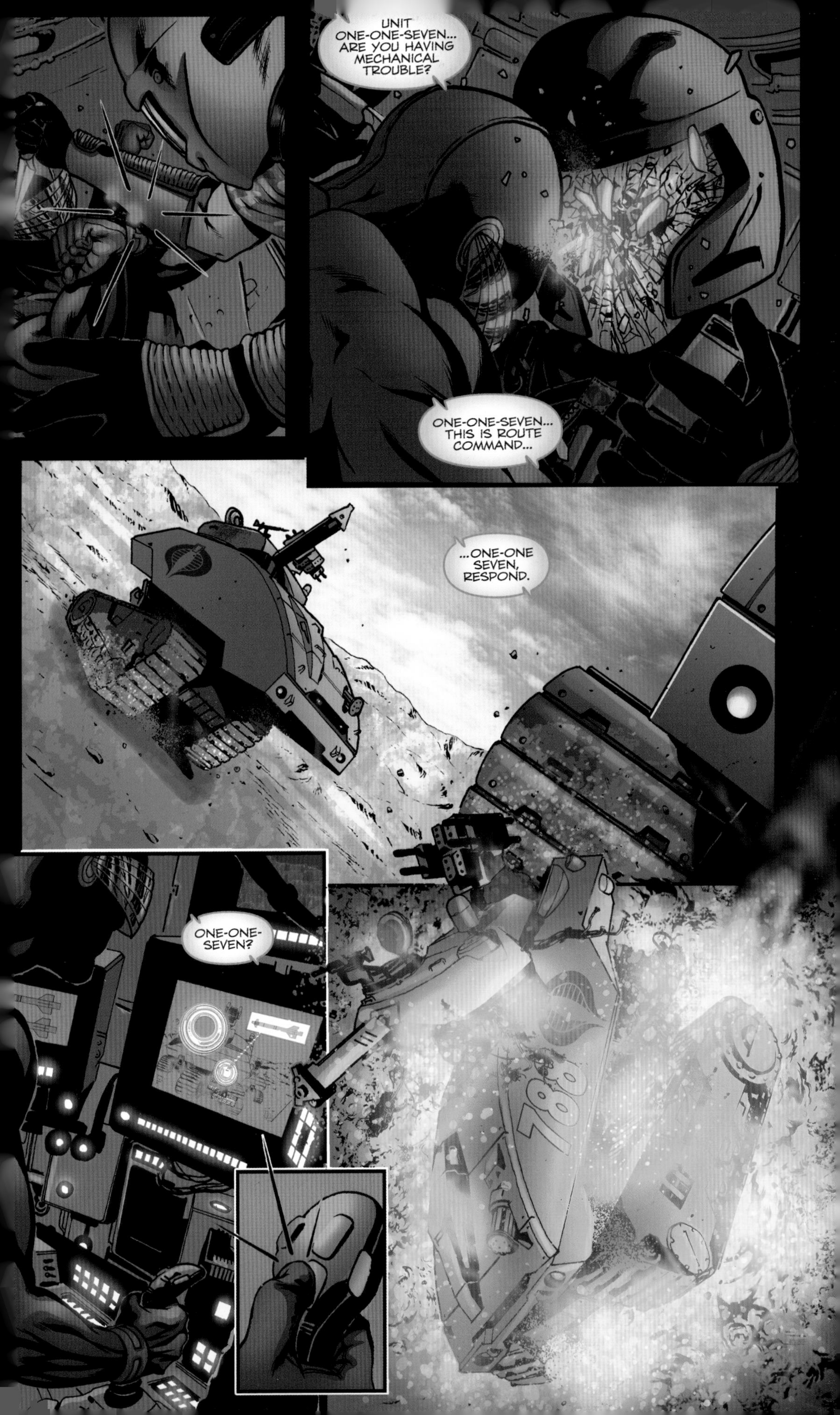
UNIT ONE-ONE-SEVEN... ARE YOU HAVING MECHANICAL TROUBLE?
ONE-ONE-SEVEN... THIS IS ROUTE COMMAND...
...ONE-ONE SEVEN, RESPOND.
ONE-ONE-SEVEN?

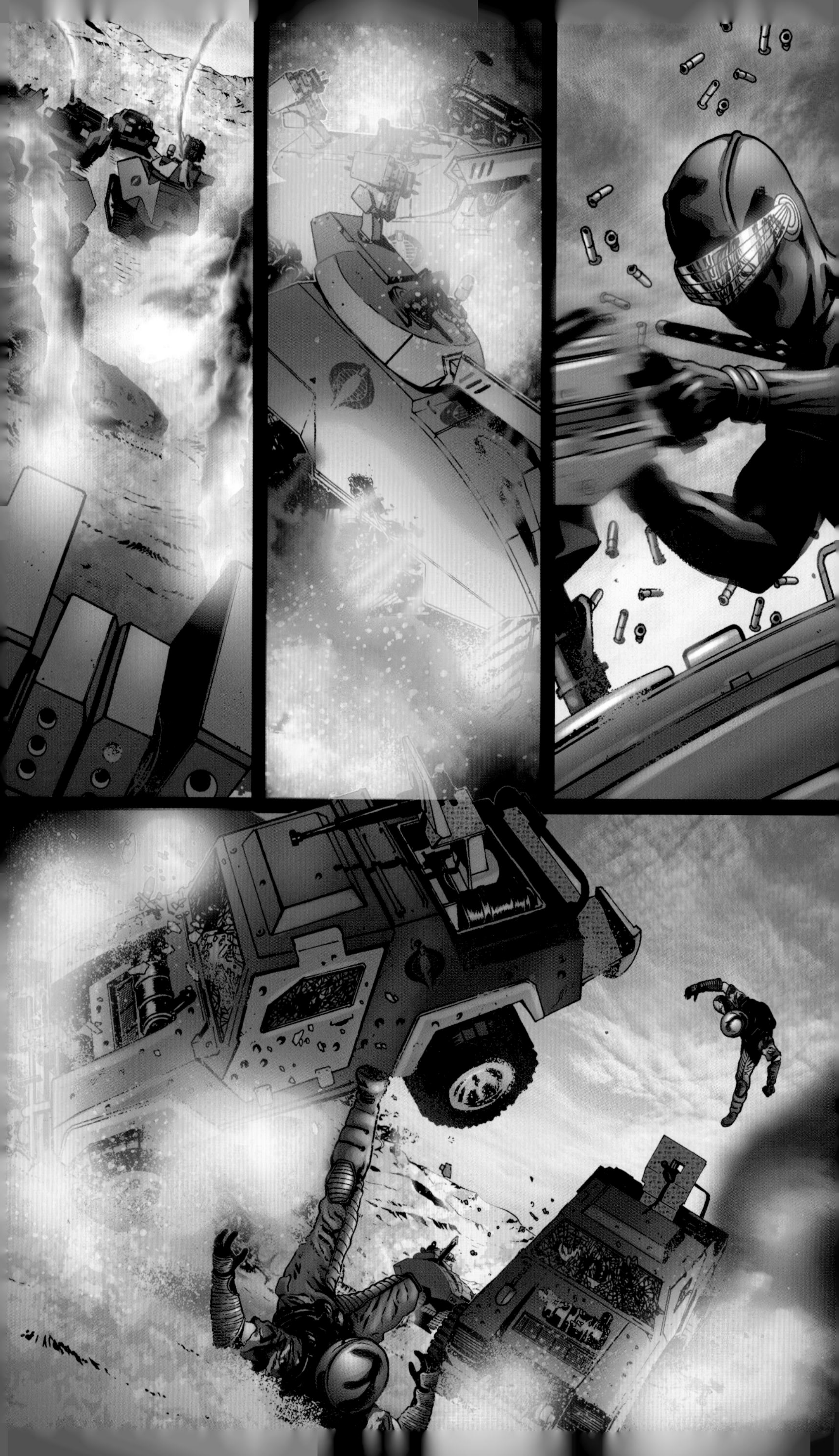

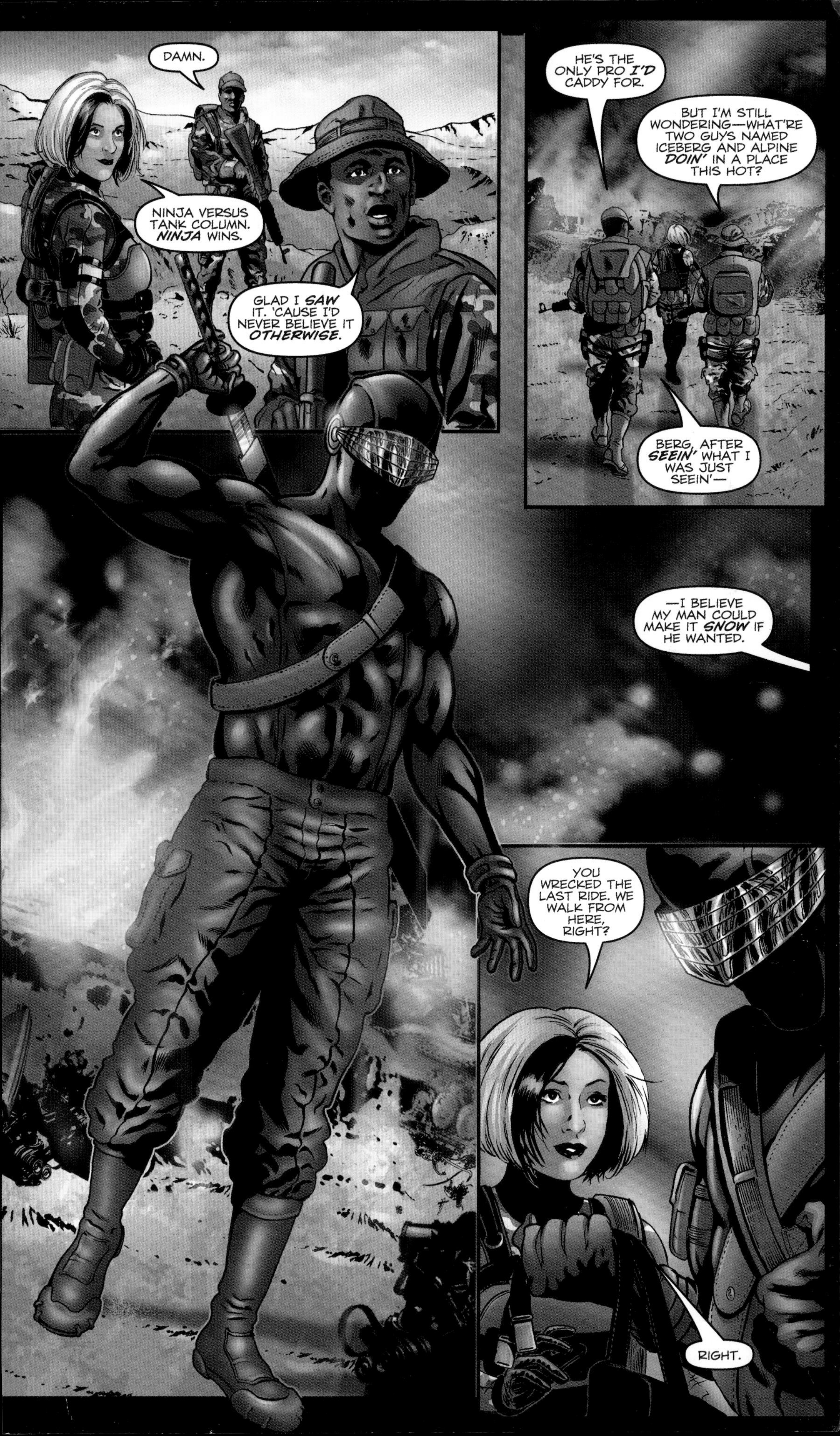
DAMN.
NINJA VERSUS TANK COLUMN. NINJA WINS.
GLAD I SAW IT. 'CAUSE I'D NEVER BELIEVE IT OTHERWISE.
HE'S THE ONLY PRO I'D CADDY FOR.
BUT I'M STILL WONDERING—WHAT'RE TWO GUYS NAMED ICEBERG AND ALPINE DOIN' IN A PLACE THIS HOT?
BERG, AFTER SEEIN' WHAT I WAS JUST SEEIN'—
—I BELIEVE MY MAN COULD MAKE IT SNOW IF HE WANTED.
YOU WRECKED THE LAST RIDE. WE WALK FROM HERE, RIGHT?
RIGHT.

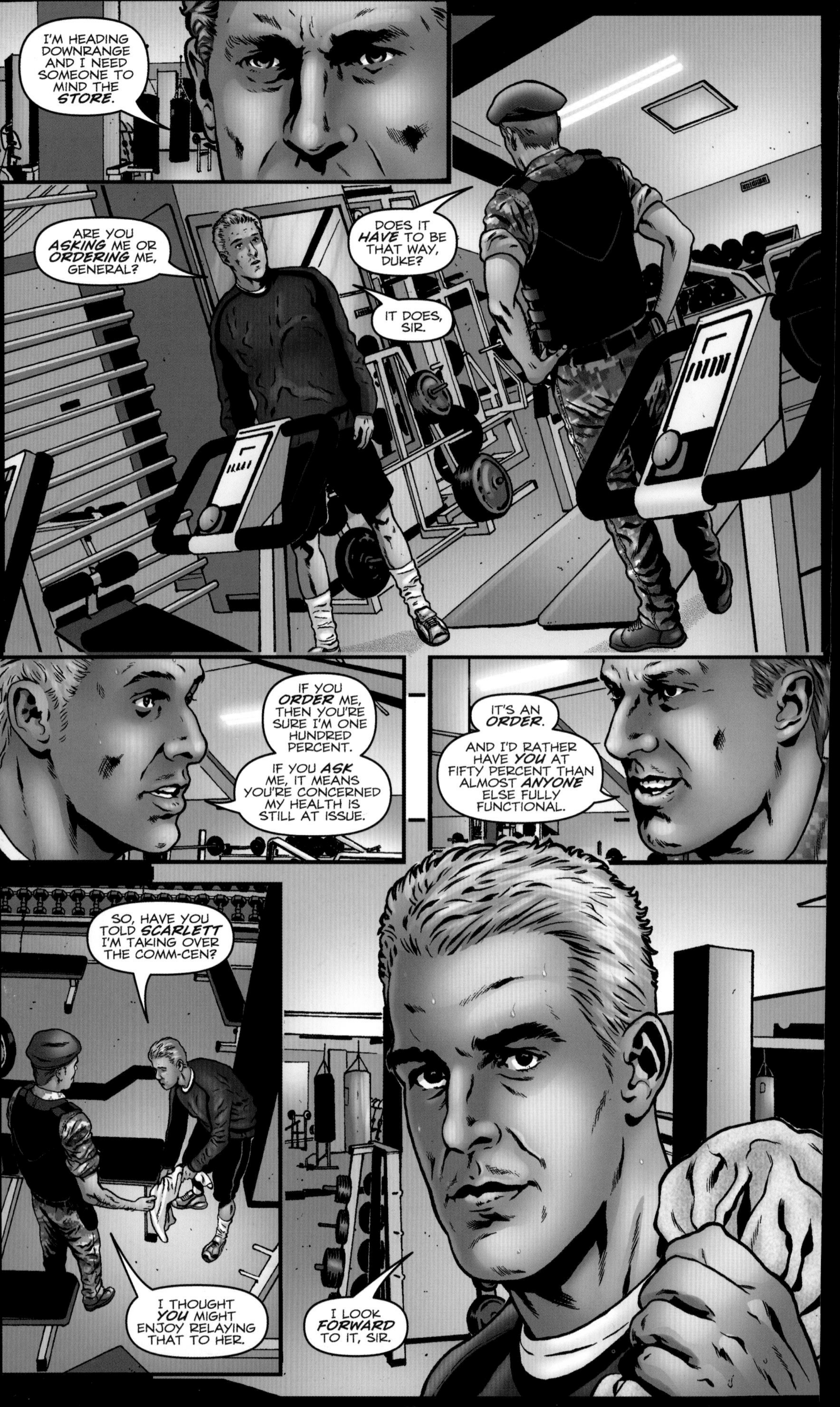
I'M HEADING DOWNRANGE AND I NEED SOMEONE TO MIND THE STORE.
ARE YOU ASKING ME OR ORDERING ME, GENERAL?
DOES IT HAVE TO BE THAT WAY, DUKE?
IT DOES, SIR.
IF YOU ORDER ME, THEN YOU'RE SURE I'M ONE HUNDRED PERCENT.
IF YOU ASK ME, IT MEANS YOU'RE CONCERNED MY HEALTH IS STILL AT ISSUE.
IT'S AN ORDER.
AND I'D RATHER HAVE YOU AT FIFTY PERCENT THAN ALMOST ANYONE ELSE FULLY FUNCTIONAL.
SO, HAVE YOU TOLD SCARLETT I'M TAKING OVER THE COMM-CEN?
I THOUGHT YOU MIGHT ENJOY RELAYING THAT TO HER.
I LOOK FORWARD TO IT, SIR.

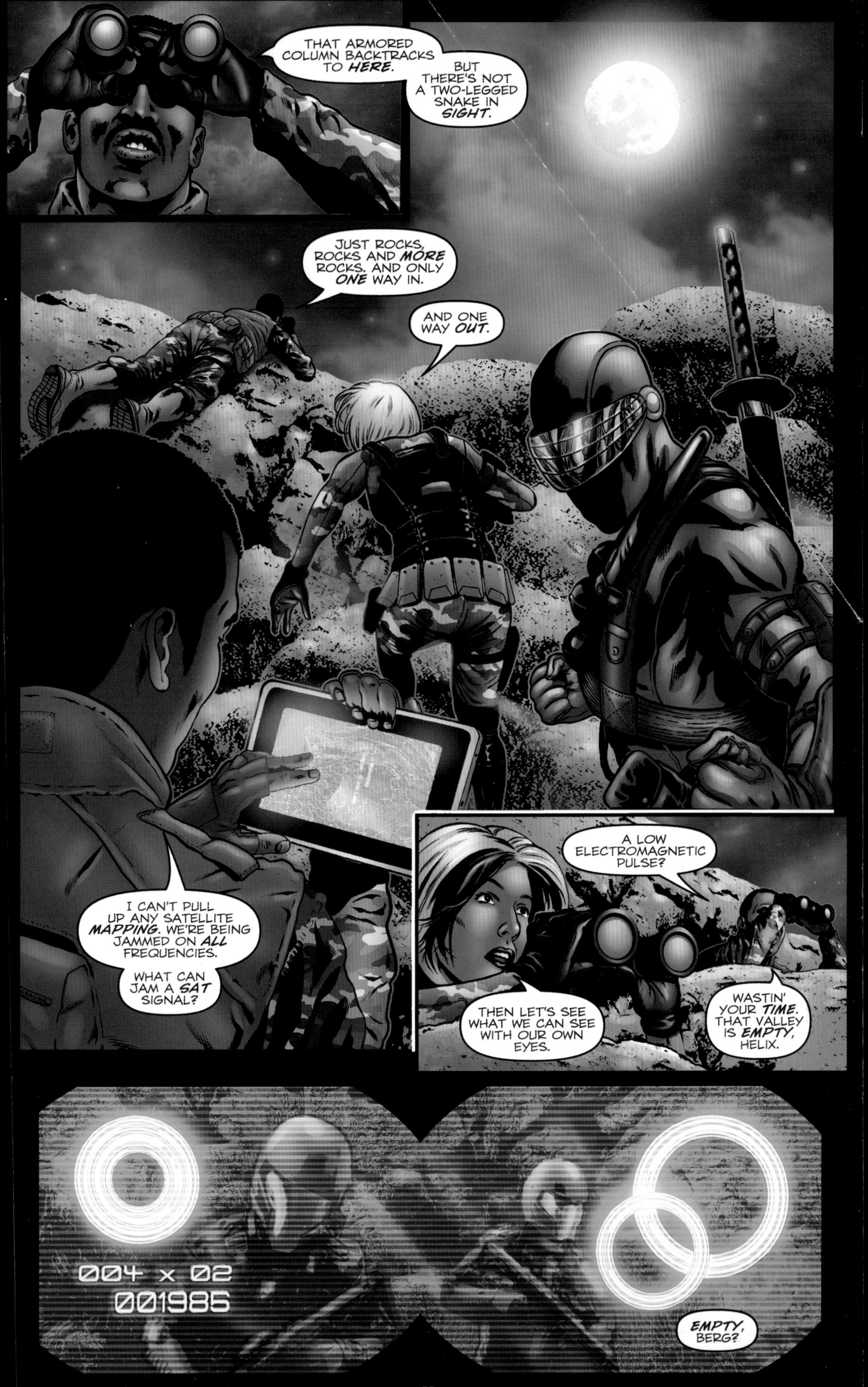
THAT ARMORED COLUMN BACKTRACKS TO *HERE*.
BUT THERE'S NOT A TWO-LEGGED SNAKE IN *SIGHT*.
JUST ROCKS, ROCKS AND *MORE* ROCKS. AND ONLY *ONE* WAY IN.
AND ONE WAY *OUT*.
I CAN'T PULL UP ANY SATELLITE *MAPPING*. WE'RE BEING JAMMED ON *ALL* FREQUENCIES.
WHAT CAN JAM A *SAT* SIGNAL?
A LOW ELECTROMAGNETIC PULSE?
THEN LET'S SEE WHAT WE CAN SEE WITH OUR OWN EYES.
WASTIN' YOUR *TIME*. THAT VALLEY IS *EMPTY*, HELIX.
004 x 02
001985
EMPTY, BERG?

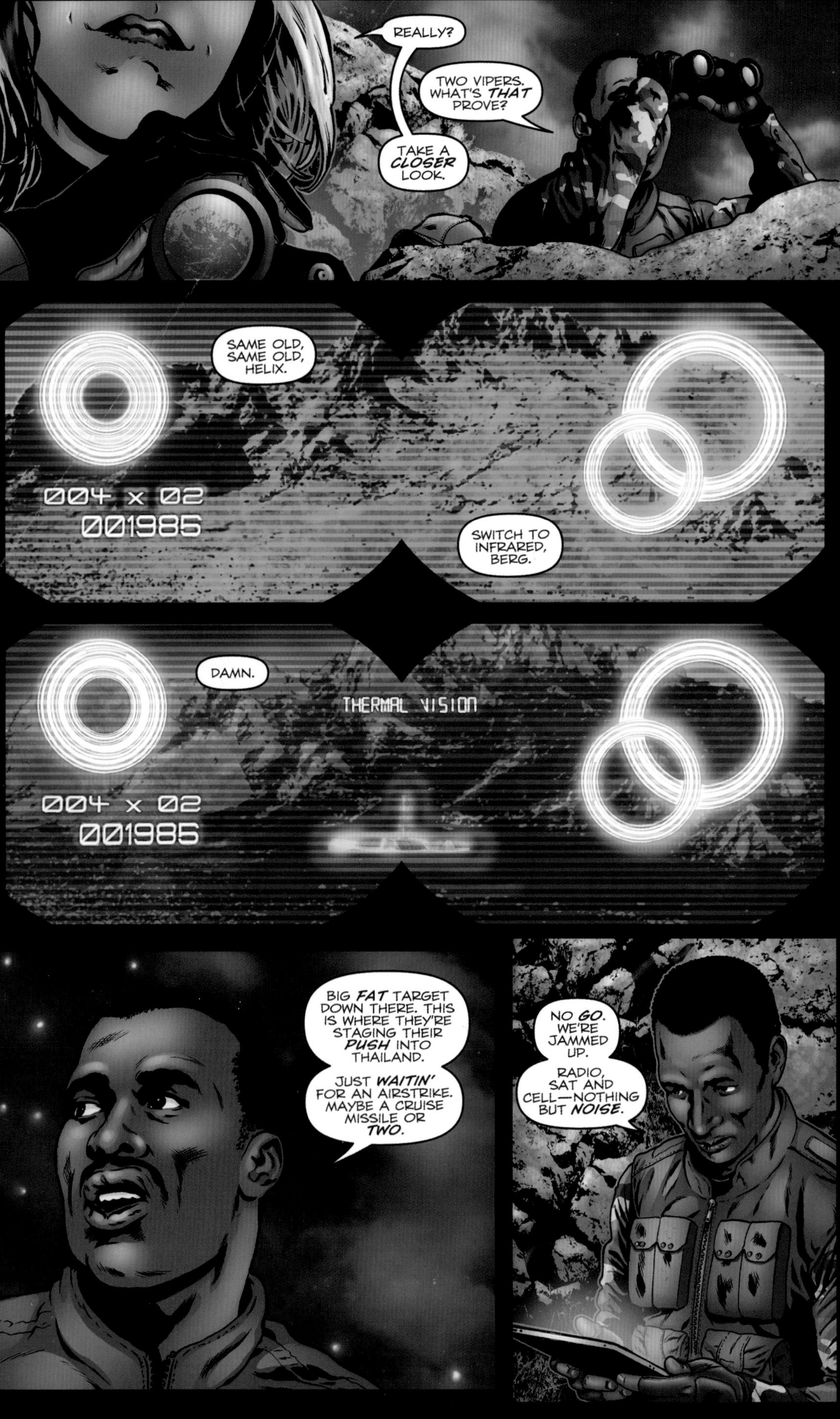
REALLY?
TWO VIPERS. WHAT'S THAT PROVE?
TAKE A CLOSER LOOK.
SAME OLD, SAME OLD, HELIX.
004 x 02
001985
SWITCH TO INFRARED, BERG.
DAMN.
THERMAL VISION
004 x 02
001985
BIG FAT TARGET DOWN THERE. THIS IS WHERE THEY'RE STAGING THEIR PUSH INTO THAILAND.
JUST WAITIN' FOR AN AIRSTRIKE. MAYBE A CRUISE MISSILE OR TWO.
NO GO. WE'RE JAMMED UP.
RADIO, SAT AND CELL—NOTHING BUT NOISE.

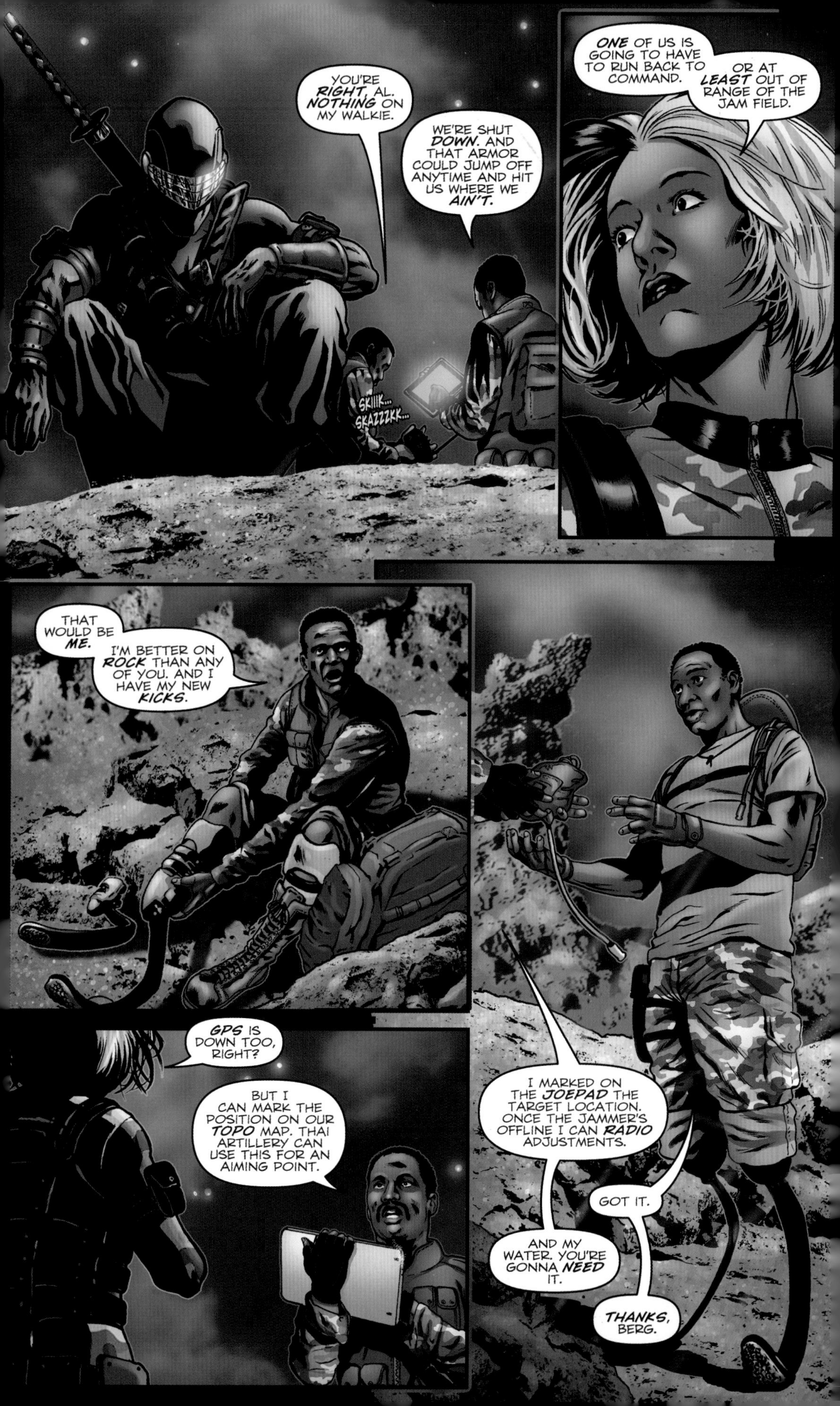

YOU'RE RIGHT, AL. NOTHING ON MY WALKIE.
WE'RE SHUT DOWN. AND THAT ARMOR COULD JUMP OFF ANYTIME AND HIT US WHERE WE AIN'T.
SKIIIK... SKAZZZZKK...
ONE OF US IS GOING TO HAVE TO RUN BACK TO COMMAND.
OR AT LEAST OUT OF RANGE OF THE JAM FIELD.
THAT WOULD BE ME.
I'M BETTER ON ROCK THAN ANY OF YOU. AND I HAVE MY NEW KICKS.
GPS IS DOWN TOO, RIGHT?
BUT I CAN MARK THE POSITION ON OUR TOPO MAP. THAI ARTILLERY CAN USE THIS FOR AN AIMING POINT.
I MARKED ON THE JOEPAD THE TARGET LOCATION. ONCE THE JAMMER'S OFFLINE I CAN RADIO ADJUSTMENTS.
GOT IT.
AND MY WATER. YOU'RE GONNA NEED IT.
THANKS, BERG.

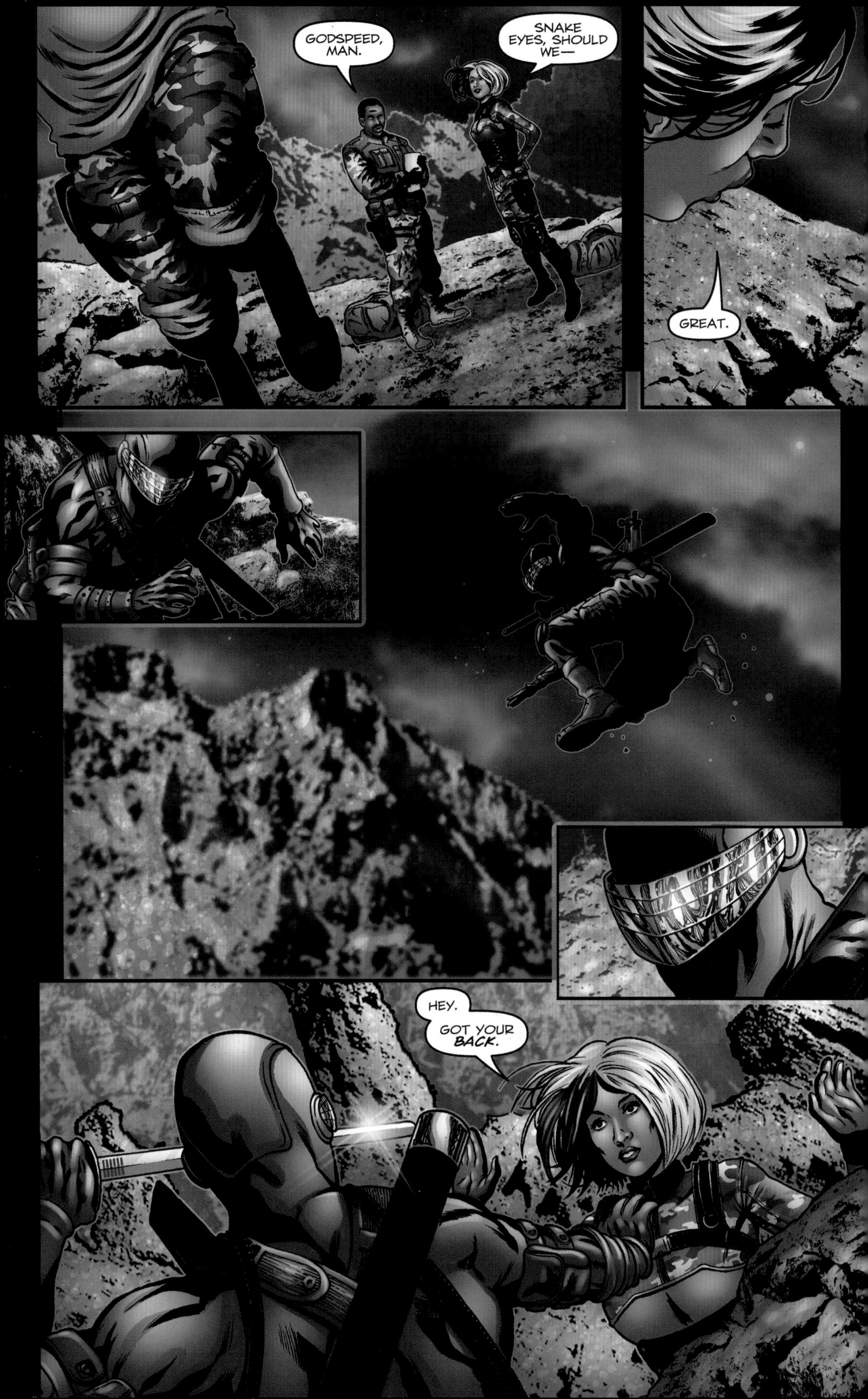
GODSPEED, MAN.
SNAKE EYES, SHOULD WE—
GREAT.
HEY.
GOT YOUR BACK.

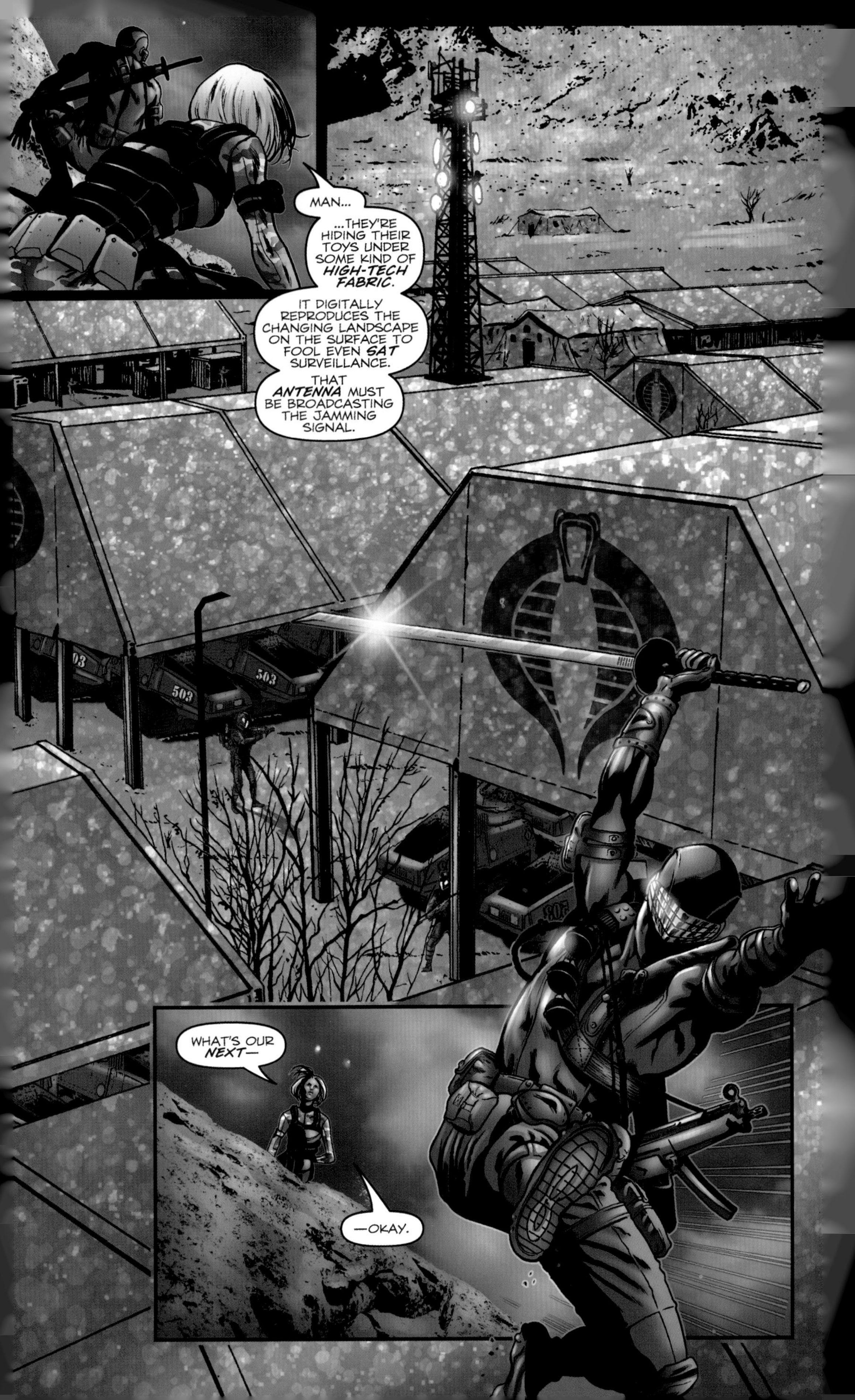
MAN...
...THEY'RE HIDING THEIR TOYS UNDER SOME KIND OF **HIGH-TECH FABRIC**.
IT DIGITALLY REPRODUCES THE CHANGING LANDSCAPE ON THE SURFACE TO FOOL EVEN **SAT** SURVEILLANCE.
THAT **ANTENNA** MUST BE BROADCASTING THE JAMMING SIGNAL.
503
503
503
WHAT'S OUR **NEXT**—
—OKAY.

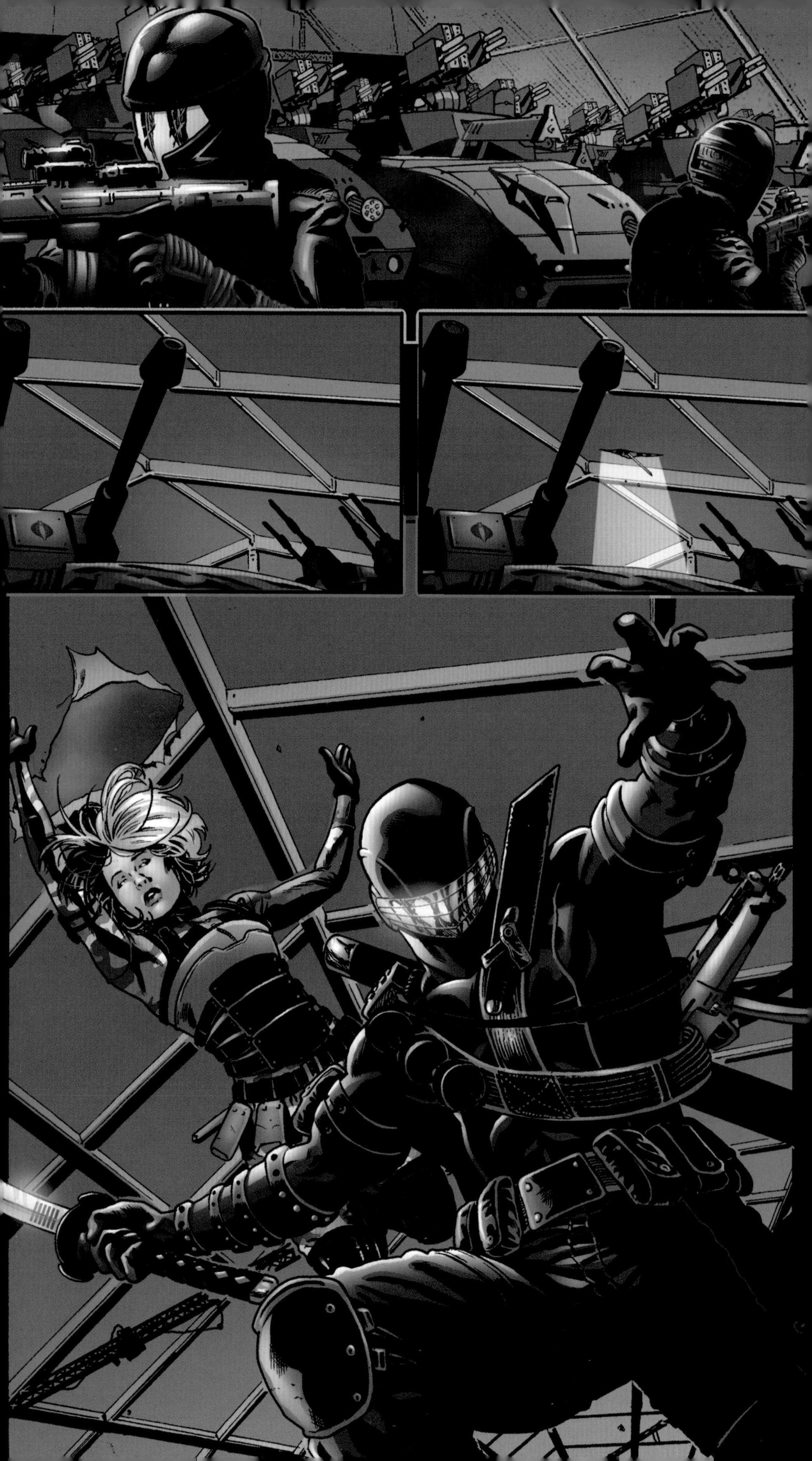

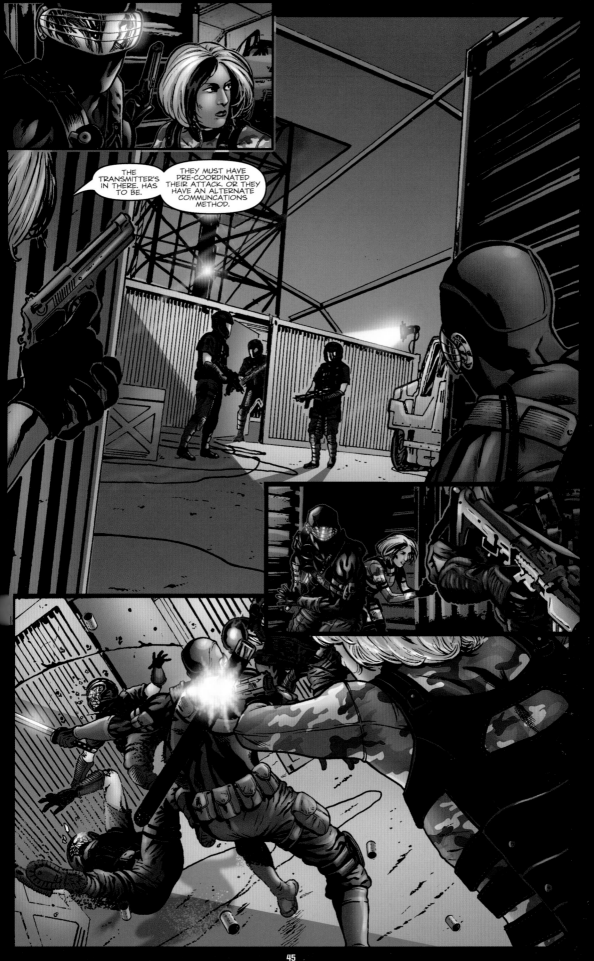

THE TRANSMITTER'S IN THERE. HAS TO BE.

THEY MUST HAVE PRE-COORDINATED THEIR ATTACK. OR THEY HAVE AN ALTERNATE COMMUNCATIONS METHOD.

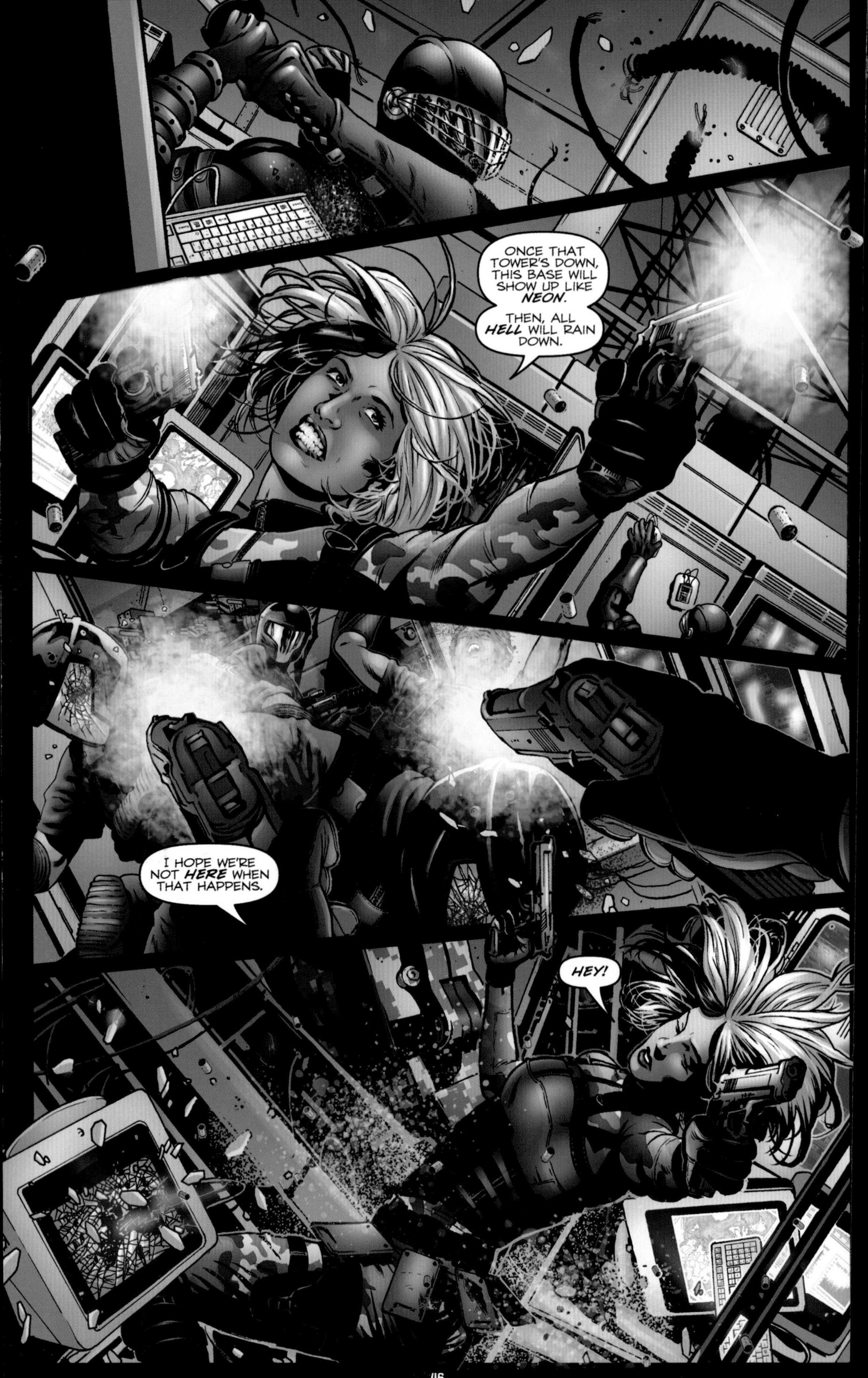
ONCE THAT TOWER'S DOWN, THIS BASE WILL SHOW UP LIKE **NEON**.
THEN, ALL **HELL** WILL RAIN DOWN.
I HOPE WE'RE NOT **HERE** WHEN THAT HAPPENS.
HEY!

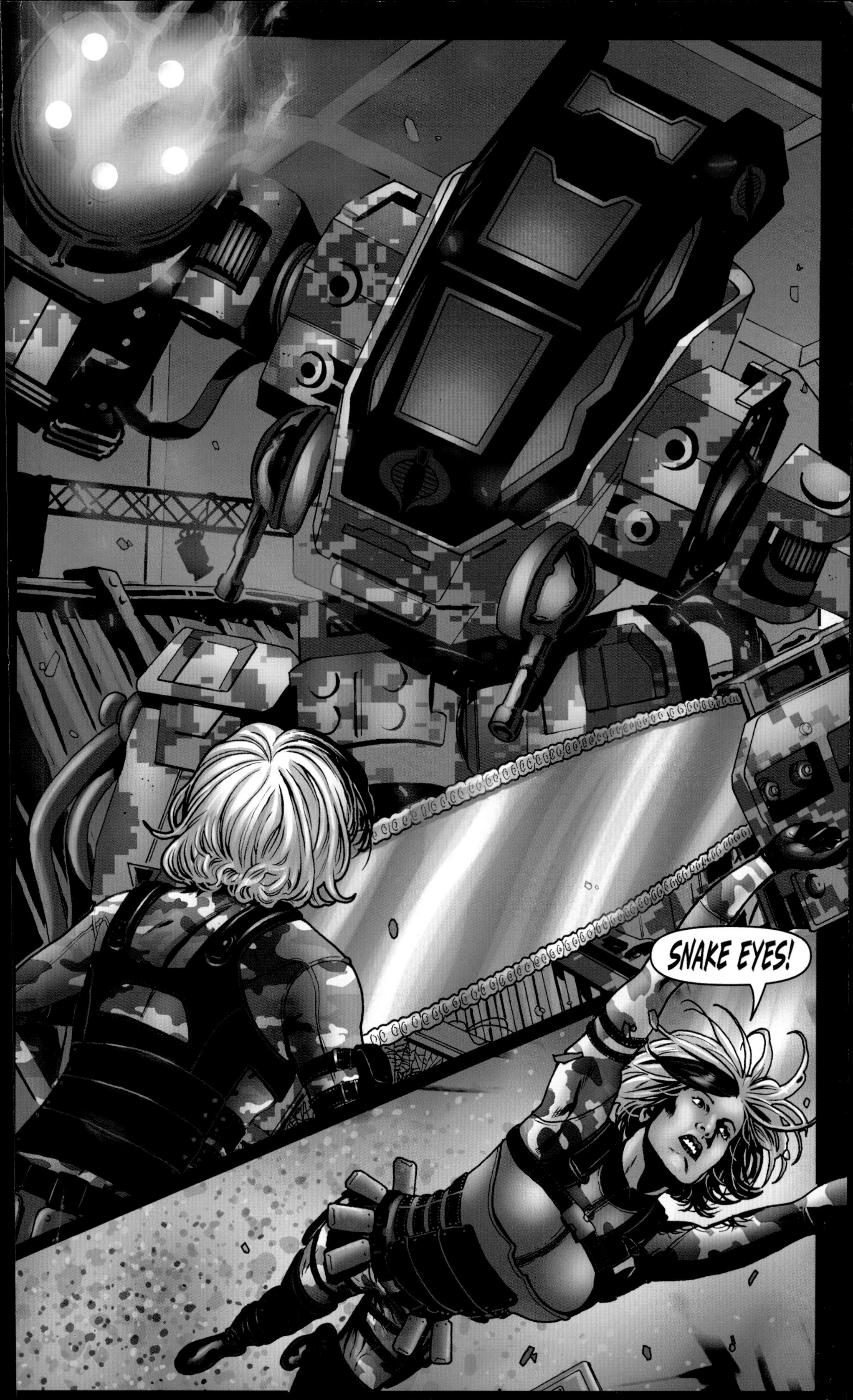
SNAKE EYES!

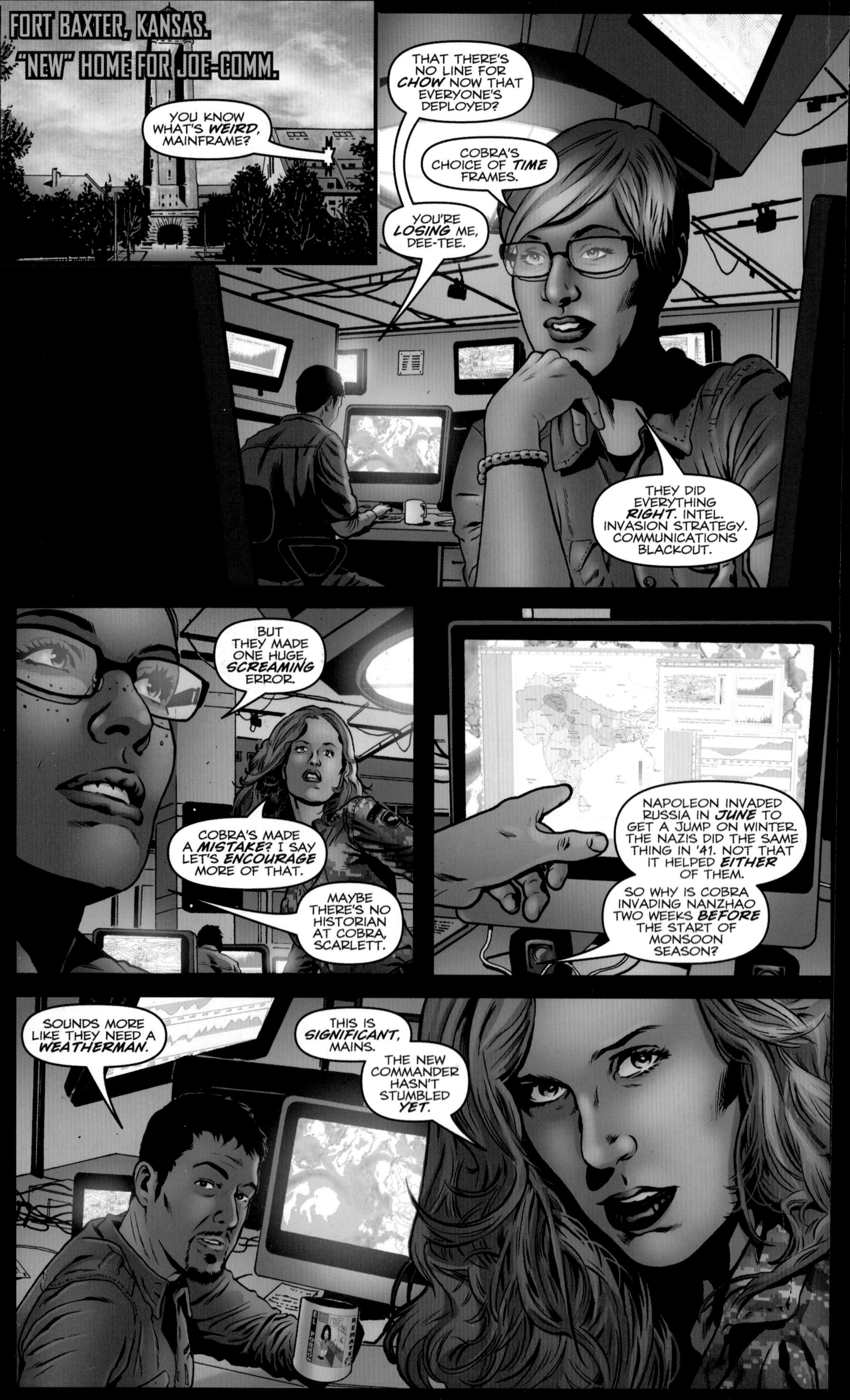
FORT BAXTER, KANSAS.
"NEW" HOME FOR JOE-COMM.
YOU KNOW WHAT'S WEIRD, MAINFRAME?
THAT THERE'S NO LINE FOR CHOW NOW THAT EVERYONE'S DEPLOYED?
COBRA'S CHOICE OF TIME FRAMES.
YOU'RE LOSING ME, DEE-TEE.
THEY DID EVERYTHING RIGHT. INTEL. INVASION STRATEGY. COMMUNICATIONS BLACKOUT.
BUT THEY MADE ONE HUGE SCREAMING ERROR.
COBRA'S MADE A MISTAKE? I SAY LET'S ENCOURAGE MORE OF THAT.
MAYBE THERE'S NO HISTORIAN AT COBRA, SCARLETT.
NAPOLEON INVADED RUSSIA IN JUNE TO GET A JUMP ON WINTER. THE NAZIS DID THE SAME THING IN '41. NOT THAT IT HELPED EITHER OF THEM.
SO WHY IS COBRA INVADING NANZHAO TWO WEEKS BEFORE THE START OF MONSOON SEASON?
SOUNDS MORE LIKE THEY NEED A WEATHERMAN.
THIS IS SIGNIFICANT, MAINS.
THE NEW COMMANDER HASN'T STUMBLED YET.

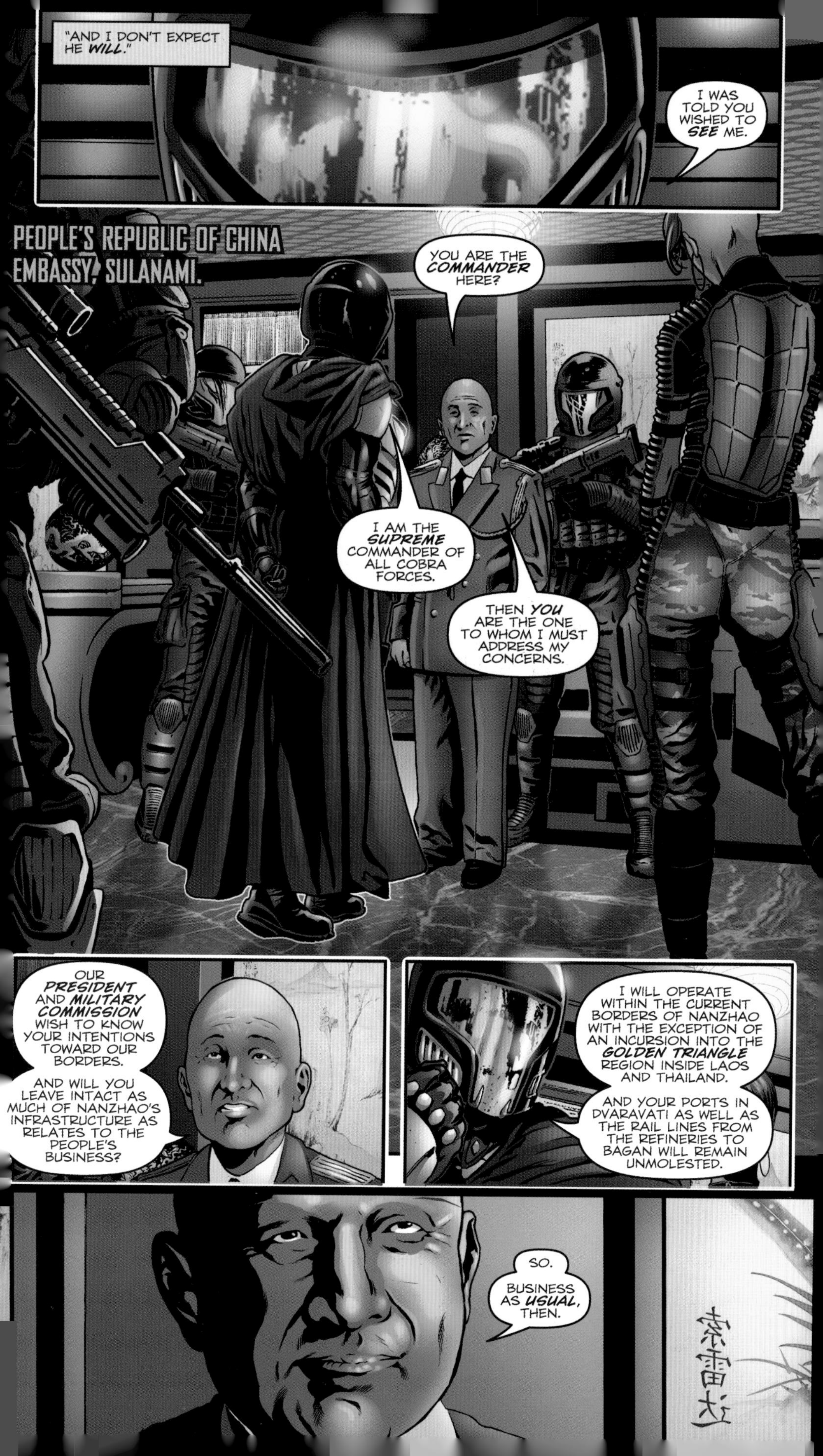

"AND I DON'T EXPECT HE *WILL*."
I WAS TOLD YOU WISHED TO *SEE* ME.
PEOPLE'S REPUBLIC OF CHINA EMBASSY, SULANAMI.
YOU ARE THE *COMMANDER* HERE?
I AM THE *SUPREME* COMMANDER OF ALL COBRA FORCES.
THEN *YOU* ARE THE ONE TO WHOM I MUST ADDRESS MY CONCERNS.
OUR *PRESIDENT* AND *MILITARY COMMISSION* WISH TO KNOW YOUR INTENTIONS TOWARD OUR BORDERS.
AND WILL YOU LEAVE INTACT AS MUCH OF NANZHAO'S INFRASTRUCTURE AS RELATES TO THE PEOPLE'S BUSINESS?
I WILL OPERATE WITHIN THE CURRENT BORDERS OF NANZHAO WITH THE EXCEPTION OF AN INCURSION INTO THE *GOLDEN TRIANGLE* REGION INSIDE LAOS AND THAILAND.
AND YOUR PORTS IN DVARAVATI AS WELL AS THE RAIL LINES FROM THE REFINERIES TO BAGAN WILL REMAIN UNMOLESTED.
SO.
BUSINESS AS *USUAL*, THEN.

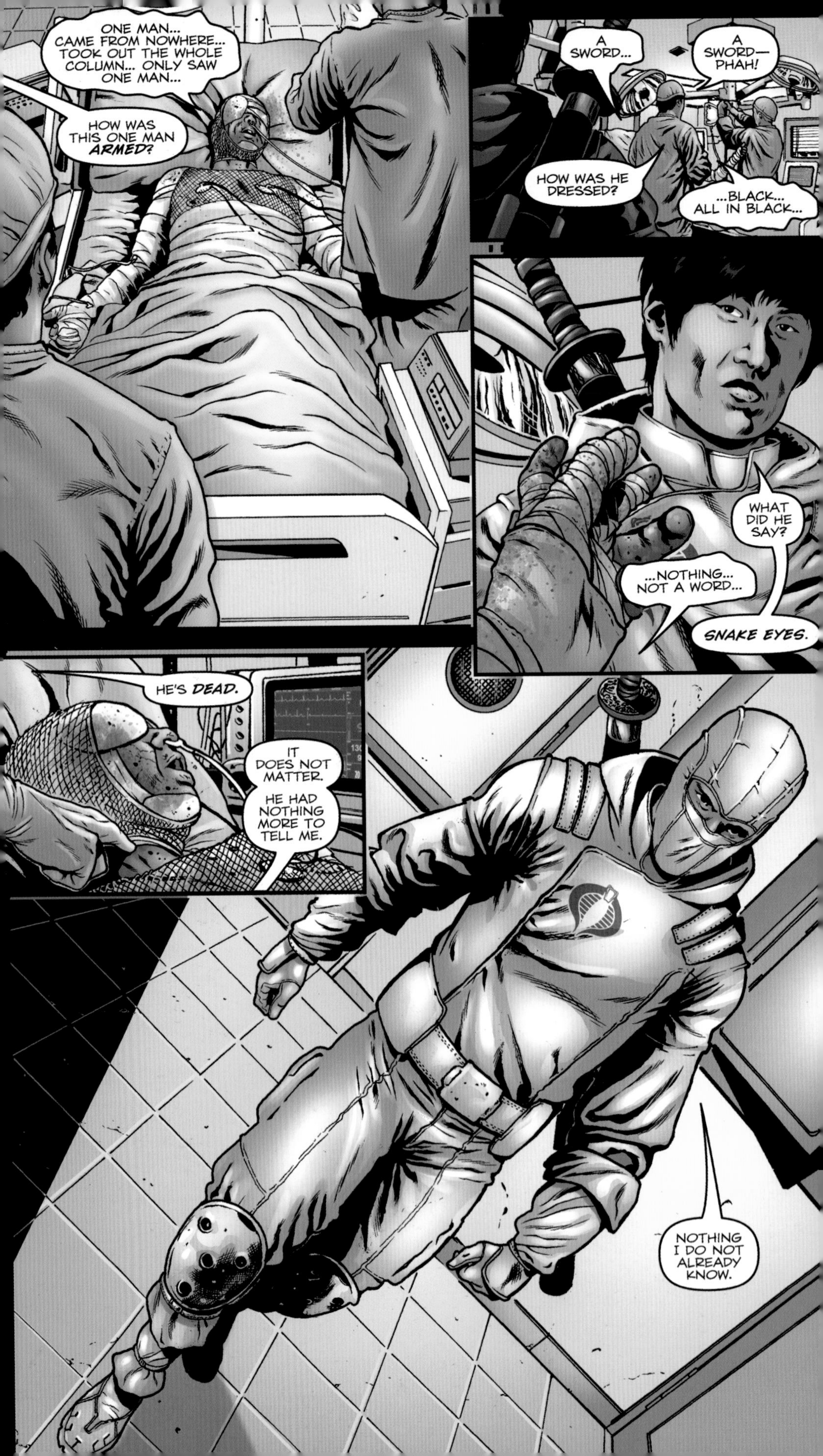
ONE MAN... CAME FROM NOWHERE... TOOK OUT THE WHOLE COLUMN... ONLY SAW ONE MAN...
HOW WAS THIS ONE MAN *ARMED*?
A SWORD...
A SWORD— PHAH!
HOW WAS HE DRESSED?
...BLACK... ALL IN BLACK...
WHAT DID HE SAY?
...NOTHING... NOT A WORD...
SNAKE EYES.
HE'S *DEAD*.
IT DOES NOT MATTER.
HE HAD NOTHING MORE TO TELL ME.
NOTHING I DO NOT ALREADY KNOW.

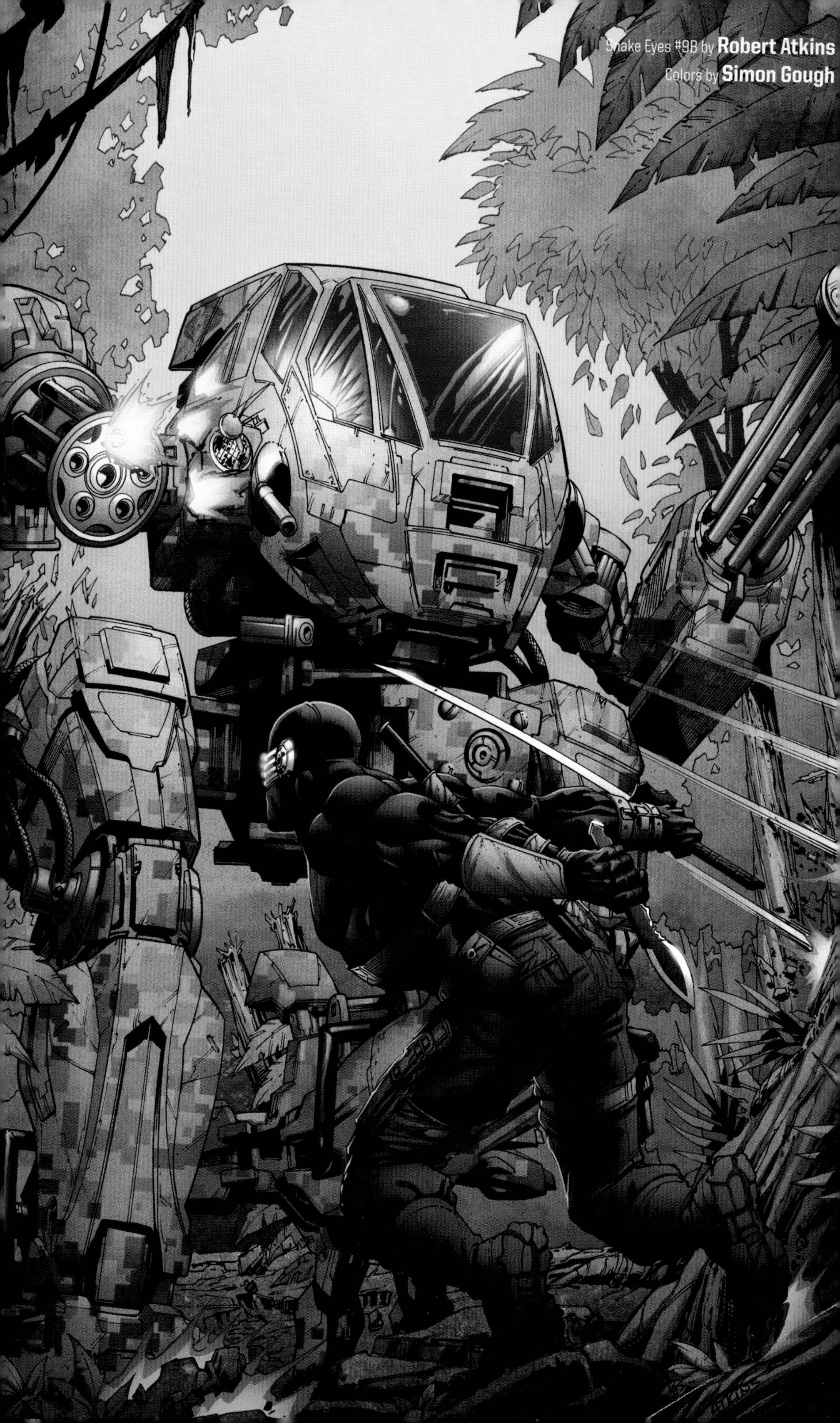

Snake Eyes #9B by **Robert Atkins**
Colors by **Simon Gough**

Cobra #9A by **Dave Wilkins**

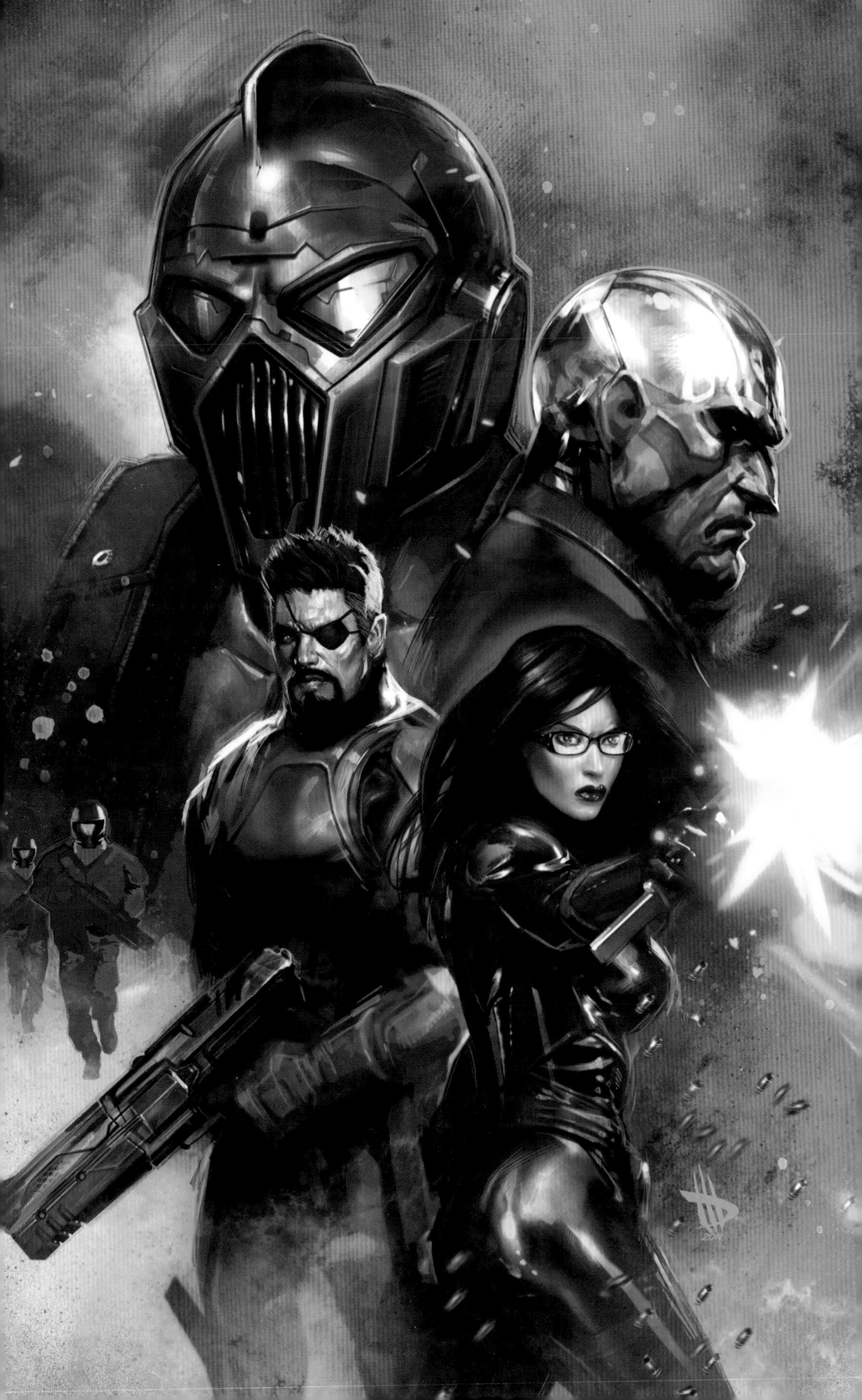

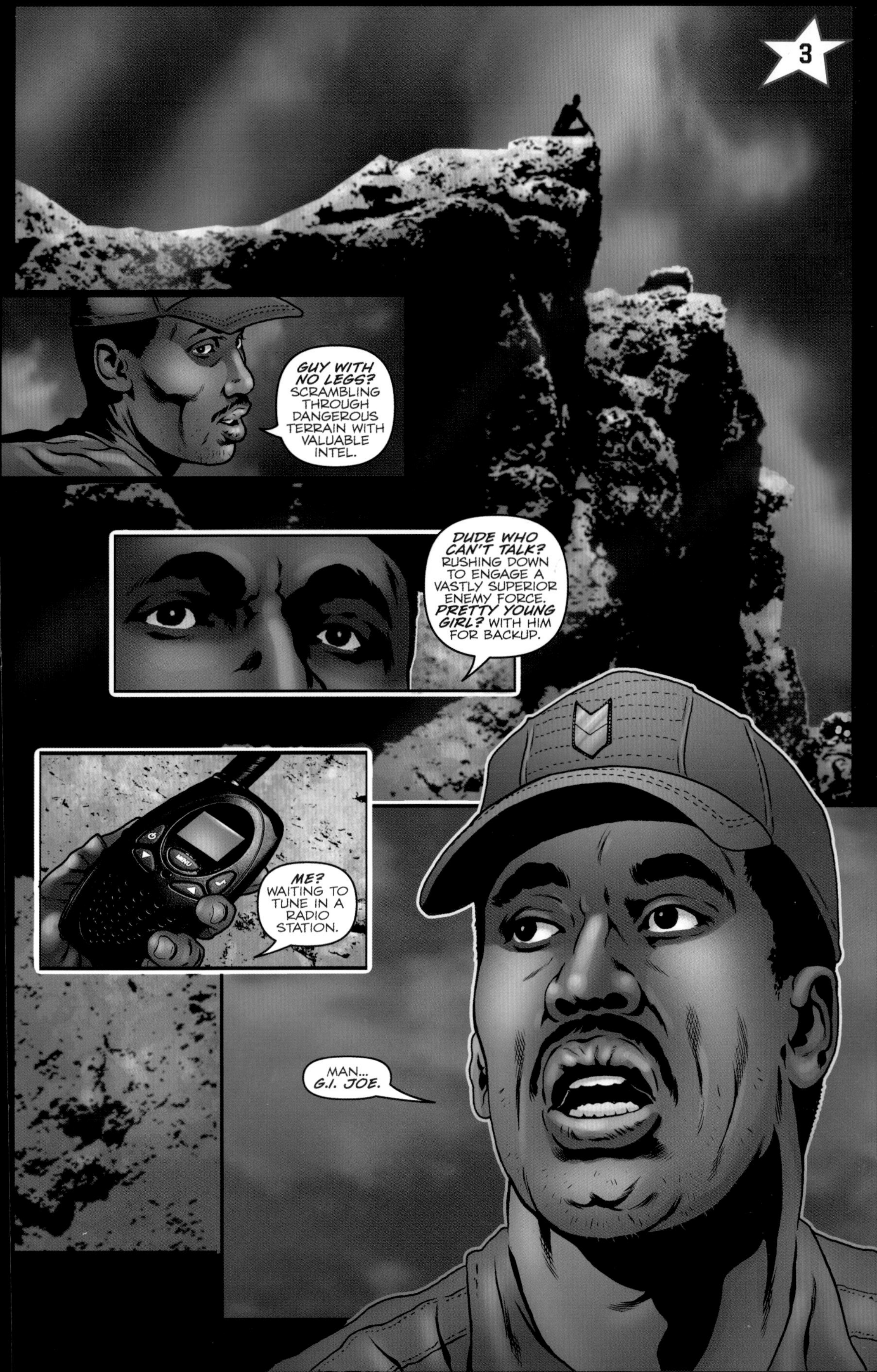
3
GUY WITH NO LEGS? SCRAMBLING THROUGH DANGEROUS TERRAIN WITH VALUABLE INTEL.
DUDE WHO CAN'T TALK? RUSHING DOWN TO ENGAGE A VASTLY SUPERIOR ENEMY FORCE. PRETTY YOUNG GIRL? WITH HIM FOR BACKUP.
ME? WAITING TO TUNE IN A RADIO STATION.
MAN... G.I. JOE.

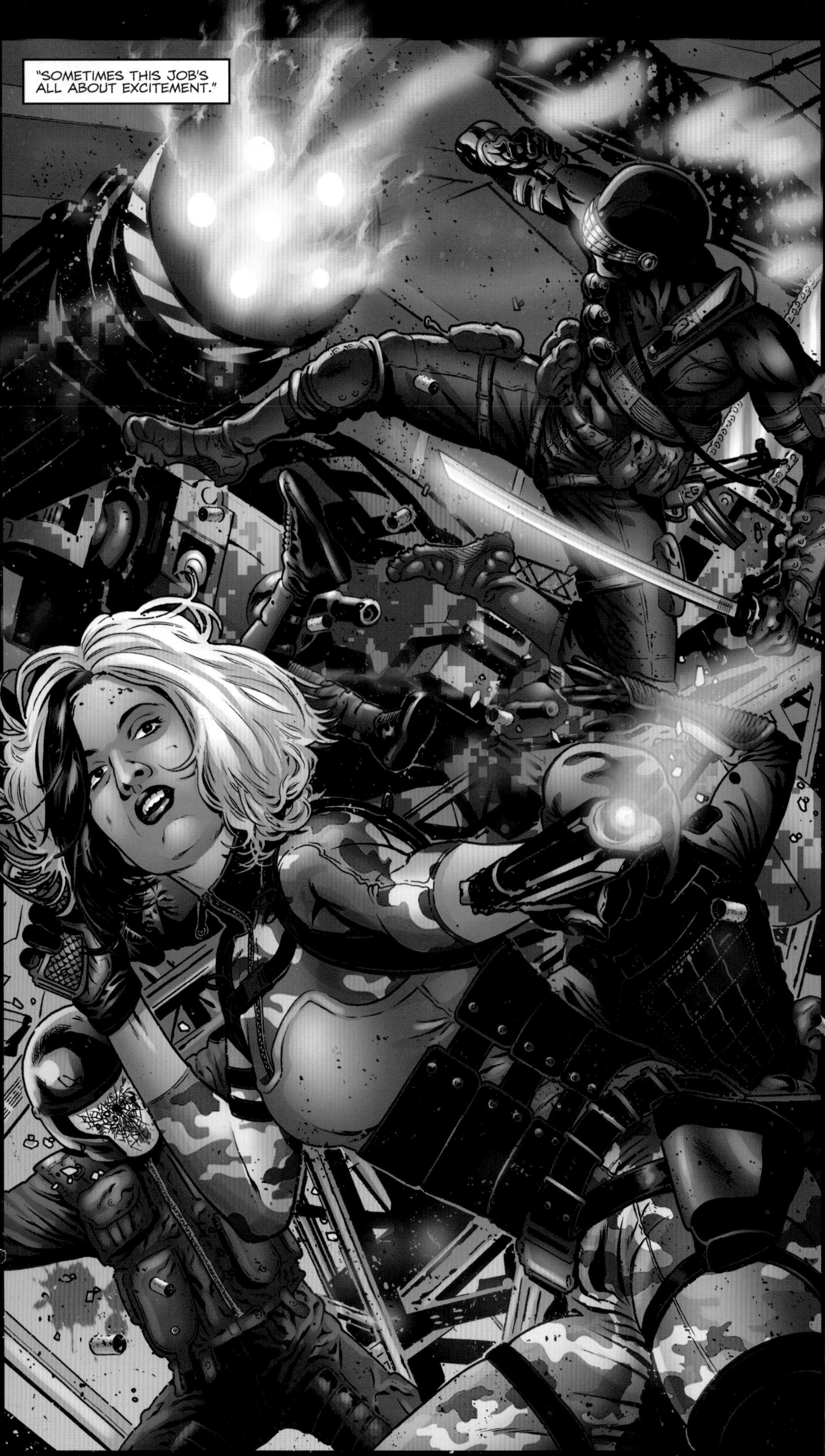
"SOMETIMES THIS JOB'S ALL ABOUT EXCITEMENT."

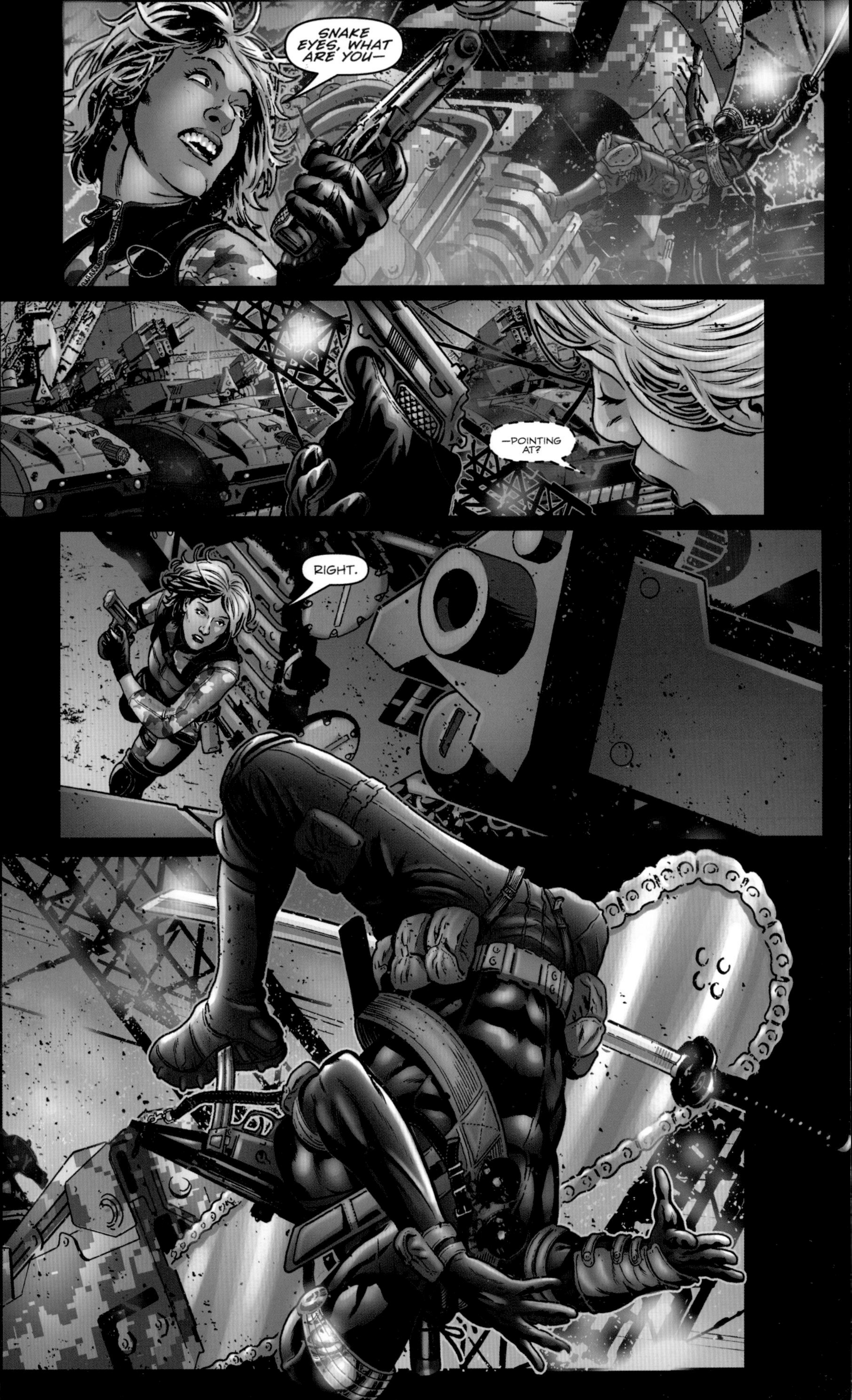
SNAKE EYES, WHAT ARE YOU—
—POINTING AT?
RIGHT.

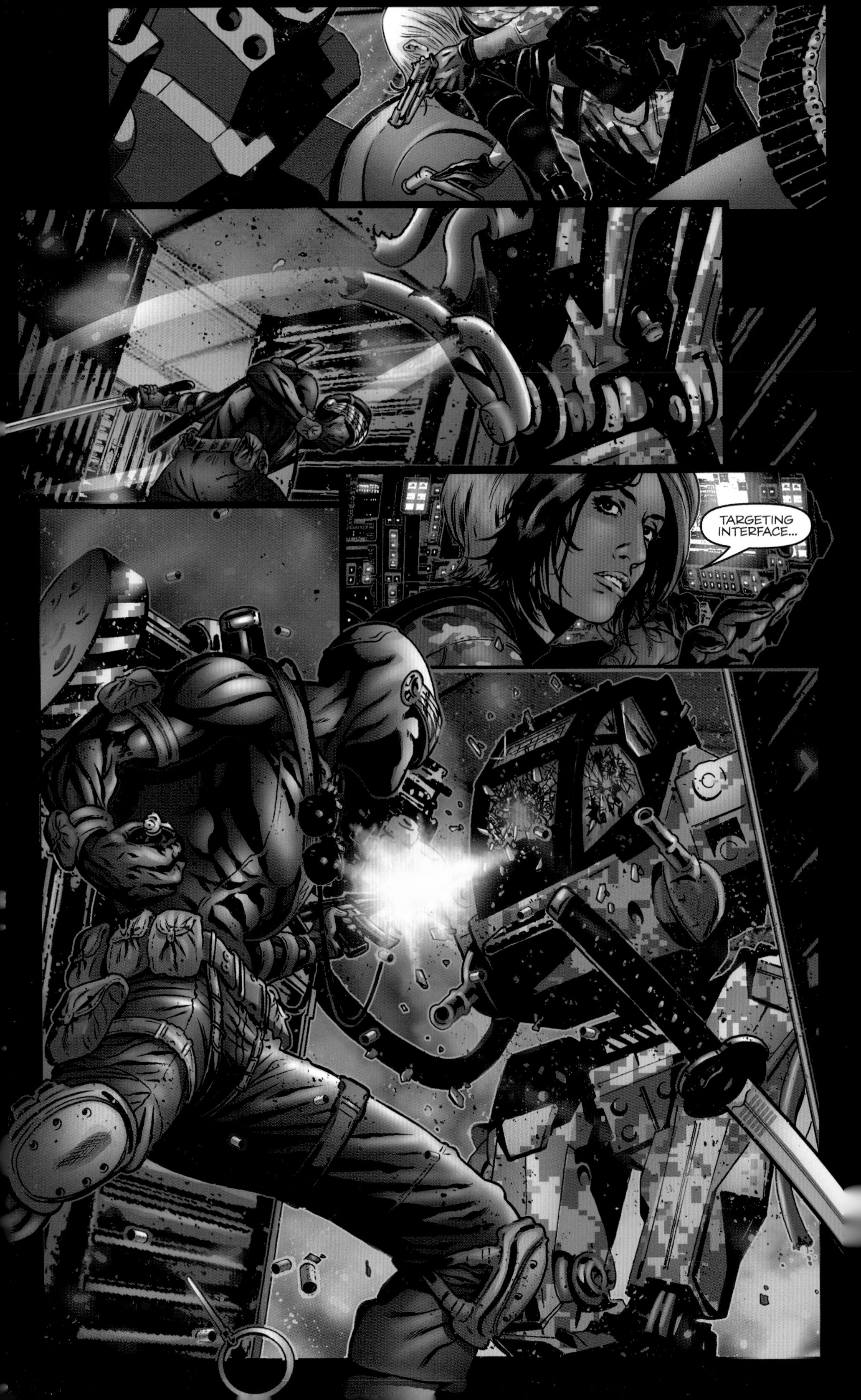
TARGETING INTERFACE...

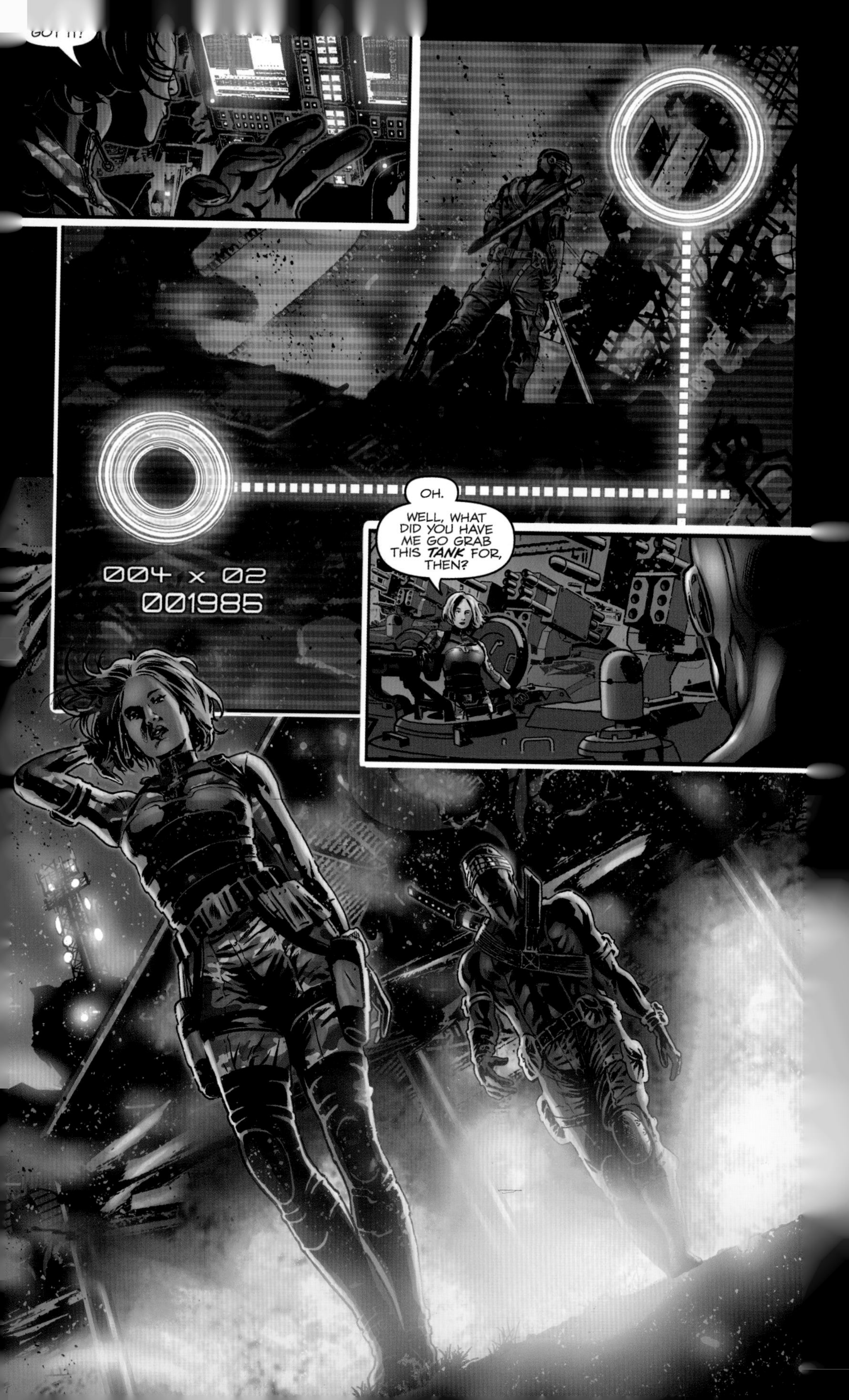
GOT IT!
004 x 02
001985
OH.
WELL, WHAT DID YOU HAVE ME GO GRAB THIS TANK FOR, THEN?

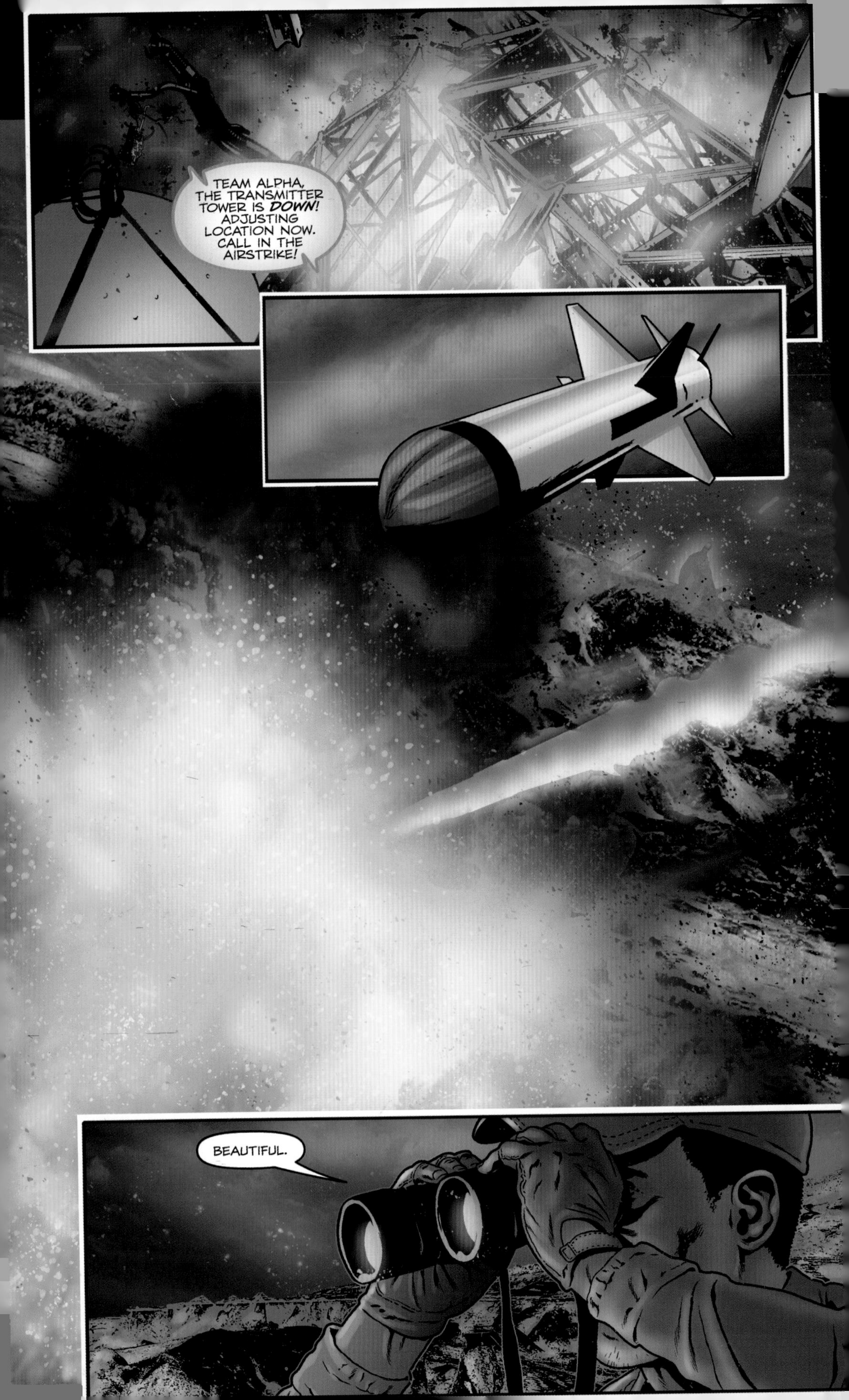
TEAM ALPHA, THE TRANSMITTER TOWER IS DOWN! ADJUSTING LOCATION NOW. CALL IN THE AIRSTRIKE!
BEAUTIFUL.

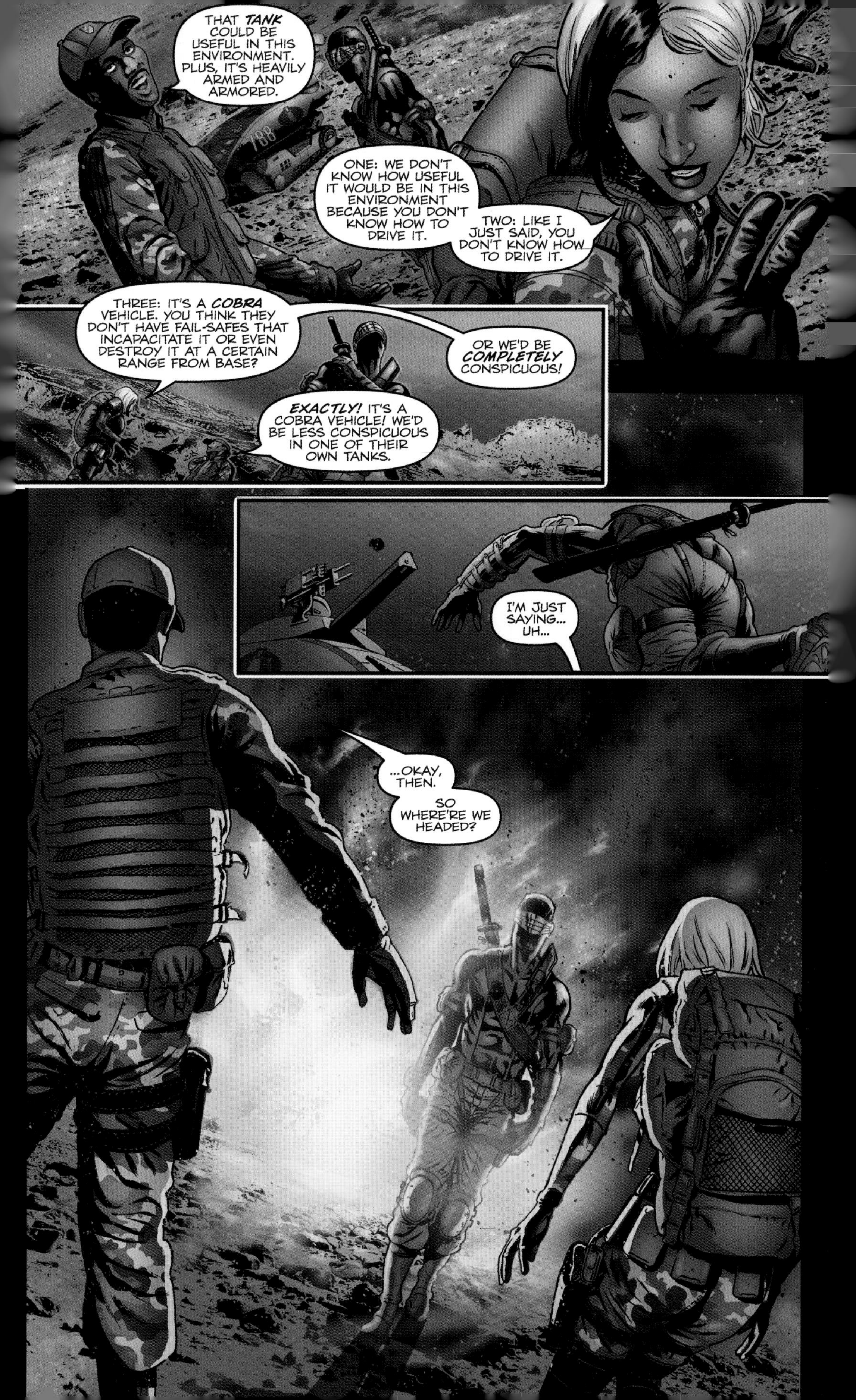
THAT TANK COULD BE USEFUL IN THIS ENVIRONMENT. PLUS, IT'S HEAVILY ARMED AND ARMORED.
ONE: WE DON'T KNOW HOW USEFUL IT WOULD BE IN THIS ENVIRONMENT BECAUSE YOU DON'T KNOW HOW TO DRIVE IT.
TWO: LIKE I JUST SAID, YOU DON'T KNOW HOW TO DRIVE IT.
THREE: IT'S A COBRA VEHICLE. YOU THINK THEY DON'T HAVE FAIL-SAFES THAT INCAPACITATE IT OR EVEN DESTROY IT AT A CERTAIN RANGE FROM BASE?
EXACTLY! IT'S A COBRA VEHICLE! WE'D BE LESS CONSPICUOUS IN ONE OF THEIR OWN TANKS.
OR WE'D BE COMPLETELY CONSPICUOUS!
I'M JUST SAYING... UH...
...OKAY, THEN.
SO WHERE'RE WE HEADED?

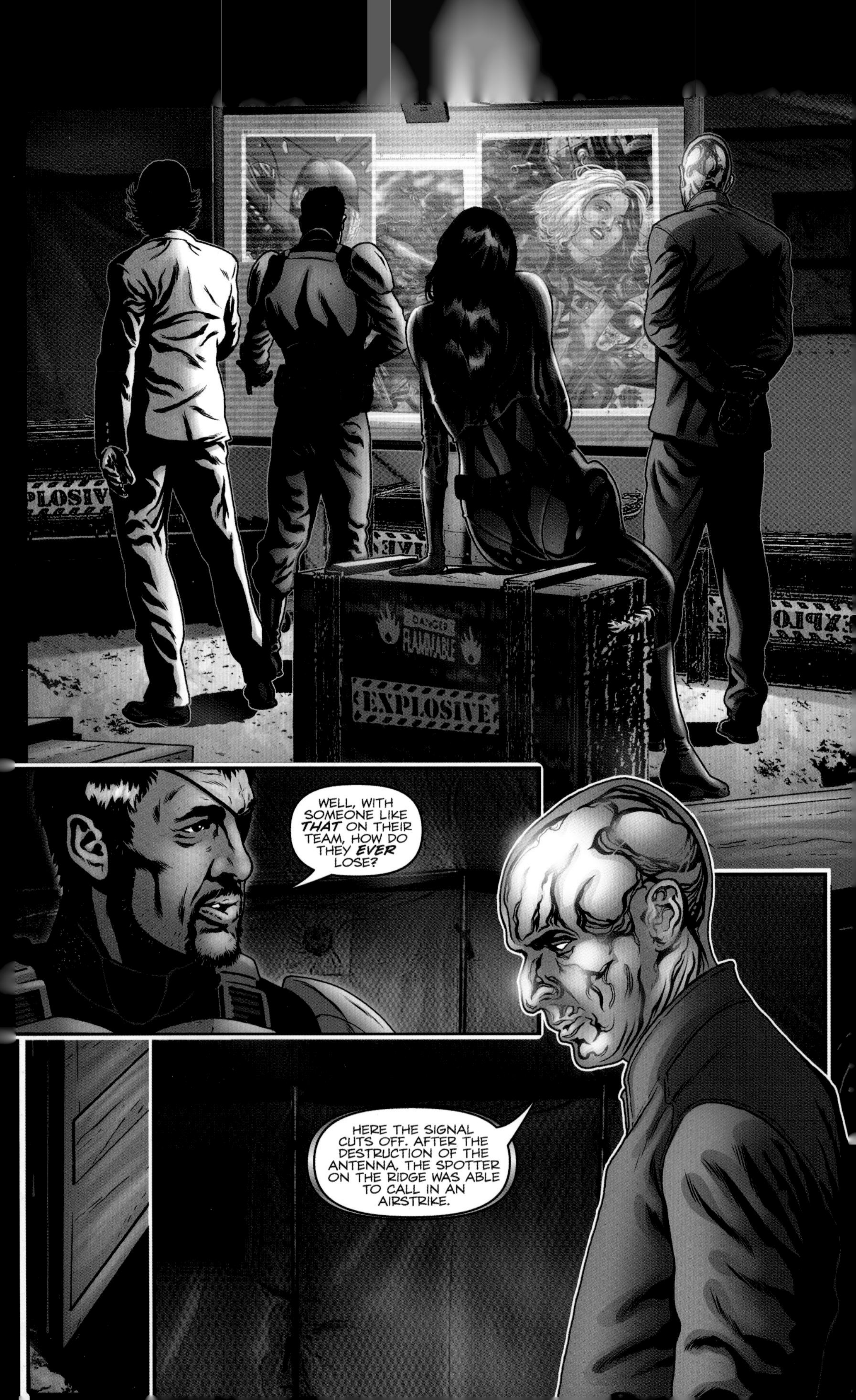
EXPLOSIVE
DANGER FLAMMABLE
EXPLOSIVE
WELL, WITH SOMEONE LIKE *THAT* ON THEIR TEAM, HOW DO THEY *EVER* LOSE?
HERE THE SIGNAL CUTS OFF. AFTER THE DESTRUCTION OF THE ANTENNA, THE SPOTTER ON THE RIDGE WAS ABLE TO CALL IN AN AIRSTRIKE.

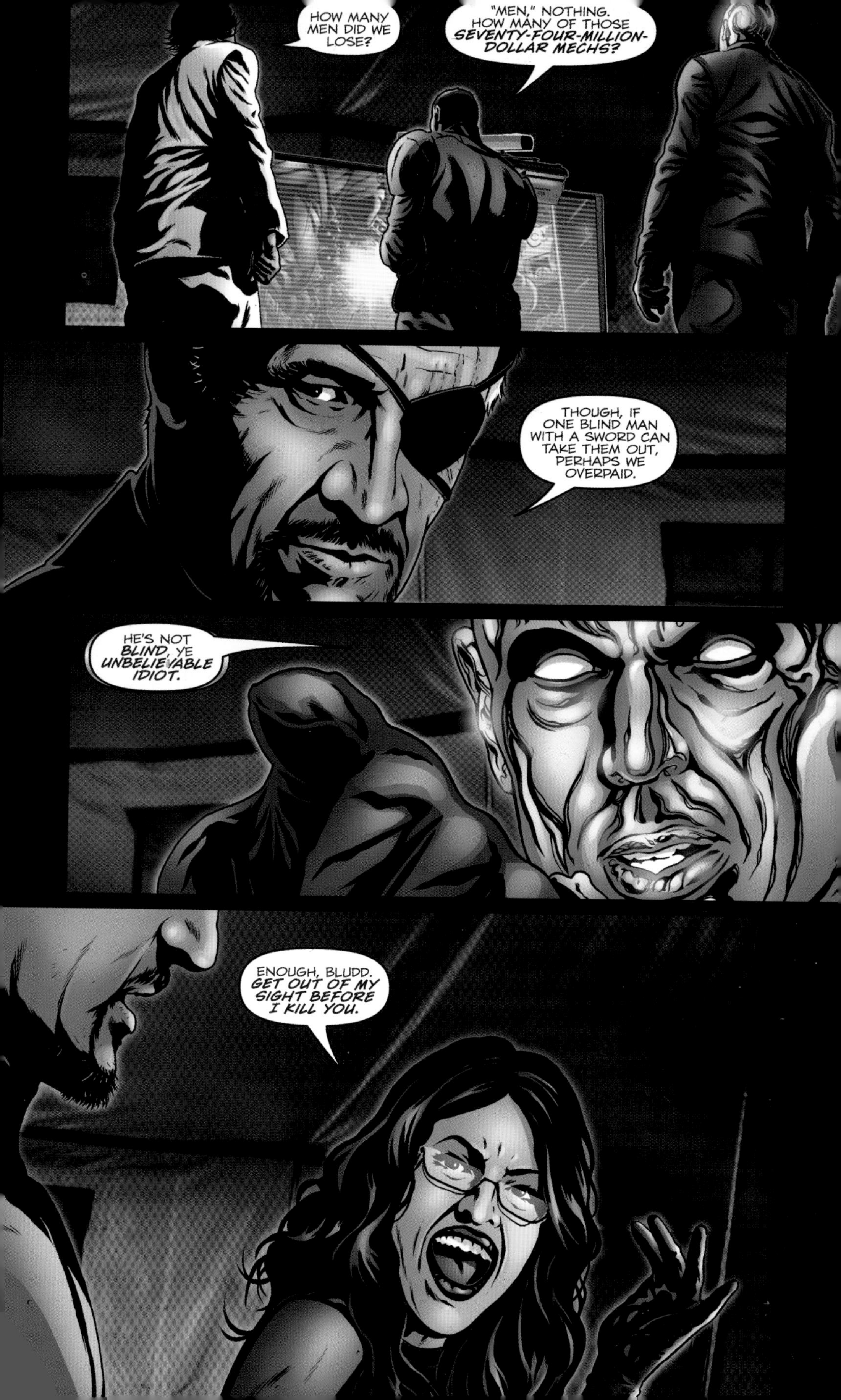
HOW MANY MEN DID WE LOSE?
"MEN," NOTHING. HOW MANY OF THOSE SEVENTY-FOUR-MILLION-DOLLAR MECHS?
THOUGH, IF ONE BLIND MAN WITH A SWORD CAN TAKE THEM OUT, PERHAPS WE OVERPAID.
HE'S NOT BLIND, YE UNBELIEVABLE IDIOT.
ENOUGH, BLUDD. GET OUT OF MY SIGHT BEFORE I KILL YOU.

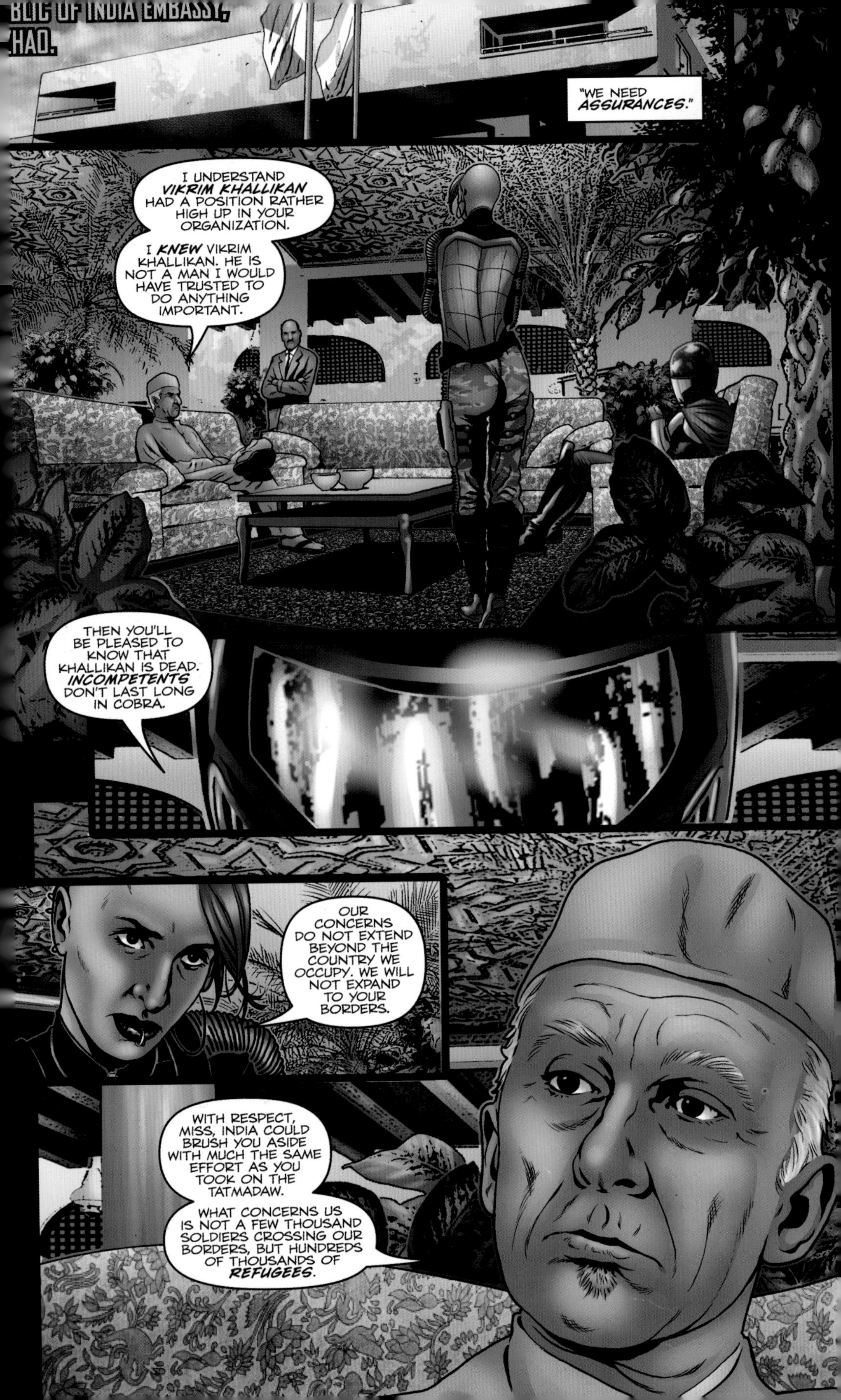
BLIC OF INDIA EMBASSY,
HAO.
"WE NEED ASSURANCES."
I UNDERSTAND VIKRIM KHALLIKAN HAD A POSITION RATHER HIGH UP IN YOUR ORGANIZATION.
I KNEW VIKRIM KHALLIKAN. HE IS NOT A MAN I WOULD HAVE TRUSTED TO DO ANYTHING IMPORTANT.
THEN YOU'LL BE PLEASED TO KNOW THAT KHALLIKAN IS DEAD. INCOMPETENTS DON'T LAST LONG IN COBRA.
OUR CONCERNS DO NOT EXTEND BEYOND THE COUNTRY WE OCCUPY. WE WILL NOT EXPAND TO YOUR BORDERS.
WITH RESPECT, MISS, INDIA COULD BRUSH YOU ASIDE WITH MUCH THE SAME EFFORT AS YOU TOOK ON THE TATMADAW.
WHAT CONCERNS US IS NOT A FEW THOUSAND SOLDIERS CROSSING OUR BORDERS, BUT HUNDREDS OF THOUSANDS OF REFUGEES.

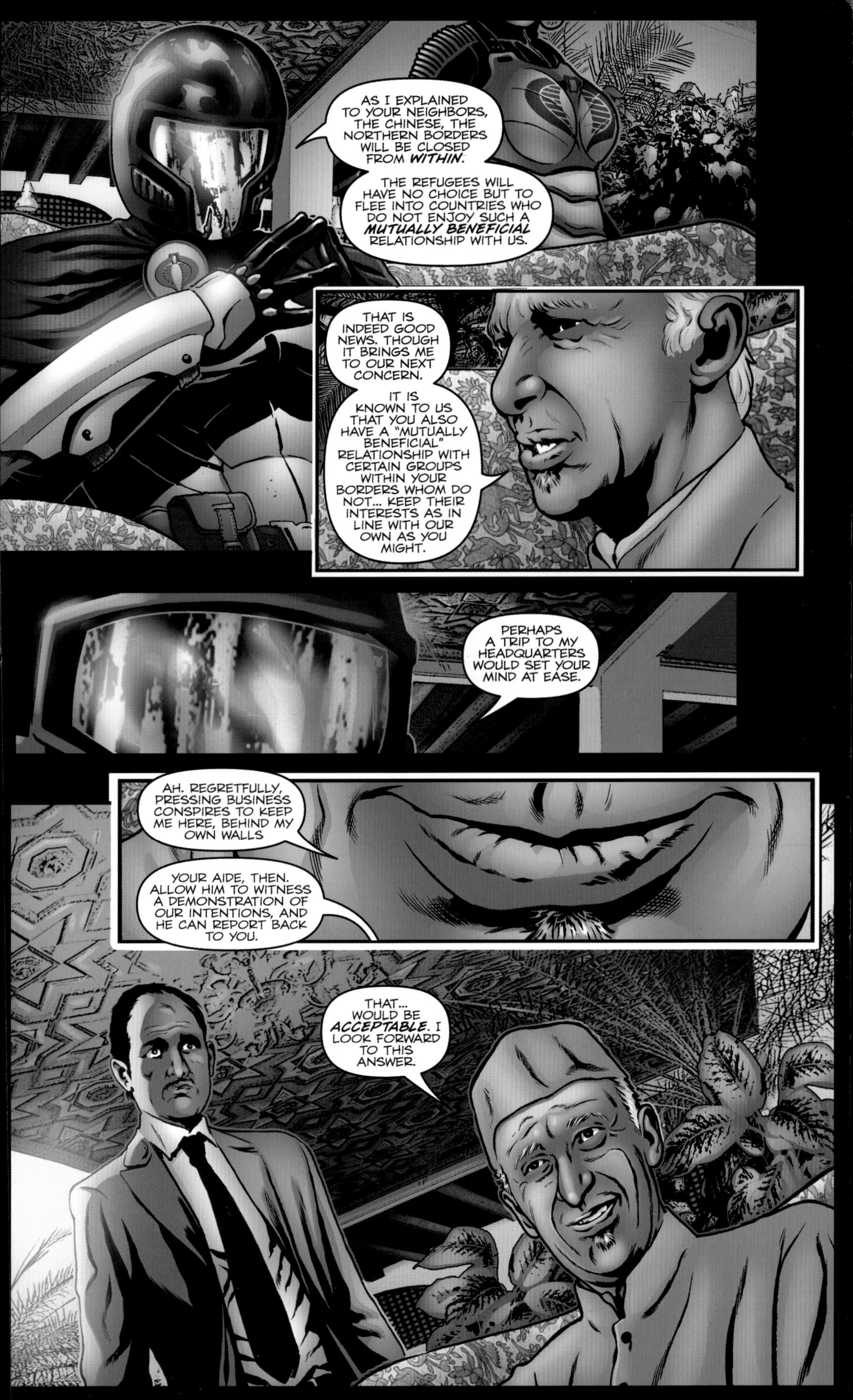
AS I EXPLAINED TO YOUR NEIGHBORS, THE CHINESE, THE NORTHERN BORDERS WILL BE CLOSED FROM *WITHIN*.
THE REFUGEES WILL HAVE NO CHOICE BUT TO FLEE INTO COUNTRIES WHO DO NOT ENJOY SUCH A ***MUTUALLY BENEFICIAL*** RELATIONSHIP WITH US.
THAT IS INDEED GOOD NEWS. THOUGH IT BRINGS ME TO OUR NEXT CONCERN.
IT IS KNOWN TO US THAT YOU ALSO HAVE A "MUTUALLY BENEFICIAL" RELATIONSHIP WITH CERTAIN GROUPS WITHIN YOUR BORDERS WHOM DO NOT... KEEP THEIR INTERESTS AS IN LINE WITH OUR OWN AS YOU MIGHT.
PERHAPS A TRIP TO MY HEADQUARTERS WOULD SET YOUR MIND AT EASE.
AH. REGRETFULLY, PRESSING BUSINESS CONSPIRES TO KEEP ME HERE, BEHIND MY OWN WALLS
YOUR AIDE, THEN. ALLOW HIM TO WITNESS A DEMONSTRATION OF OUR INTENTIONS, AND HE CAN REPORT BACK TO YOU.
THAT... WOULD BE ***ACCEPTABLE***. I LOOK FORWARD TO THIS ANSWER.

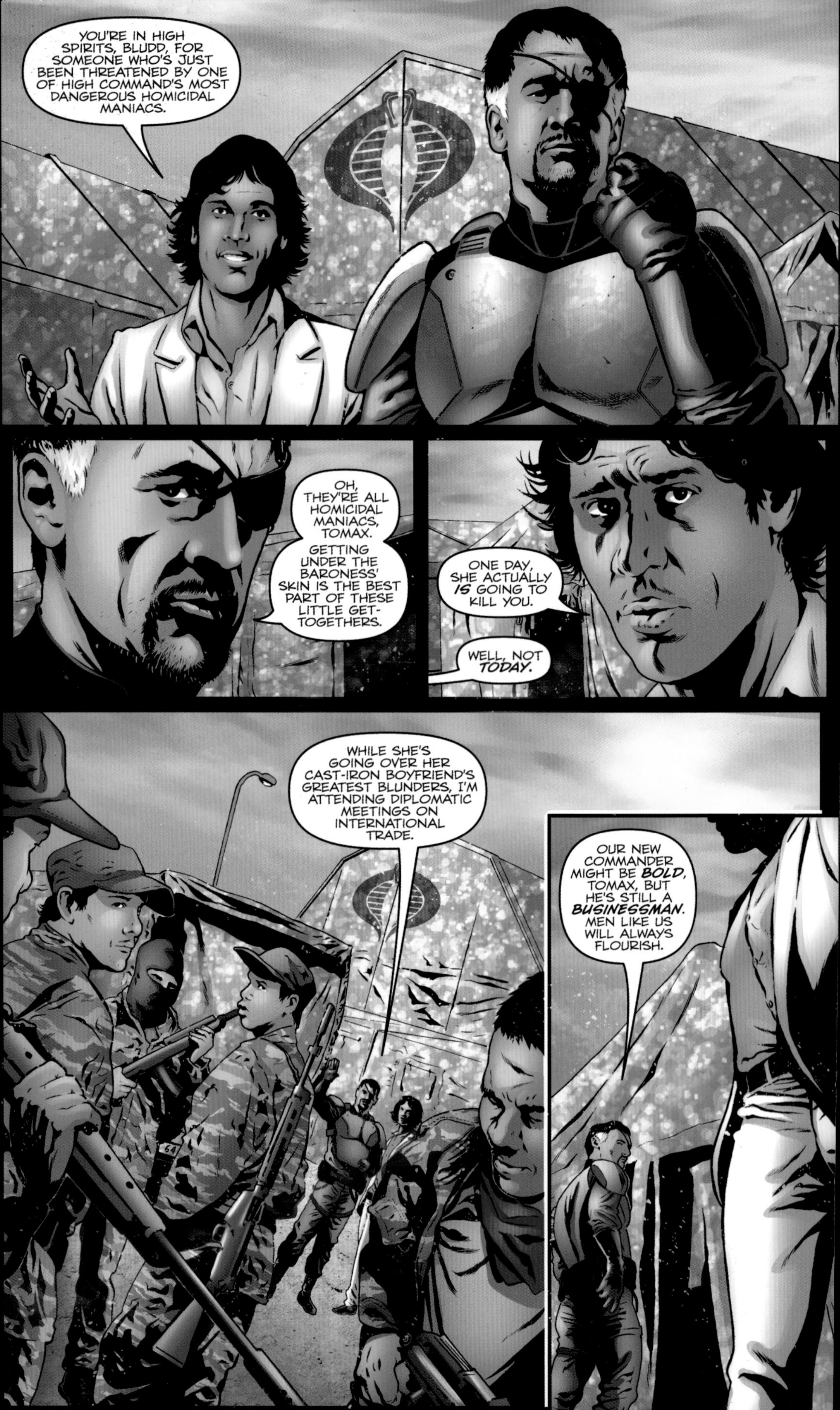
YOU'RE IN HIGH SPIRITS, BLUDD, FOR SOMEONE WHO'S JUST BEEN THREATENED BY ONE OF HIGH COMMAND'S MOST DANGEROUS HOMICIDAL MANIACS.
OH, THEY'RE ALL HOMICIDAL MANIACS, TOMAX.
GETTING UNDER THE BARONESS' SKIN IS THE BEST PART OF THESE LITTLE GET-TOGETHERS.
ONE DAY, SHE ACTUALLY *IS* GOING TO KILL YOU.
WELL, NOT *TODAY*.
WHILE SHE'S GOING OVER HER CAST-IRON BOYFRIEND'S GREATEST BLUNDERS, I'M ATTENDING DIPLOMATIC MEETINGS ON INTERNATIONAL TRADE.
OUR NEW COMMANDER MIGHT BE *BOLD*, TOMAX, BUT HE'S STILL A *BUSINESSMAN*. MEN LIKE US WILL ALWAYS FLOURISH.

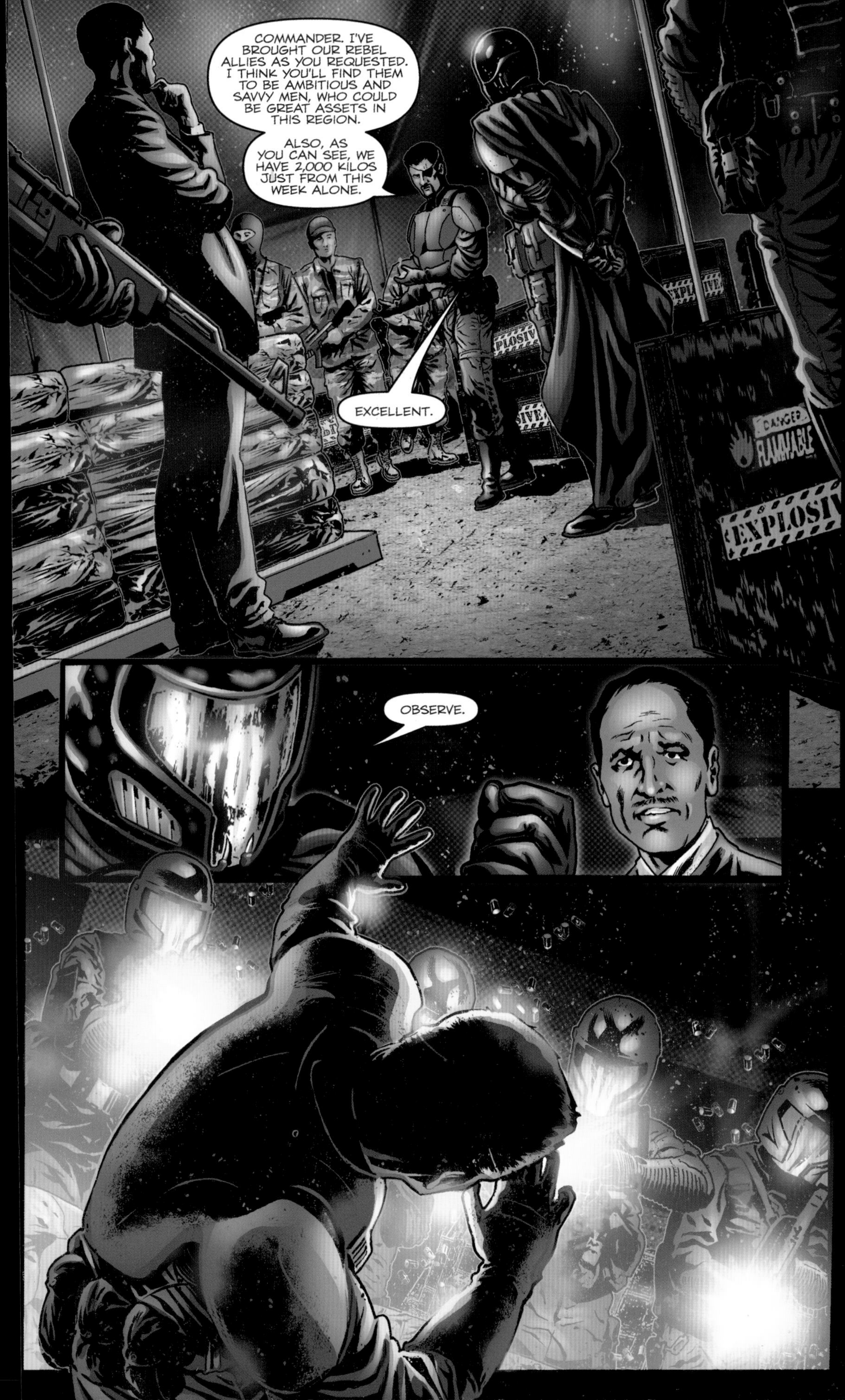
COMMANDER. I'VE BROUGHT OUR REBEL ALLIES AS YOU REQUESTED. I THINK YOU'LL FIND THEM TO BE AMBITIOUS AND SAVVY MEN, WHO COULD BE GREAT ASSETS IN THIS REGION.
ALSO, AS YOU CAN SEE, WE HAVE 2,000 KILOS JUST FROM THIS WEEK ALONE.
EXCELLENT.
DANGER
FLAMMABLE
EXPLOSIV
OBSERVE.

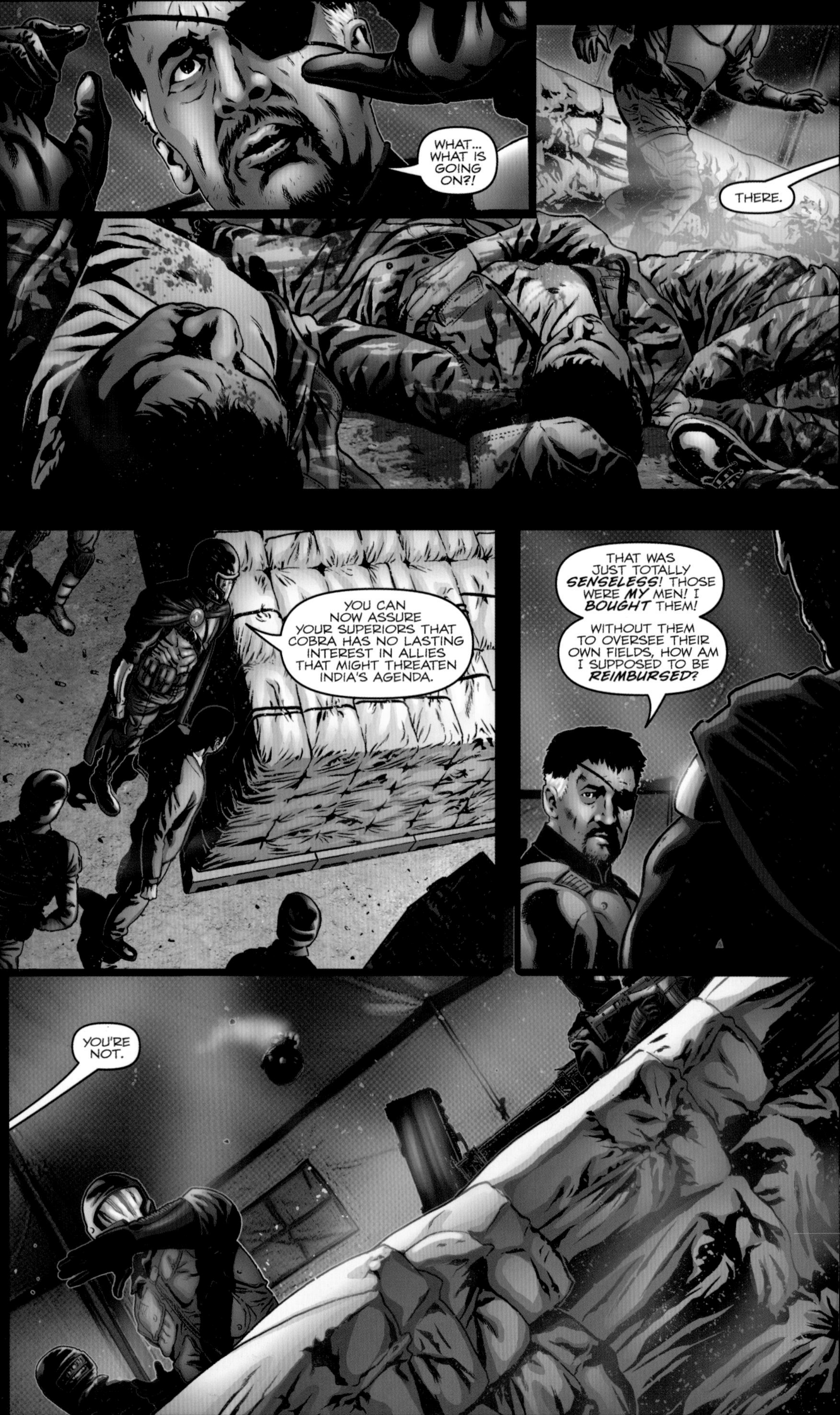
WHAT... WHAT IS GOING ON?!
THERE.
YOU CAN NOW ASSURE YOUR SUPERIORS THAT COBRA HAS NO LASTING INTEREST IN ALLIES THAT MIGHT THREATEN INDIA'S AGENDA.
THAT WAS JUST TOTALLY SENSELESS! THOSE WERE MY MEN! I BOUGHT THEM!
WITHOUT THEM TO OVERSEE THEIR OWN FIELDS, HOW AM I SUPPOSED TO BE REIMBURSED?
YOU'RE NOT.

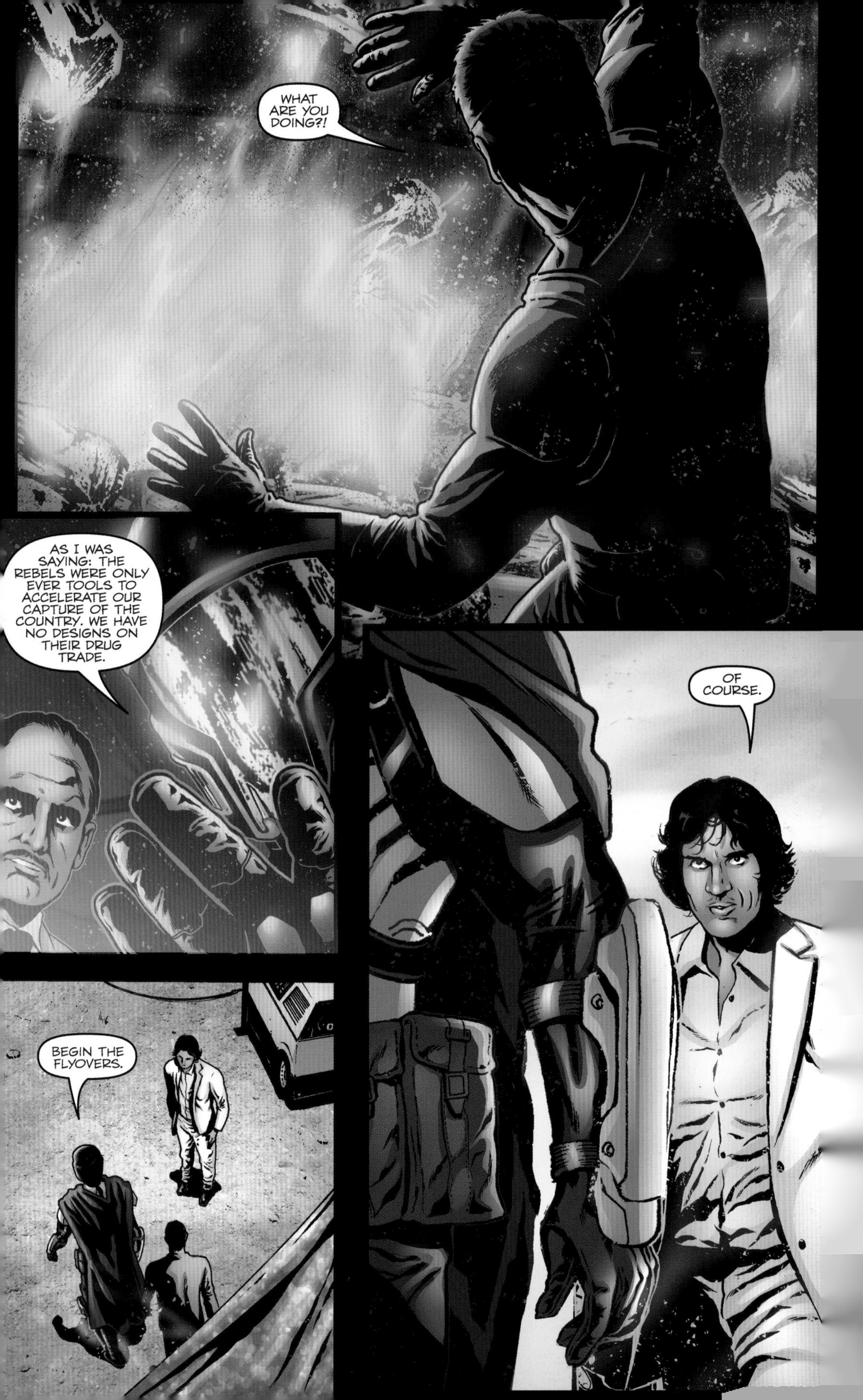
WHAT ARE YOU DOING?!
AS I WAS SAYING: THE REBELS WERE ONLY EVER TOOLS TO ACCELERATE OUR CAPTURE OF THE COUNTRY. WE HAVE NO DESIGNS ON THEIR DRUG TRADE.
OF COURSE.
BEGIN THE FLYOVERS.

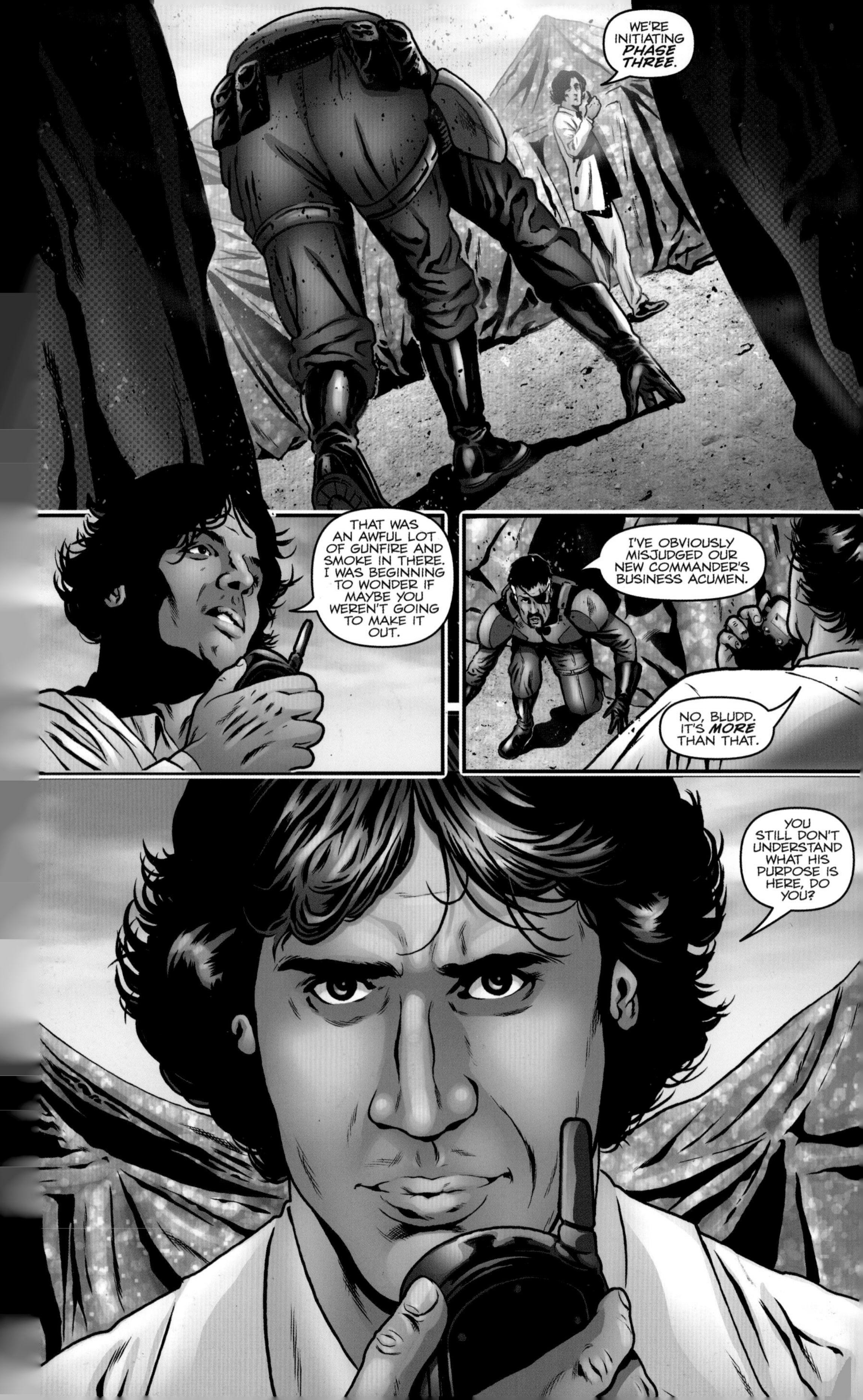
WE'RE INITIATING PHASE THREE.
THAT WAS AN AWFUL LOT OF GUNFIRE AND SMOKE IN THERE. I WAS BEGINNING TO WONDER IF MAYBE YOU WEREN'T GOING TO MAKE IT OUT.
I'VE OBVIOUSLY MISJUDGED OUR NEW COMMANDER'S BUSINESS ACUMEN.
NO, BLUDD. IT'S MORE THAN THAT.
YOU STILL DON'T UNDERSTAND WHAT HIS PURPOSE IS HERE, DO YOU?

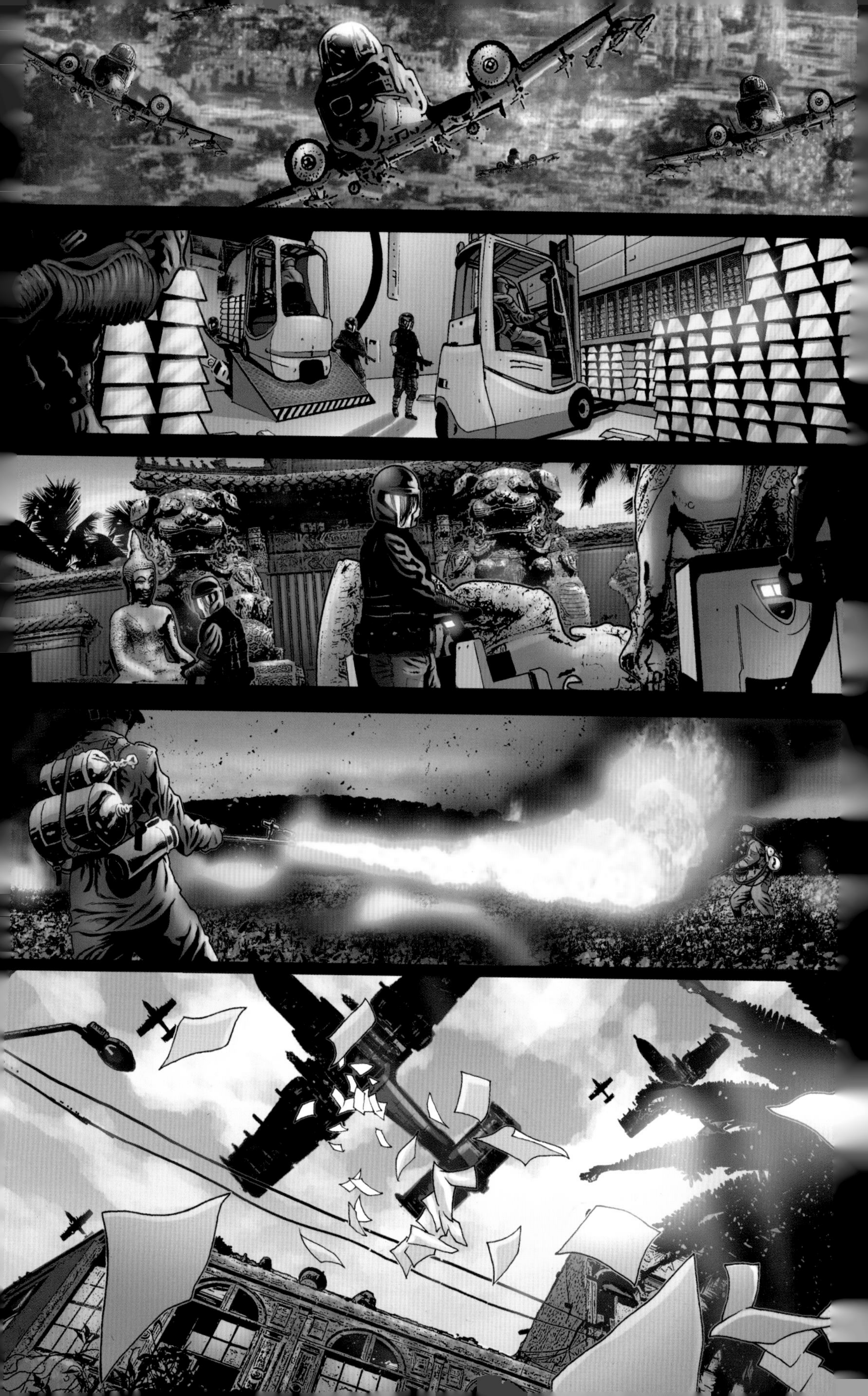

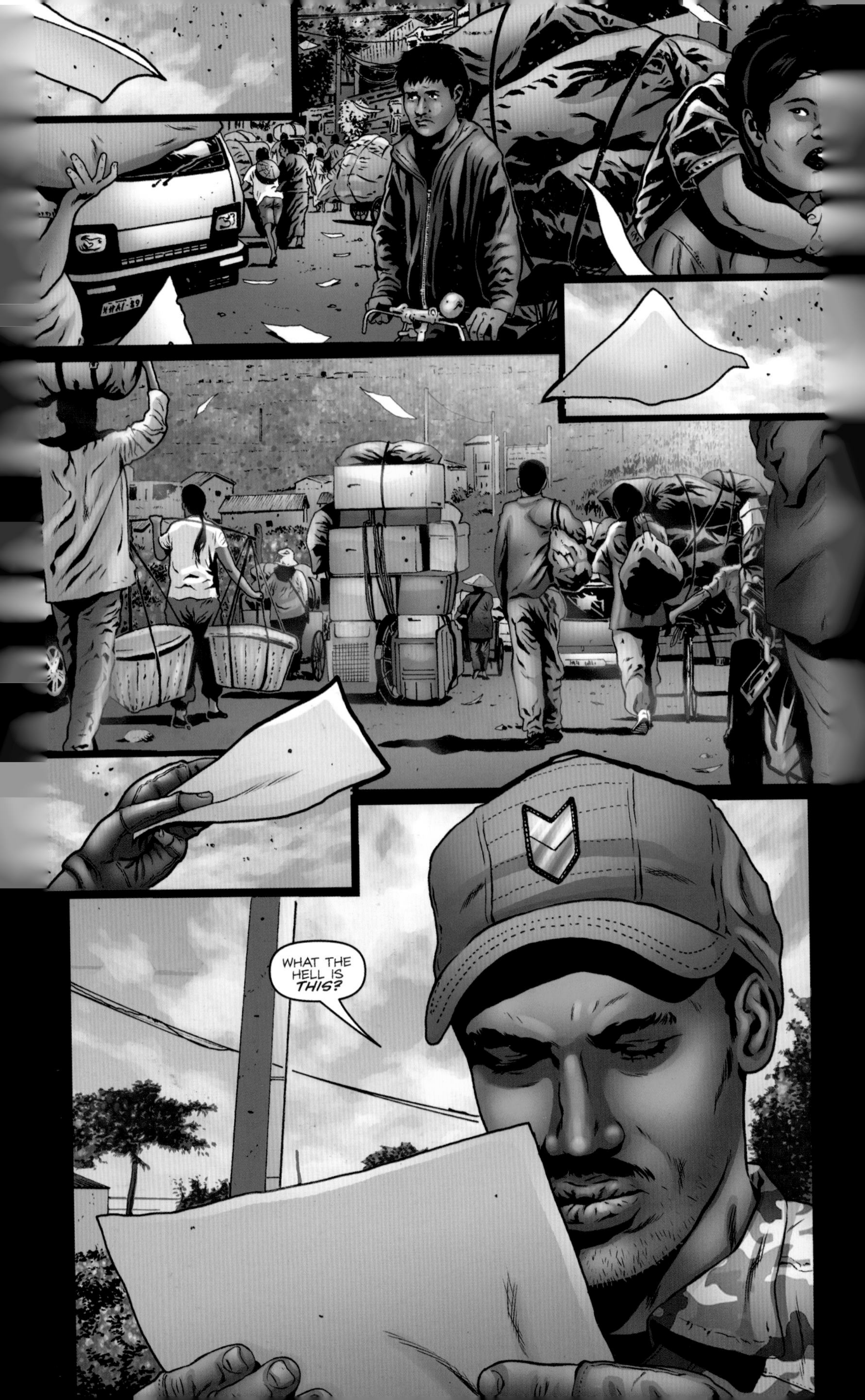
WHAT THE HELL IS THIS?

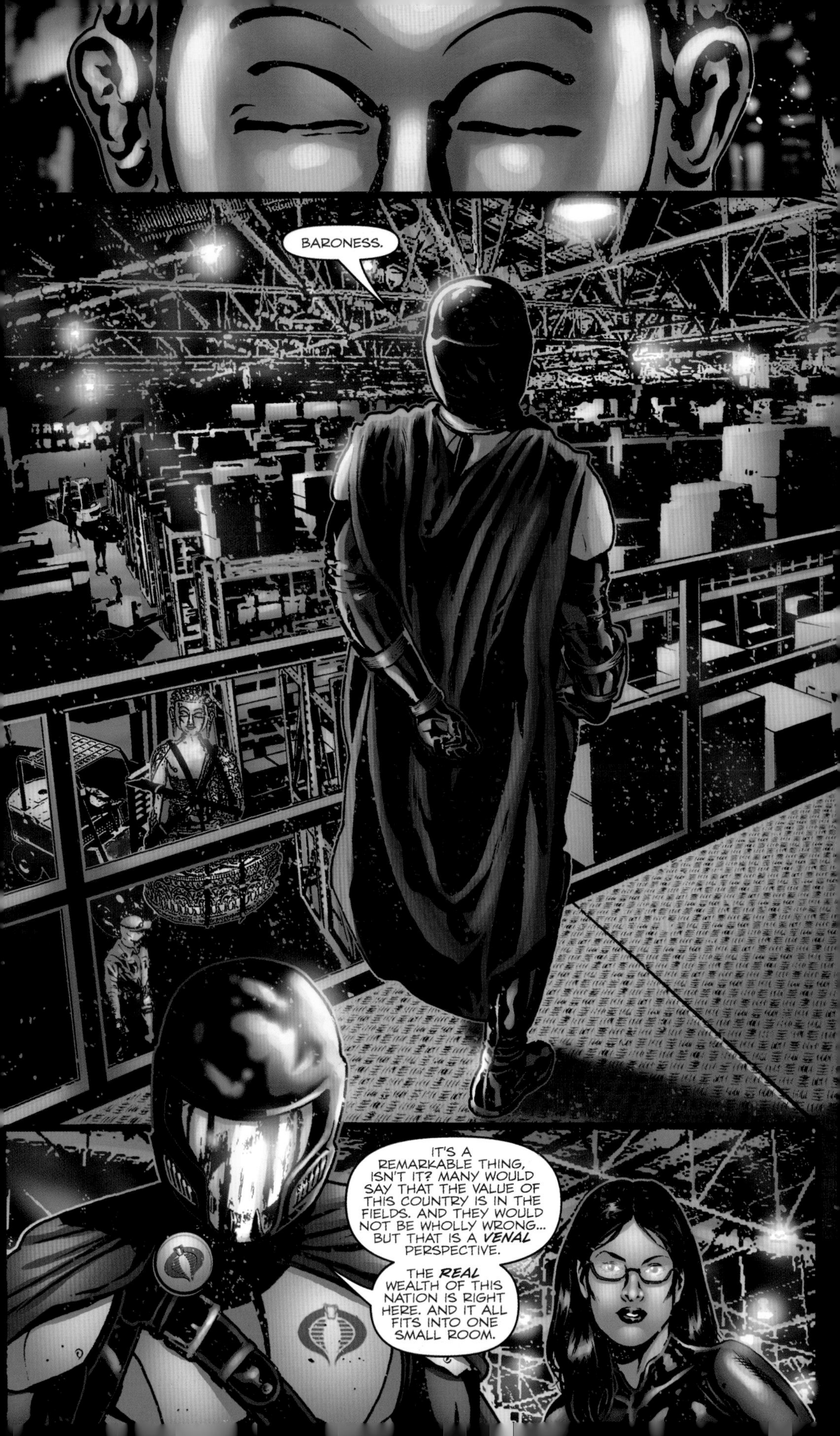
BARONESS.
IT'S A REMARKABLE THING, ISN'T IT? MANY WOULD SAY THAT THE VALUE OF THIS COUNTRY IS IN THE FIELDS. AND THEY WOULD NOT BE WHOLLY WRONG... BUT THAT IS A *VENAL* PERSPECTIVE.
THE *REAL* WEALTH OF THIS NATION IS RIGHT HERE. AND IT ALL FITS INTO ONE SMALL ROOM.

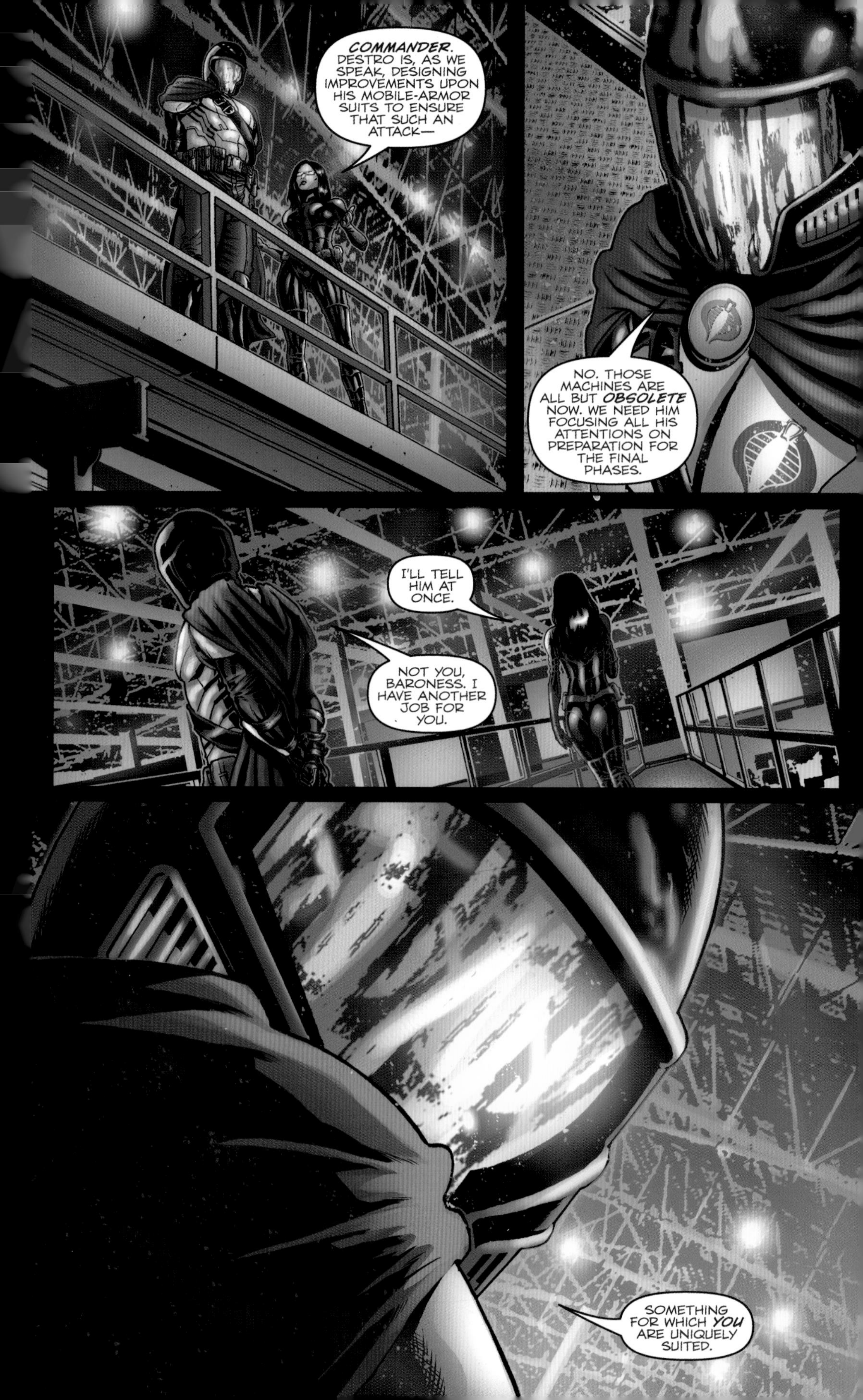
COMMANDER. DESTRO IS, AS WE SPEAK, DESIGNING IMPROVEMENTS UPON HIS MOBILE-ARMOR SUITS TO ENSURE THAT SUCH AN ATTACK—
NO. THOSE MACHINES ARE ALL BUT OBSOLETE NOW. WE NEED HIM FOCUSING ALL HIS ATTENTIONS ON PREPARATION FOR THE FINAL PHASES.
I'LL TELL HIM AT ONCE.
NOT YOU, BARONESS. I HAVE ANOTHER JOB FOR YOU.
SOMETHING FOR WHICH YOU ARE UNIQUELY SUITED.

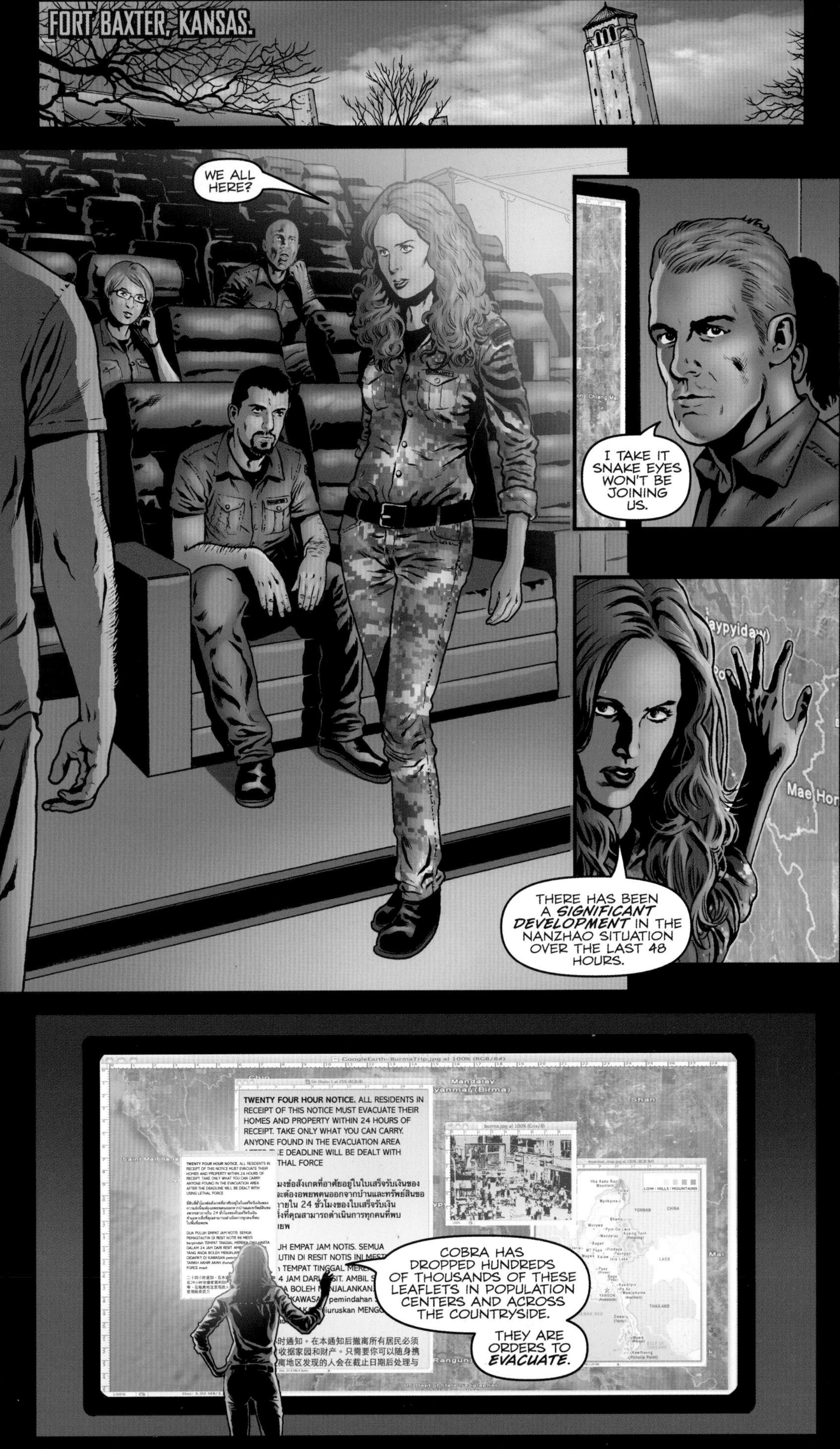
FORT BAXTER, KANSAS.
WE ALL HERE?
I TAKE IT SNAKE EYES WON'T BE JOINING US.
THERE HAS BEEN A *SIGNIFICANT DEVELOPMENT* IN THE NANZHAO SITUATION OVER THE LAST 48 HOURS.
TWENTY FOUR HOUR NOTICE. ALL RESIDENTS IN RECEIPT OF THIS NOTICE MUST EVACUATE THEIR HOMES AND PROPERTY WITHIN 24 HOURS OF RECEIPT. TAKE ONLY WHAT YOU CAN CARRY. ANYONE FOUND IN THE EVACUATION AREA
Mandalay
Shan
COBRA HAS DROPPED HUNDREDS OF THOUSANDS OF THESE LEAFLETS IN POPULATION CENTERS AND ACROSS THE COUNTRYSIDE.
THEY ARE ORDERS TO *EVACUATE*.

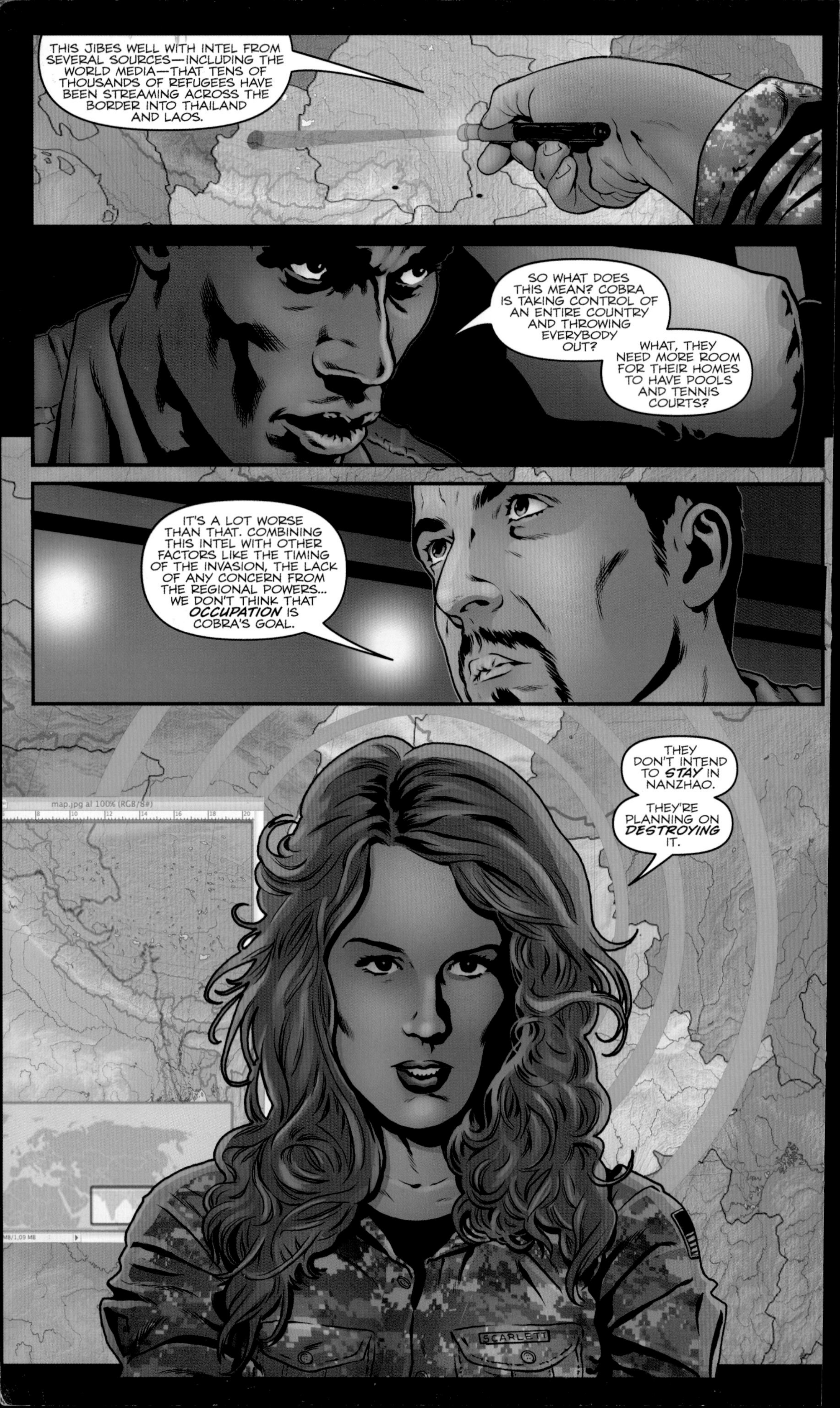
THIS JIBES WELL WITH INTEL FROM SEVERAL SOURCES—INCLUDING THE WORLD MEDIA—THAT TENS OF THOUSANDS OF REFUGEES HAVE BEEN STREAMING ACROSS THE BORDER INTO THAILAND AND LAOS.
SO WHAT DOES THIS MEAN? COBRA IS TAKING CONTROL OF AN ENTIRE COUNTRY AND THROWING EVERYBODY OUT?
WHAT, THEY NEED MORE ROOM FOR THEIR HOMES TO HAVE POOLS AND TENNIS COURTS?
IT'S A LOT WORSE THAN THAT. COMBINING THIS INTEL WITH OTHER FACTORS LIKE THE TIMING OF THE INVASION, THE LACK OF ANY CONCERN FROM THE REGIONAL POWERS... WE DON'T THINK THAT *OCCUPATION* IS COBRA'S GOAL.
map.jpg al 100% (RGB/8#)
THEY DON'T INTEND TO *STAY* IN NANZHAO.
THEY'RE PLANNING ON *DESTROYING* IT.
SCARLETT

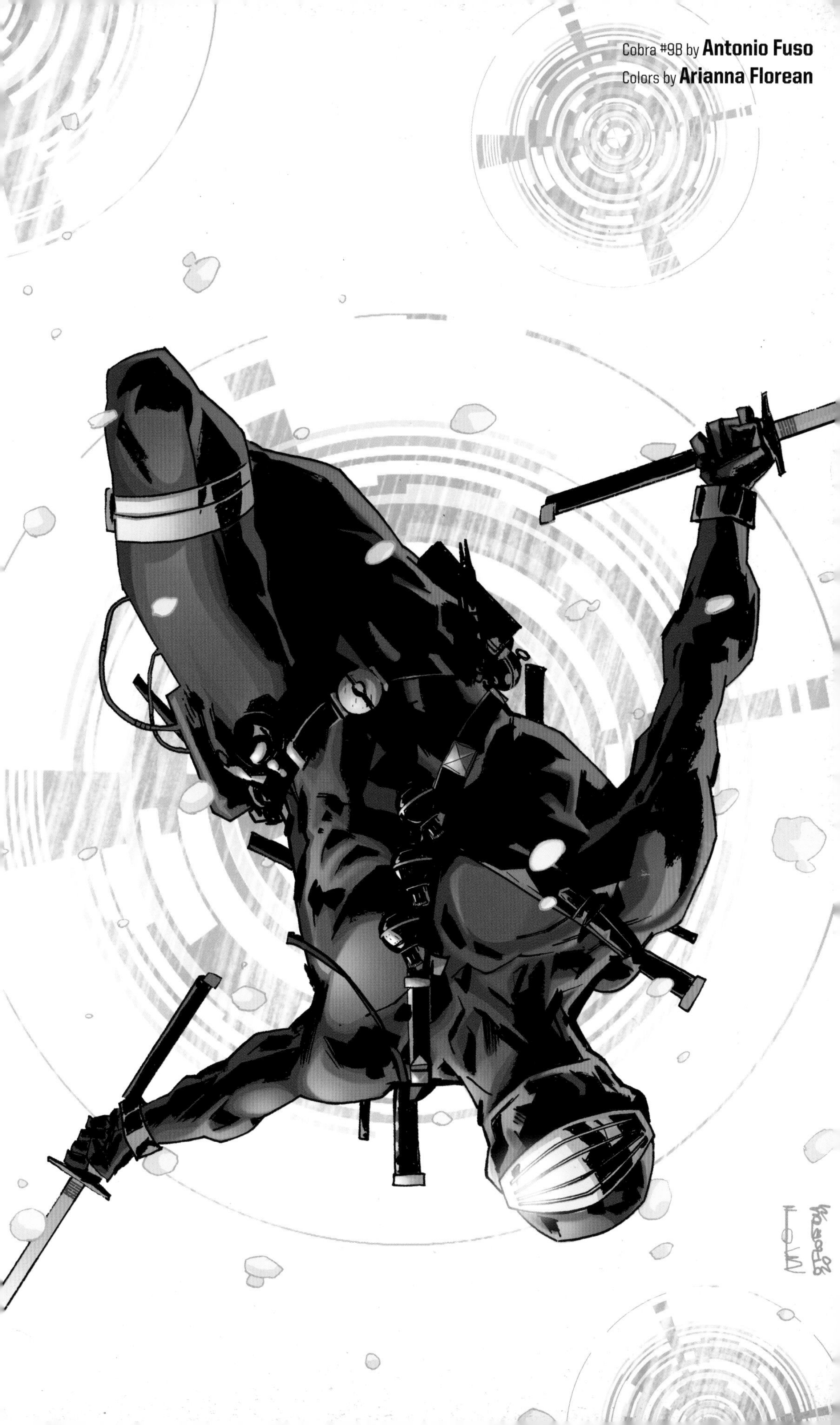

Cobra #9B by **Antonio Fuso**
Colors by **Arianna Florean**

GI JOE #10B by **Wil Rosado**
Colors by **Romulo Fajardo, Jr.**

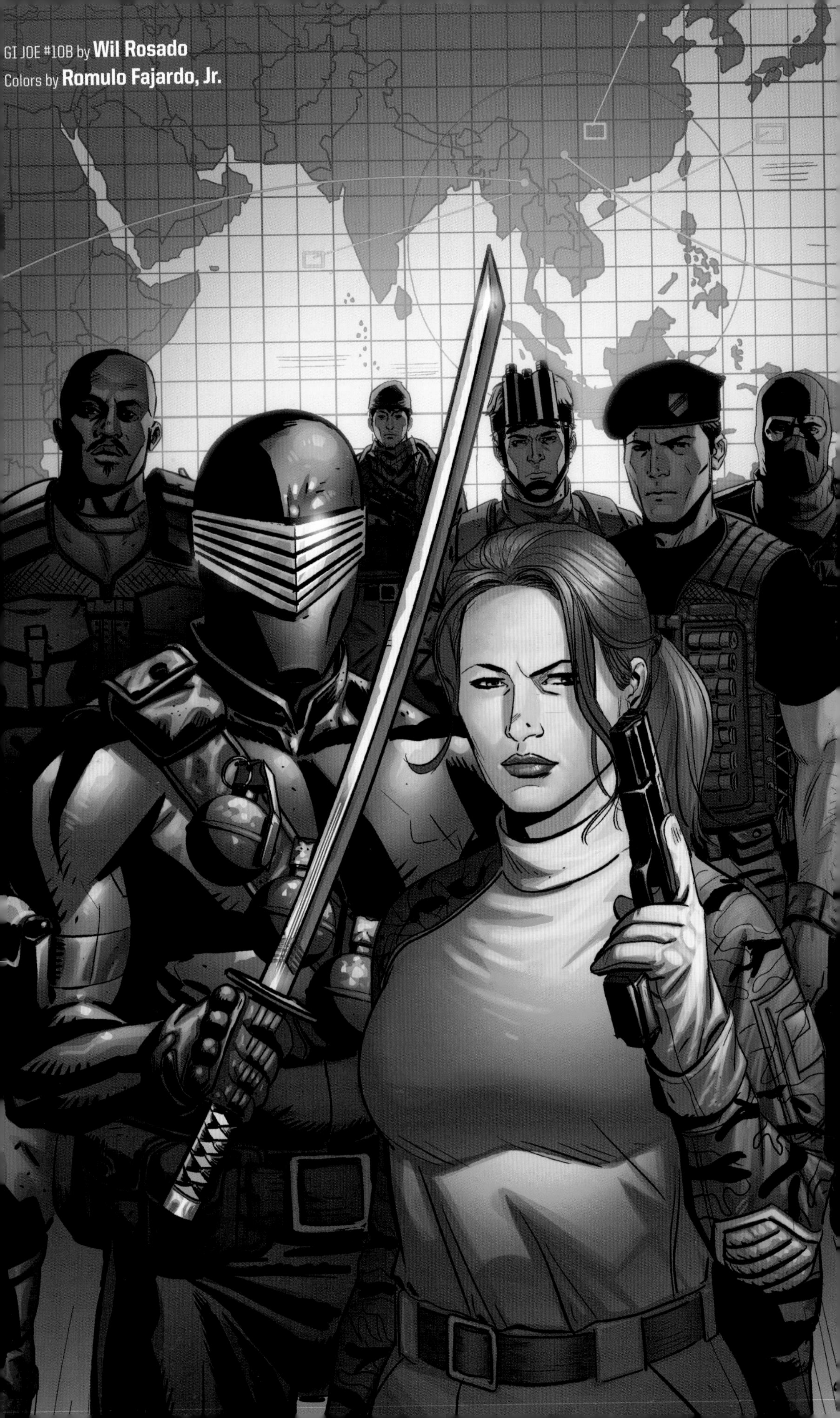

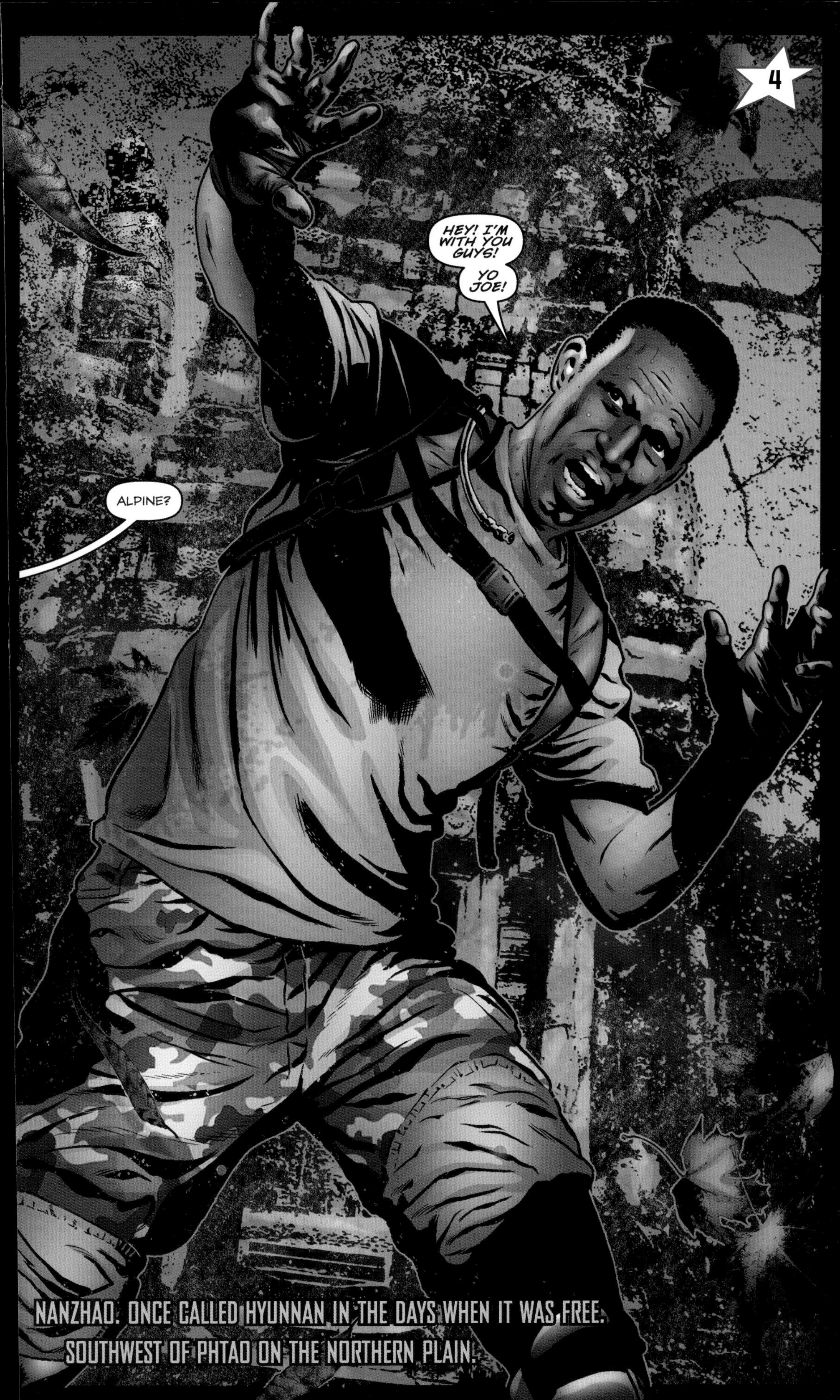
4
HEY! I'M WITH YOU GUYS!
YO JOE!
ALPINE?
NANZHAO. ONCE CALLED HYUNNAN IN THE DAYS WHEN IT WAS FREE.
SOUTHWEST OF PHTAO ON THE NORTHERN PLAIN.

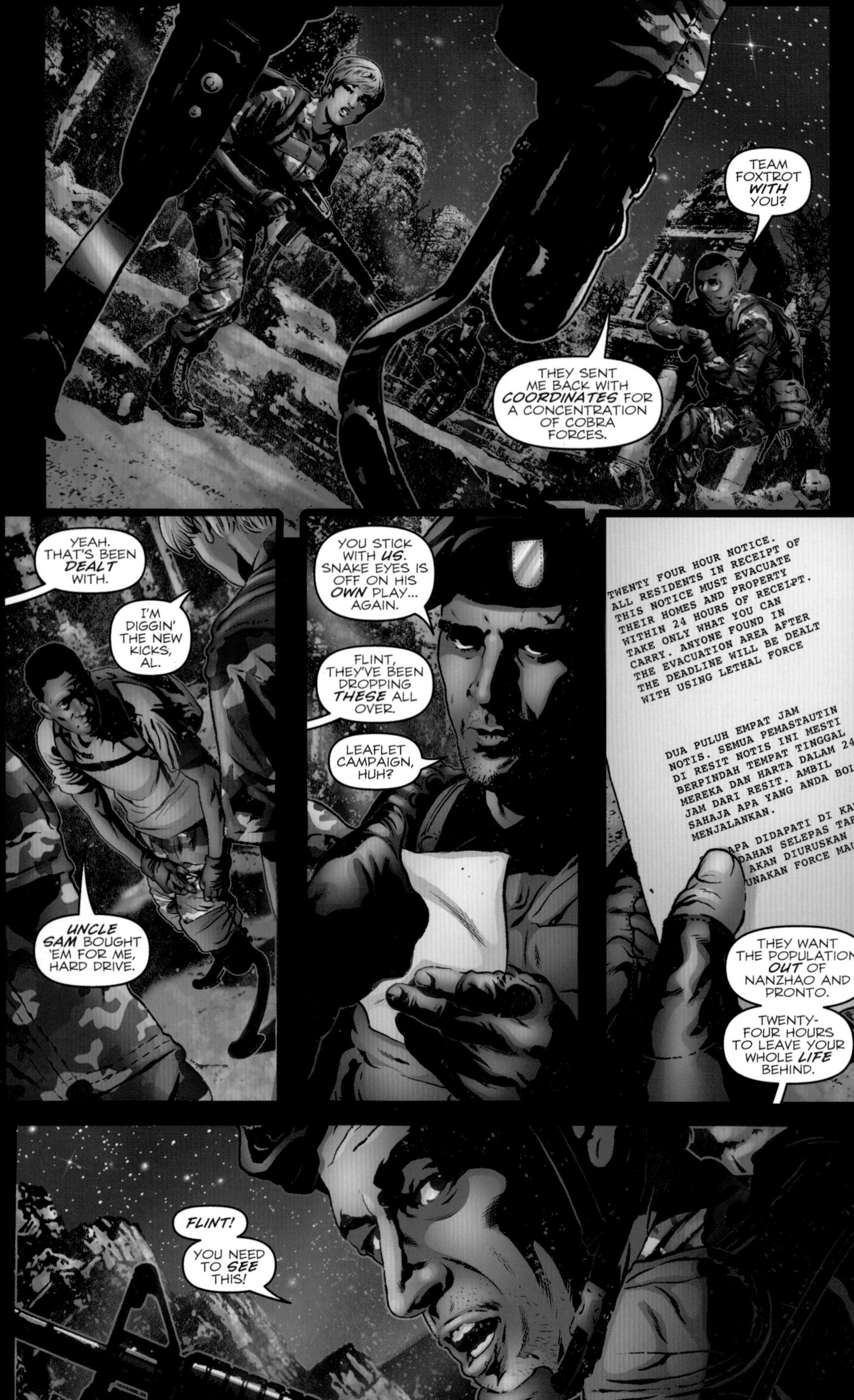

TEAM FOXTROT WITH YOU?
THEY SENT ME BACK WITH COORDINATES FOR A CONCENTRATION OF COBRA FORCES.
YEAH. THAT'S BEEN DEALT WITH.
I'M DIGGIN' THE NEW KICKS, AL.
UNCLE SAM BOUGHT 'EM FOR ME, HARD DRIVE.
YOU STICK WITH US. SNAKE EYES IS OFF ON HIS OWN PLAY... AGAIN.
FLINT, THEY'VE BEEN DROPPING THESE ALL OVER.
LEAFLET CAMPAIGN, HUH?
TWENTY FOUR HOUR NOTICE. ALL RESIDENTS IN RECEIPT OF THIS NOTICE MUST EVACUATE THEIR HOMES AND PROPERTY WITHIN 24 HOURS OF RECEIPT. TAKE ONLY WHAT YOU CAN CARRY. ANYONE FOUND IN THE EVACUATION AREA AFTER THE DEADLINE WILL BE DEALT WITH USING LETHAL FORCE
DUA PULUH EMPAT JAM NOTIS. SEMUA PEMASTAUTIN DI RESIT NOTIS INI MESTI BERPINDAH TEMPAT TINGGAL MEREKA DAN HARTA DALAM 24 JAM DARI RESIT. AMBIL SAHAJA APA YANG ANDA BOLE MENJALANKAN.
APA DIDAPATI DI KAWA DAHAN SELEPAS TARI AKAN DIURUSKAN UNAKAN FORCE MAUT
THEY WANT THE POPULATION OUT OF NANZHAO AND PRONTO.
TWENTY-FOUR HOURS TO LEAVE YOUR WHOLE LIFE BEHIND.
FLINT!
YOU NEED TO SEE THIS!

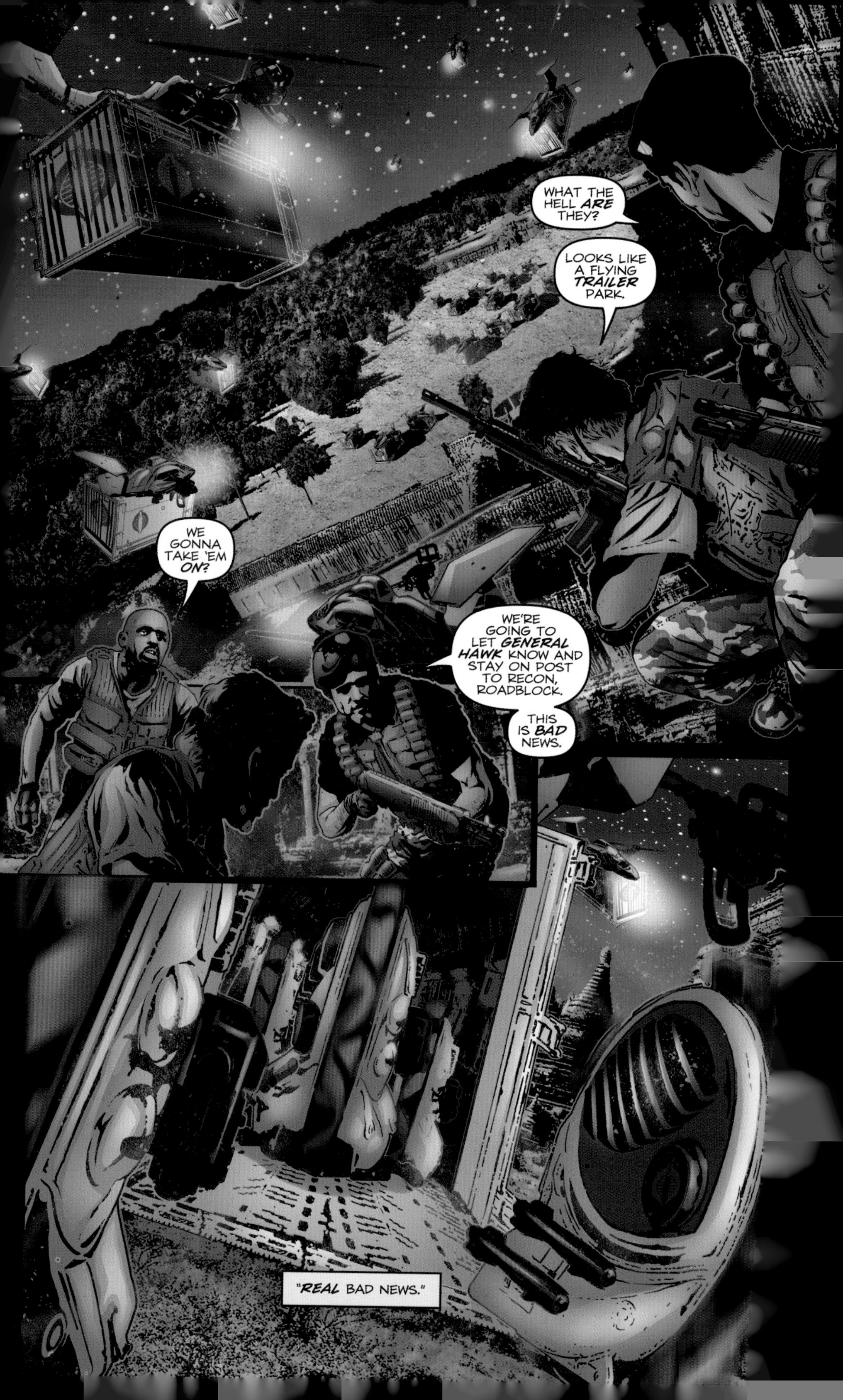

WHAT THE HELL **ARE** THEY?
LOOKS LIKE A FLYING **TRAILER** PARK.
WE GONNA TAKE 'EM **ON**?
WE'RE GOING TO LET **GENERAL HAWK** KNOW AND STAY ON POST TO RECON, ROADBLOCK.
THIS IS **BAD** NEWS.
"**REAL** BAD NEWS."

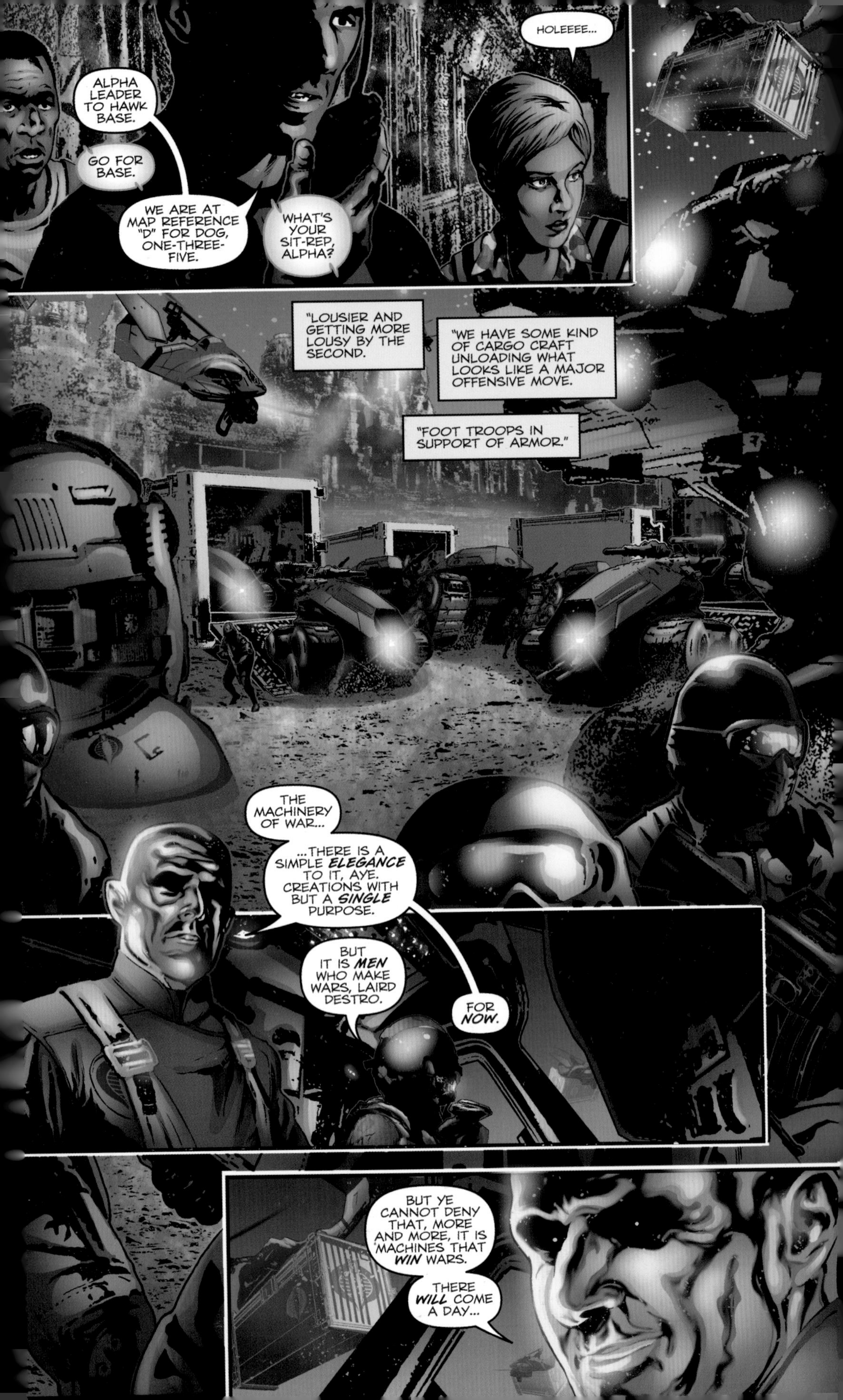
ALPHA LEADER TO HAWK BASE.
GO FOR BASE.
WE ARE AT MAP REFERENCE "D" FOR DOG, ONE-THREE-FIVE.
WHAT'S YOUR SIT-REP, ALPHA?
HOLEEEE...
"LOUSIER AND GETTING MORE LOUSY BY THE SECOND.
"WE HAVE SOME KIND OF CARGO CRAFT UNLOADING WHAT LOOKS LIKE A MAJOR OFFENSIVE MOVE.
"FOOT TROOPS IN SUPPORT OF ARMOR."
THE MACHINERY OF WAR...
...THERE IS A SIMPLE ELEGANCE TO IT, AYE. CREATIONS WITH BUT A SINGLE PURPOSE.
BUT IT IS MEN WHO MAKE WARS, LAIRD DESTRO.
FOR NOW.
BUT YE CANNOT DENY THAT, MORE AND MORE, IT IS MACHINES THAT WIN WARS.
THERE WILL COME A DAY...

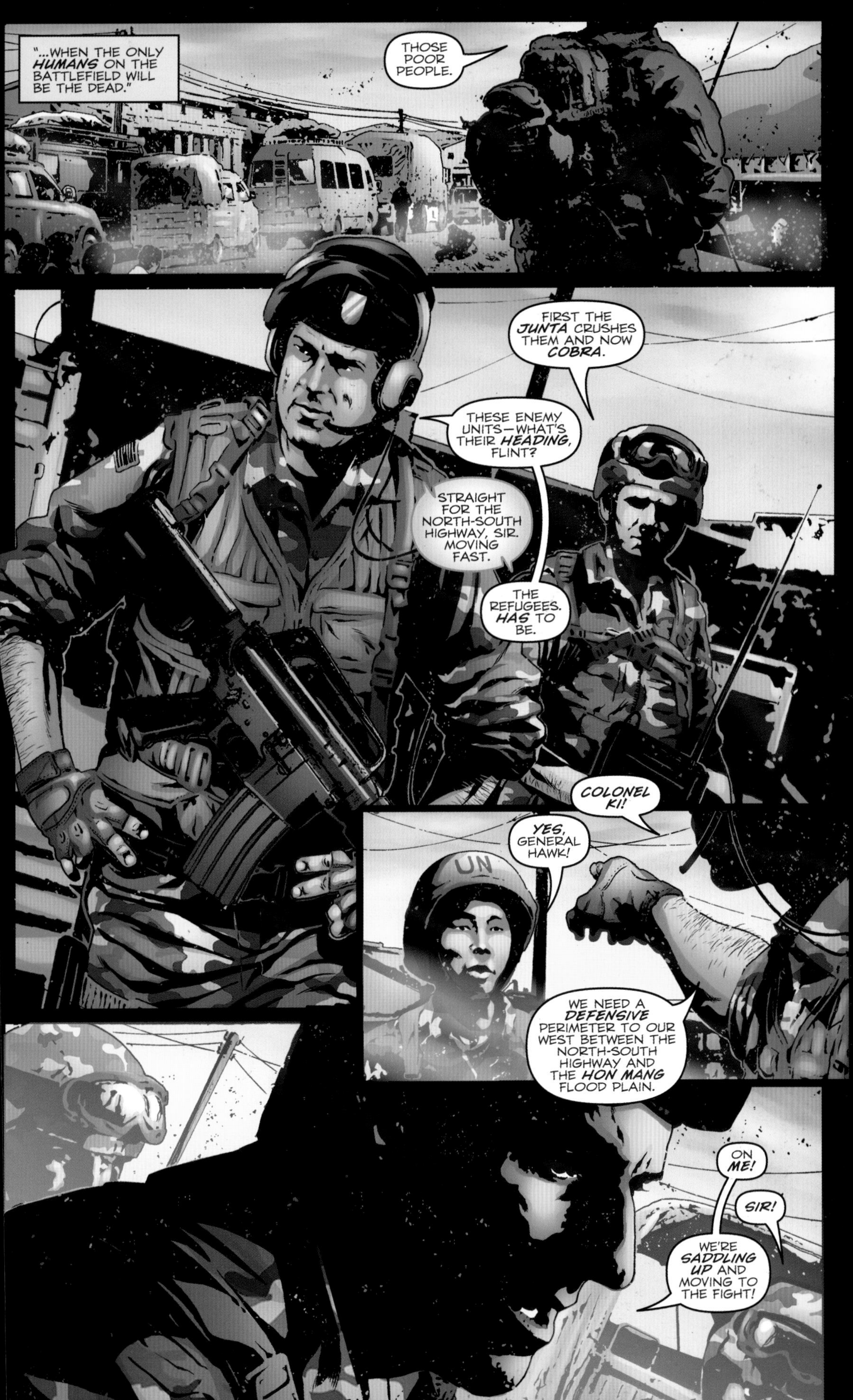
"...WHEN THE ONLY HUMANS ON THE BATTLEFIELD WILL BE THE DEAD."
THOSE POOR PEOPLE.
FIRST THE JUNTA CRUSHES THEM AND NOW COBRA.
THESE ENEMY UNITS—WHAT'S THEIR HEADING, FLINT?
STRAIGHT FOR THE NORTH-SOUTH HIGHWAY, SIR. MOVING FAST.
THE REFUGEES. HAS TO BE.
COLONEL KI!
YES, GENERAL HAWK!
UN
WE NEED A DEFENSIVE PERIMETER TO OUR WEST BETWEEN THE NORTH-SOUTH HIGHWAY AND THE HON MANG FLOOD PLAIN.
ON ME!
SIR!
WE'RE SADDLING UP AND MOVING TO THE FIGHT!

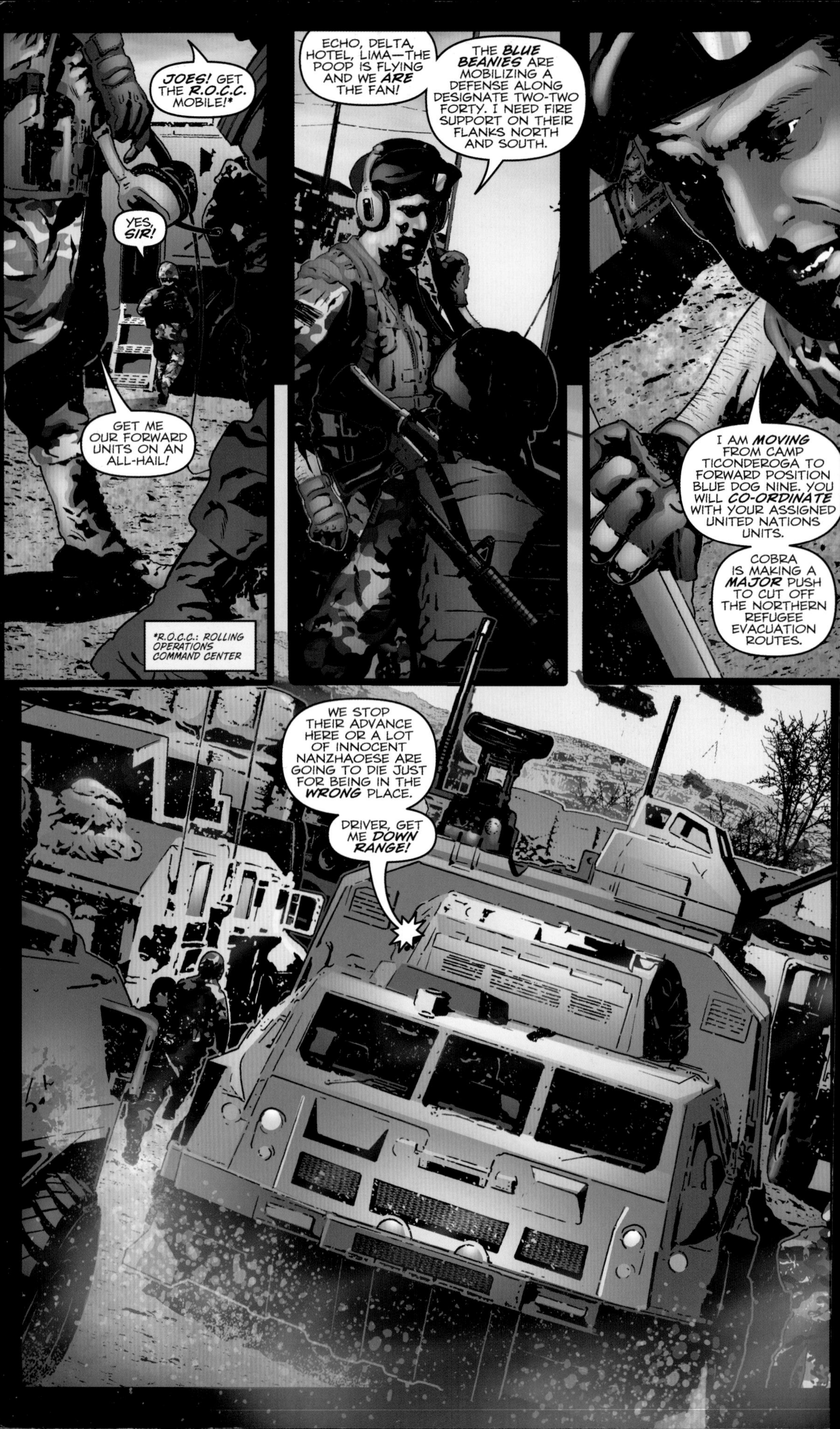
JOES! GET THE R.O.C.C. MOBILE!*
YES, SIR!
GET ME OUR FORWARD UNITS ON AN ALL-HAIL!
*R.O.C.C.: ROLLING OPERATIONS COMMAND CENTER
ECHO, DELTA, HOTEL, LIMA—THE POOP IS FLYING AND WE ARE THE FAN!
THE BLUE BEANIES ARE MOBILIZING A DEFENSE ALONG DESIGNATE TWO-TWO FORTY. I NEED FIRE SUPPORT ON THEIR FLANKS NORTH AND SOUTH.
I AM MOVING FROM CAMP TICONDEROGA TO FORWARD POSITION BLUE DOG NINE. YOU WILL CO-ORDINATE WITH YOUR ASSIGNED UNITED NATIONS UNITS.
COBRA IS MAKING A MAJOR PUSH TO CUT OFF THE NORTHERN REFUGEE EVACUATION ROUTES.
WE STOP THEIR ADVANCE HERE OR A LOT OF INNOCENT NANZHAOESE ARE GOING TO DIE JUST FOR BEING IN THE WRONG PLACE.
DRIVER, GET ME DOWN RANGE!

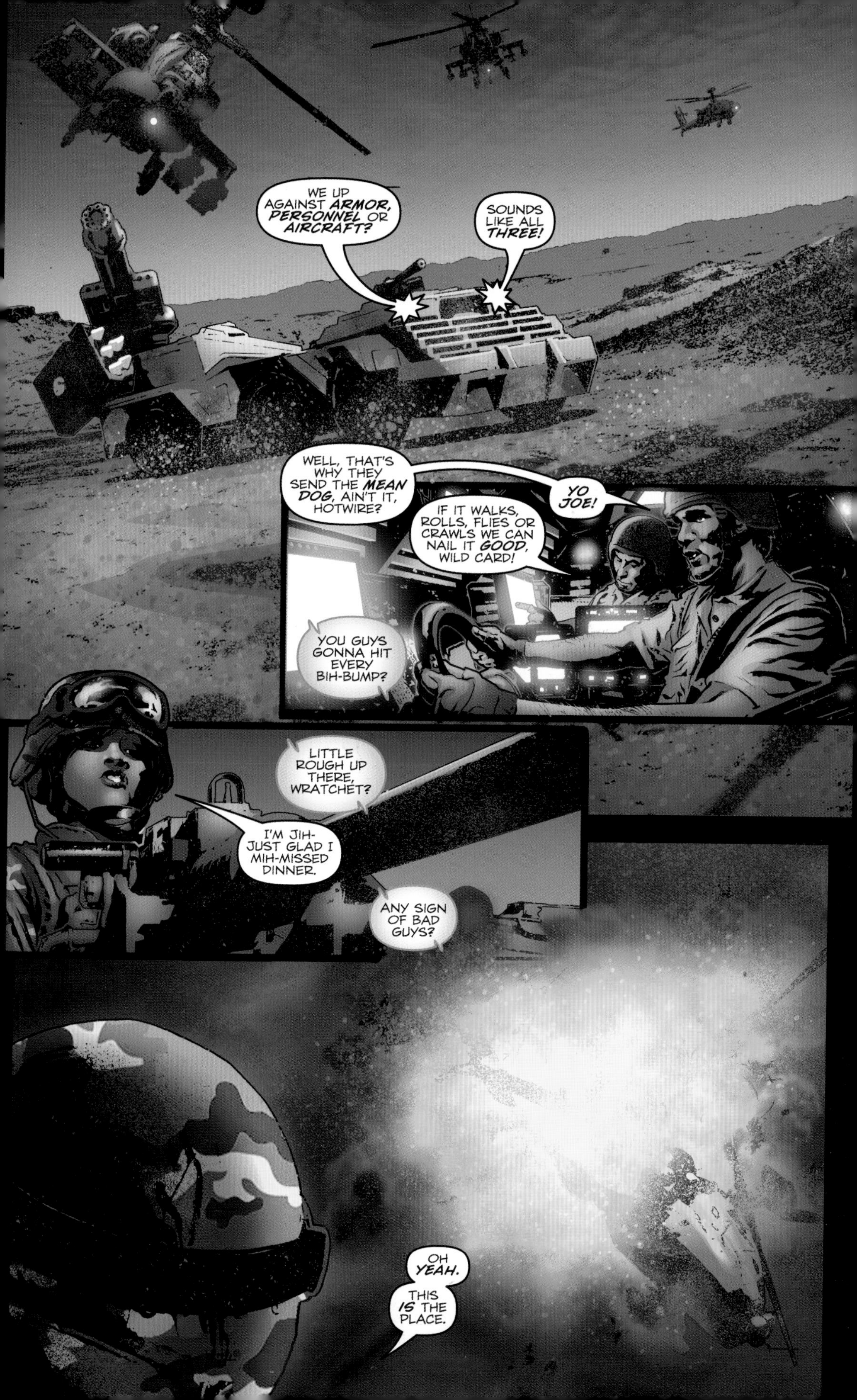
WE UP AGAINST **ARMOR, PERSONNEL** OR **AIRCRAFT?**
SOUNDS LIKE ALL **THREE!**
WELL, THAT'S WHY THEY SEND THE **MEAN DOG**, AIN'T IT, HOTWIRE?
YO JOE!
IF IT WALKS, ROLLS, FLIES OR CRAWLS WE CAN NAIL IT **GOOD**, WILD CARD!
YOU GUYS GONNA HIT EVERY BIH-BUMP?
LITTLE ROUGH UP THERE, WRATCHET?
I'M JIH-JUST GLAD I MIH-MISSED DINNER.
ANY SIGN OF BAD GUYS?
OH **YEAH.**
THIS **IS** THE PLACE.

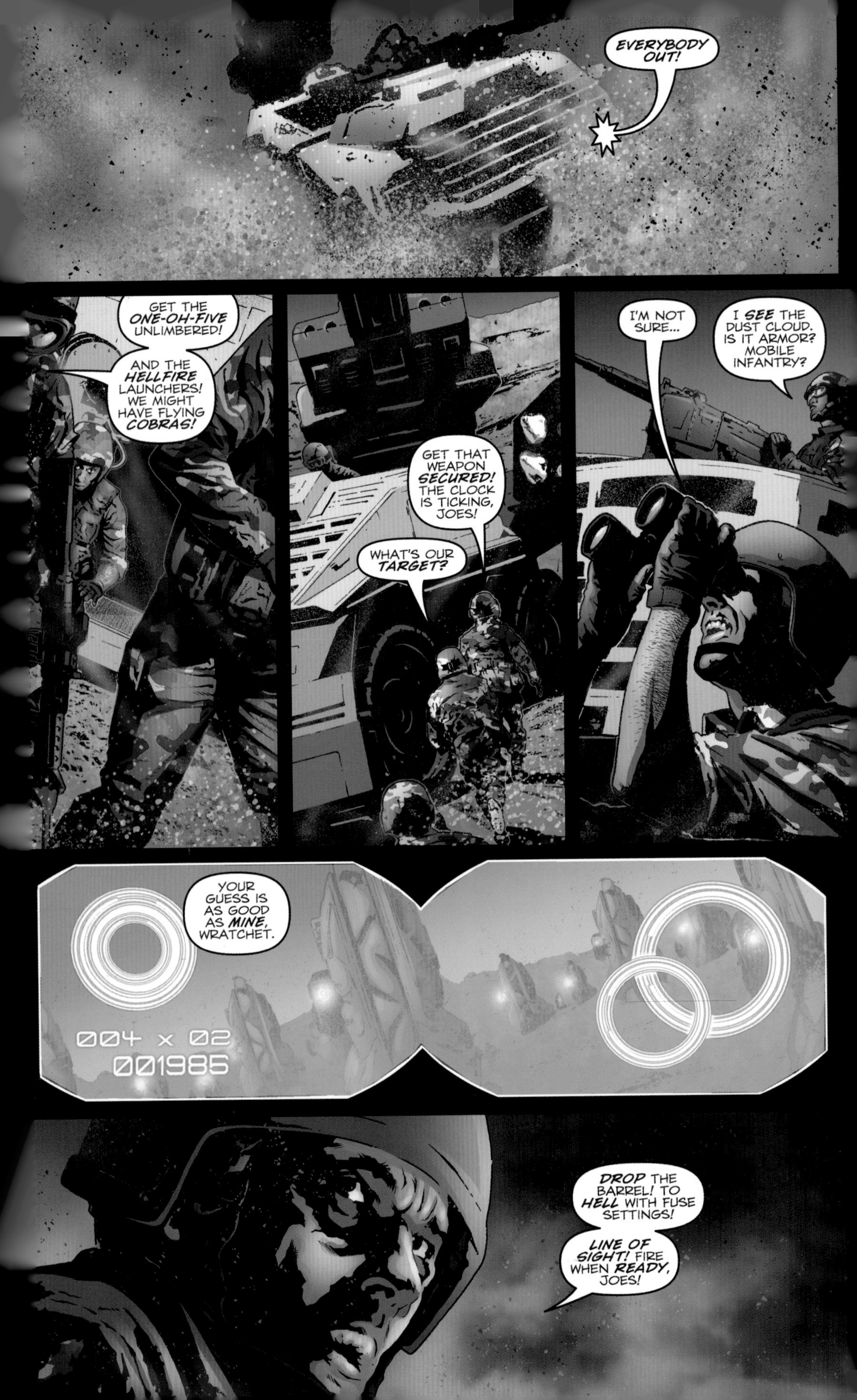
EVERYBODY OUT!
GET THE ONE-OH-FIVE UNLIMBERED!
AND THE HELLFIRE LAUNCHERS! WE MIGHT HAVE FLYING COBRAS!
GET THAT WEAPON SECURED! THE CLOCK IS TICKING, JOES!
WHAT'S OUR TARGET?
I'M NOT SURE...
I SEE THE DUST CLOUD. IS IT ARMOR? MOBILE INFANTRY?
YOUR GUESS IS AS GOOD AS MINE, WRATCHET.
004 x 02
001985
DROP THE BARREL! TO HELL WITH FUSE SETTINGS!
LINE OF SIGHT! FIRE WHEN READY, JOES!

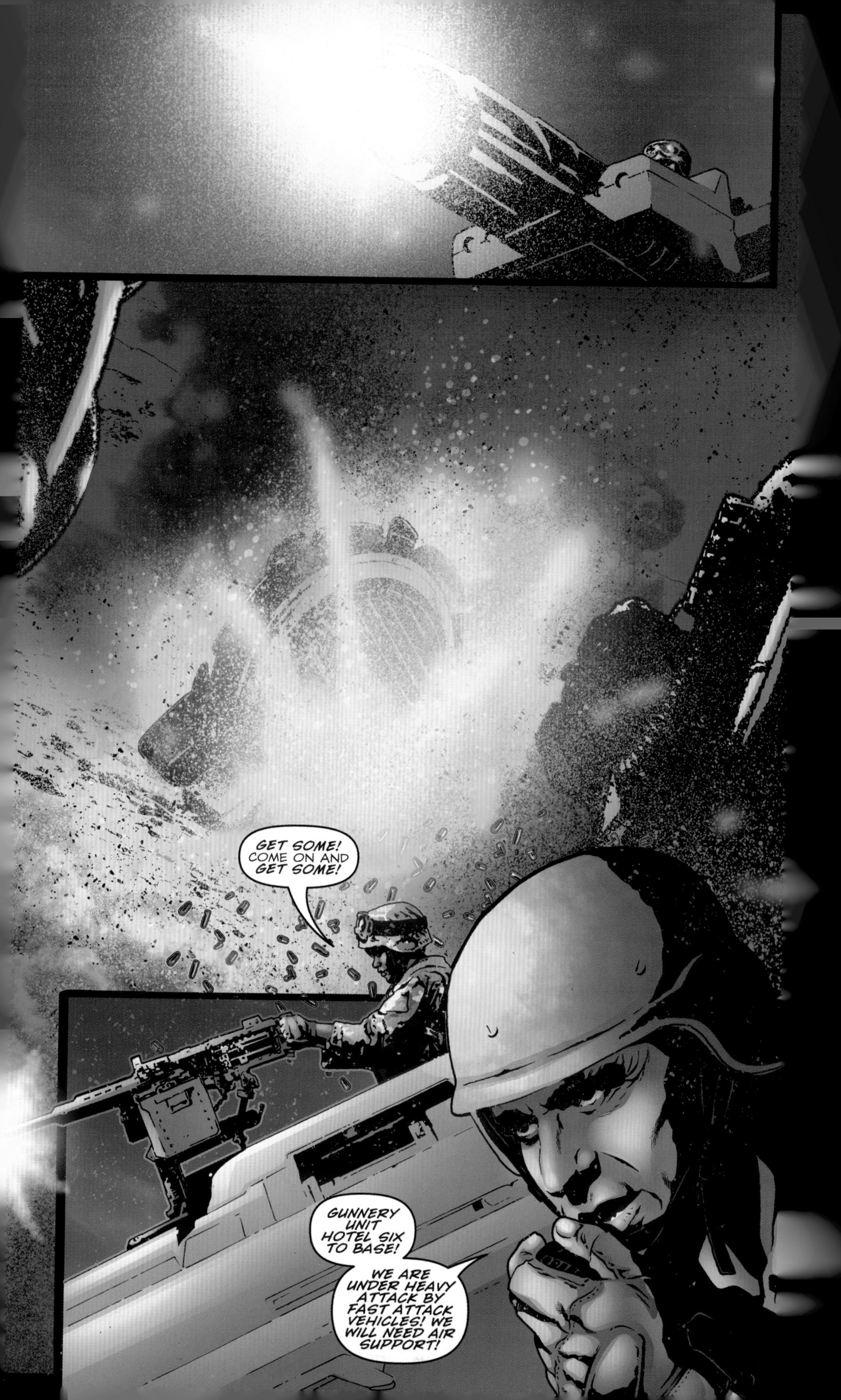
GET SOME! COME ON AND GET SOME!
GUNNERY UNIT HOTEL SIX TO BASE!
WE ARE UNDER HEAVY ATTACK BY FAST ATTACK VEHICLES! WE WILL NEED AIR SUPPORT!

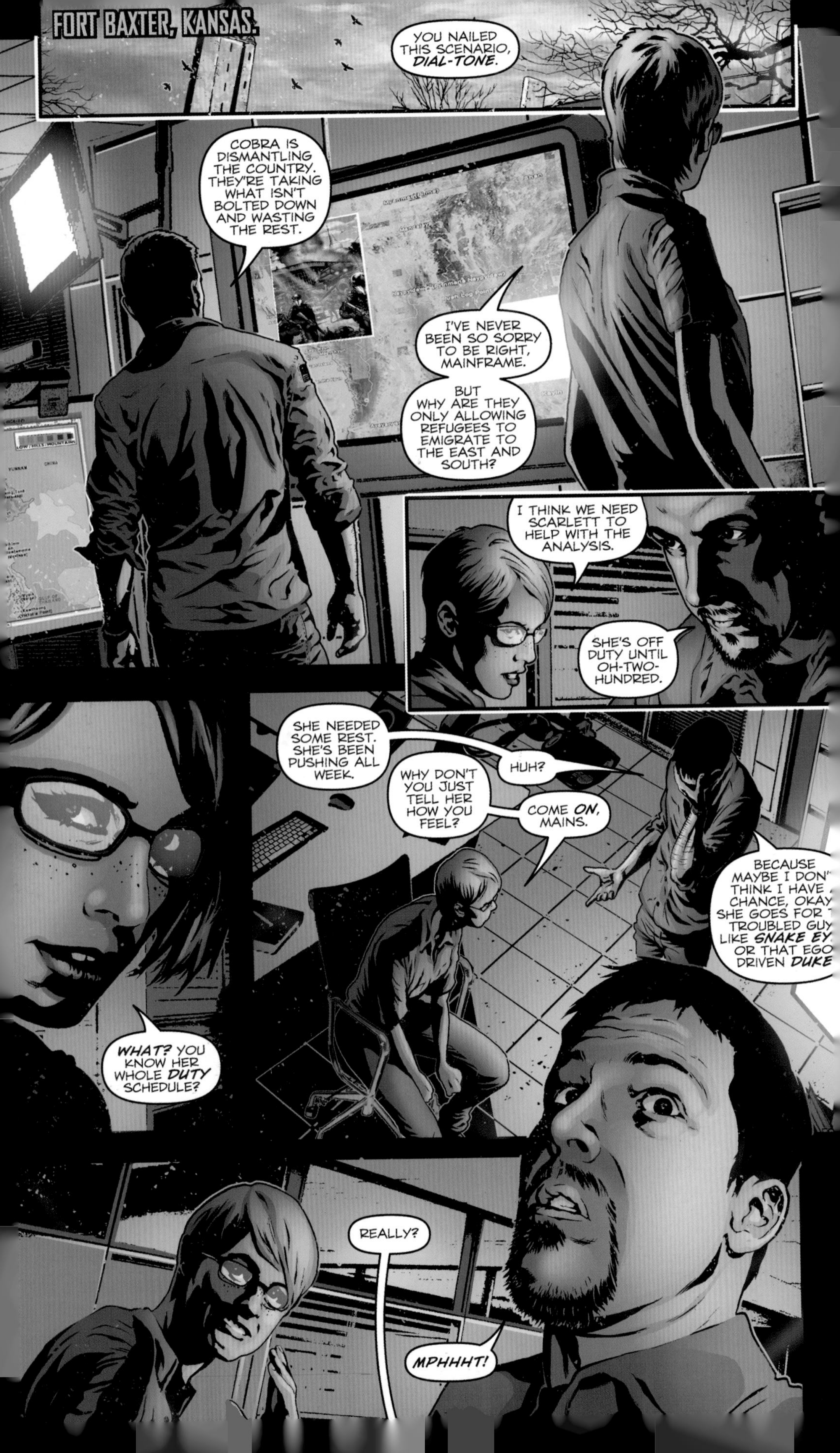

FORT BAXTER, KANSAS.
YOU NAILED THIS SCENARIO, DIAL-TONE.
COBRA IS DISMANTLING THE COUNTRY. THEY'RE TAKING WHAT ISN'T BOLTED DOWN AND WASTING THE REST.
I'VE NEVER BEEN SO SORRY TO BE RIGHT, MAINFRAME.
BUT WHY ARE THEY ONLY ALLOWING REFUGEES TO EMIGRATE TO THE EAST AND SOUTH?
I THINK WE NEED SCARLETT TO HELP WITH THE ANALYSIS.
SHE'S OFF DUTY UNTIL OH-TWO-HUNDRED.
WHAT? YOU KNOW HER WHOLE DUTY SCHEDULE?
SHE NEEDED SOME REST. SHE'S BEEN PUSHING ALL WEEK.
HUH?
WHY DON'T YOU JUST TELL HER HOW YOU FEEL?
COME ON, MAINS.
BECAUSE MAYBE I DON' THINK I HAVE CHANCE, OKAY SHE GOES FOR TROUBLED GUY LIKE SNAKE EY OR THAT EGO DRIVEN DUKE
REALLY?
MPHHHT!

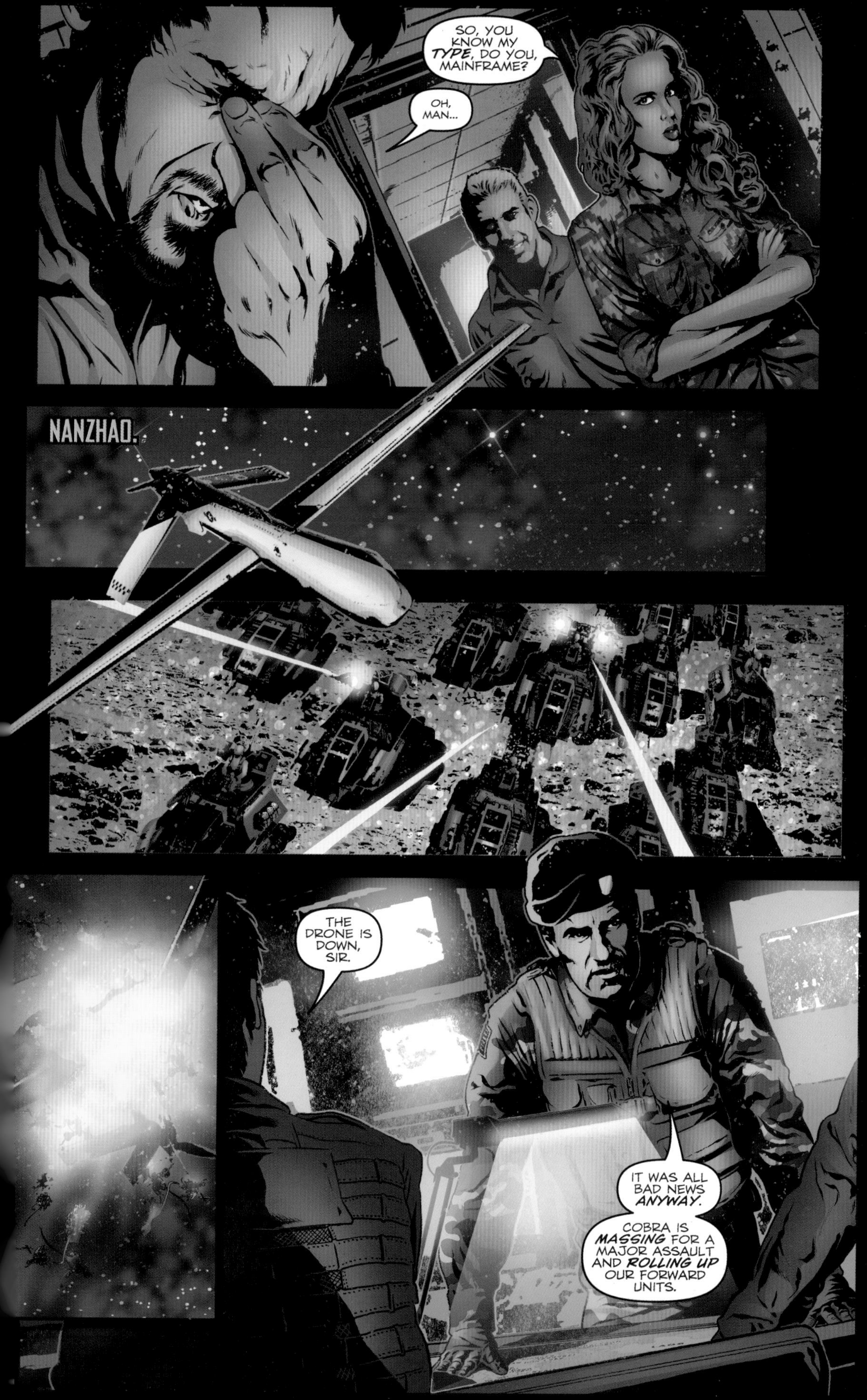
SO, YOU KNOW MY TYPE, DO YOU, MAINFRAME?
OH, MAN...
NANZHAO.
THE DRONE IS DOWN, SIR.
IT WAS ALL BAD NEWS ANYWAY.
COBRA IS MASSING FOR A MAJOR ASSAULT AND ROLLING UP OUR FORWARD UNITS.

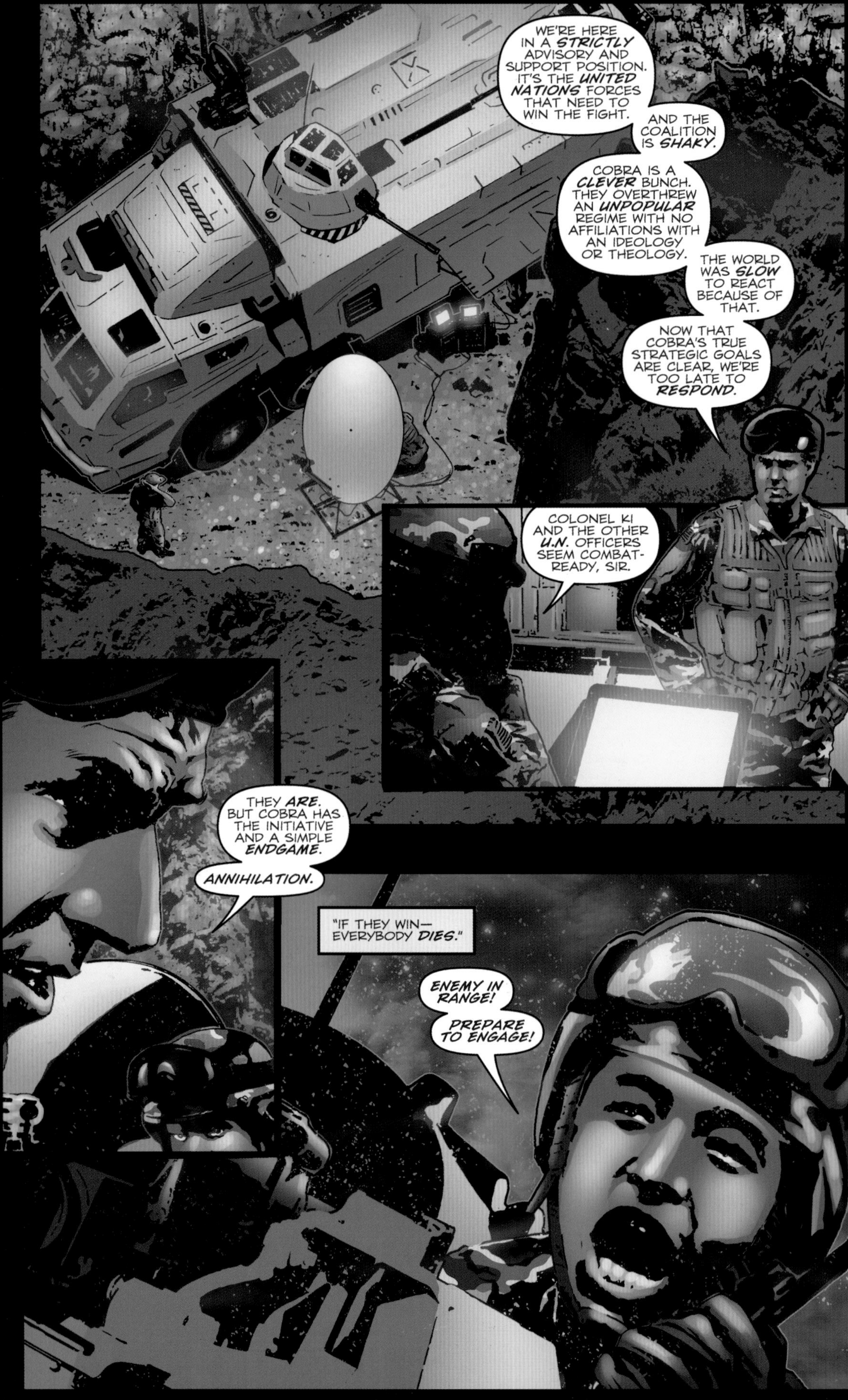
WE'RE HERE IN A STRICTLY ADVISORY AND SUPPORT POSITION. IT'S THE UNITED NATIONS FORCES THAT NEED TO WIN THE FIGHT.
AND THE COALITION IS SHAKY.
COBRA IS A CLEVER BUNCH. THEY OVERTHREW AN UNPOPULAR REGIME WITH NO AFFILIATIONS WITH AN IDEOLOGY OR THEOLOGY.
THE WORLD WAS SLOW TO REACT BECAUSE OF THAT.
NOW THAT COBRA'S TRUE STRATEGIC GOALS ARE CLEAR, WE'RE TOO LATE TO RESPOND.
COLONEL KI AND THE OTHER U.N. OFFICERS SEEM COMBAT-READY, SIR.
THEY ARE. BUT COBRA HAS THE INITIATIVE AND A SIMPLE ENDGAME.
ANNIHILATION.
"IF THEY WIN— EVERYBODY DIES."
ENEMY IN RANGE!
PREPARE TO ENGAGE!

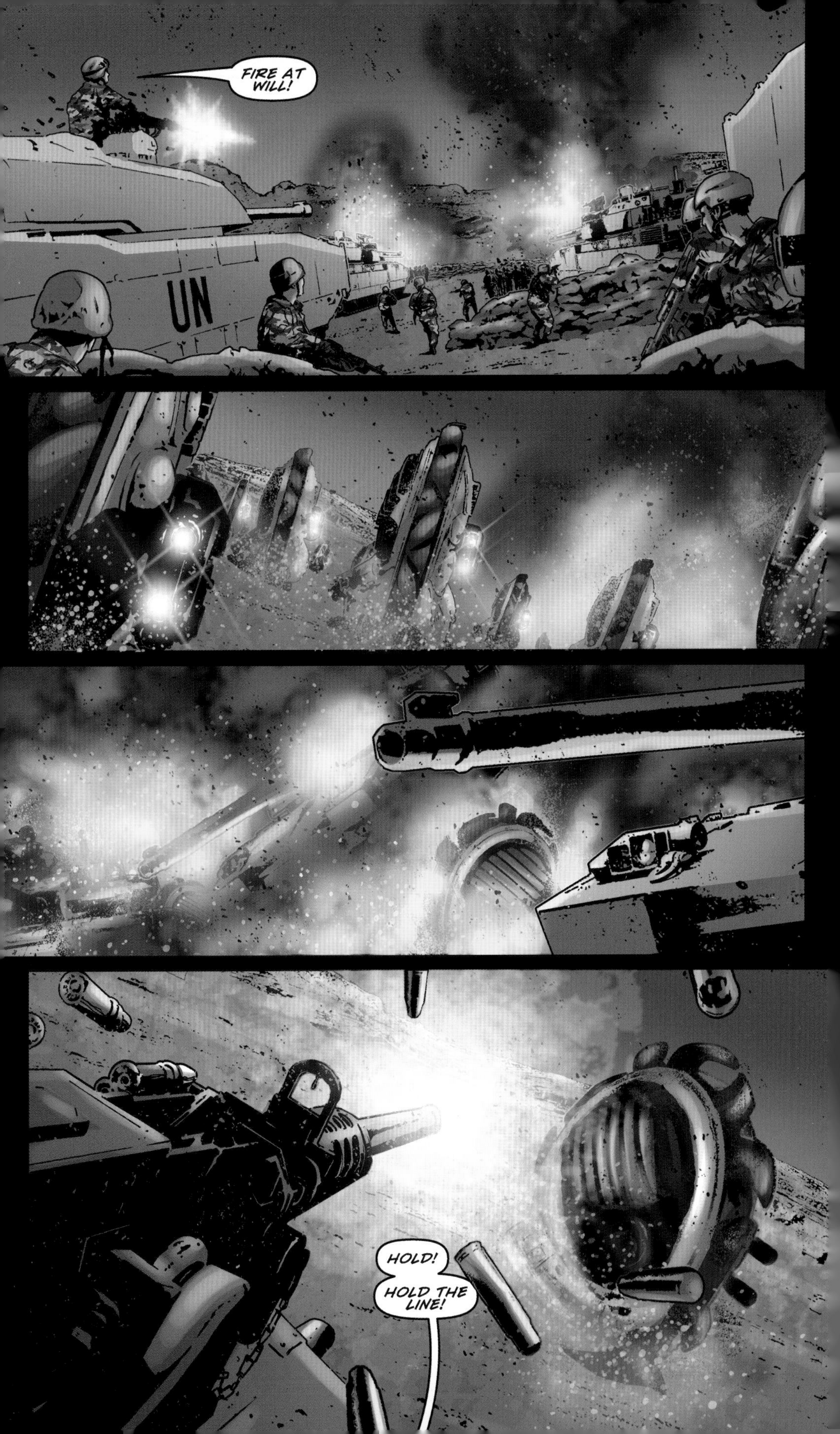
FIRE AT WILL!
HOLD!
HOLD THE LINE!

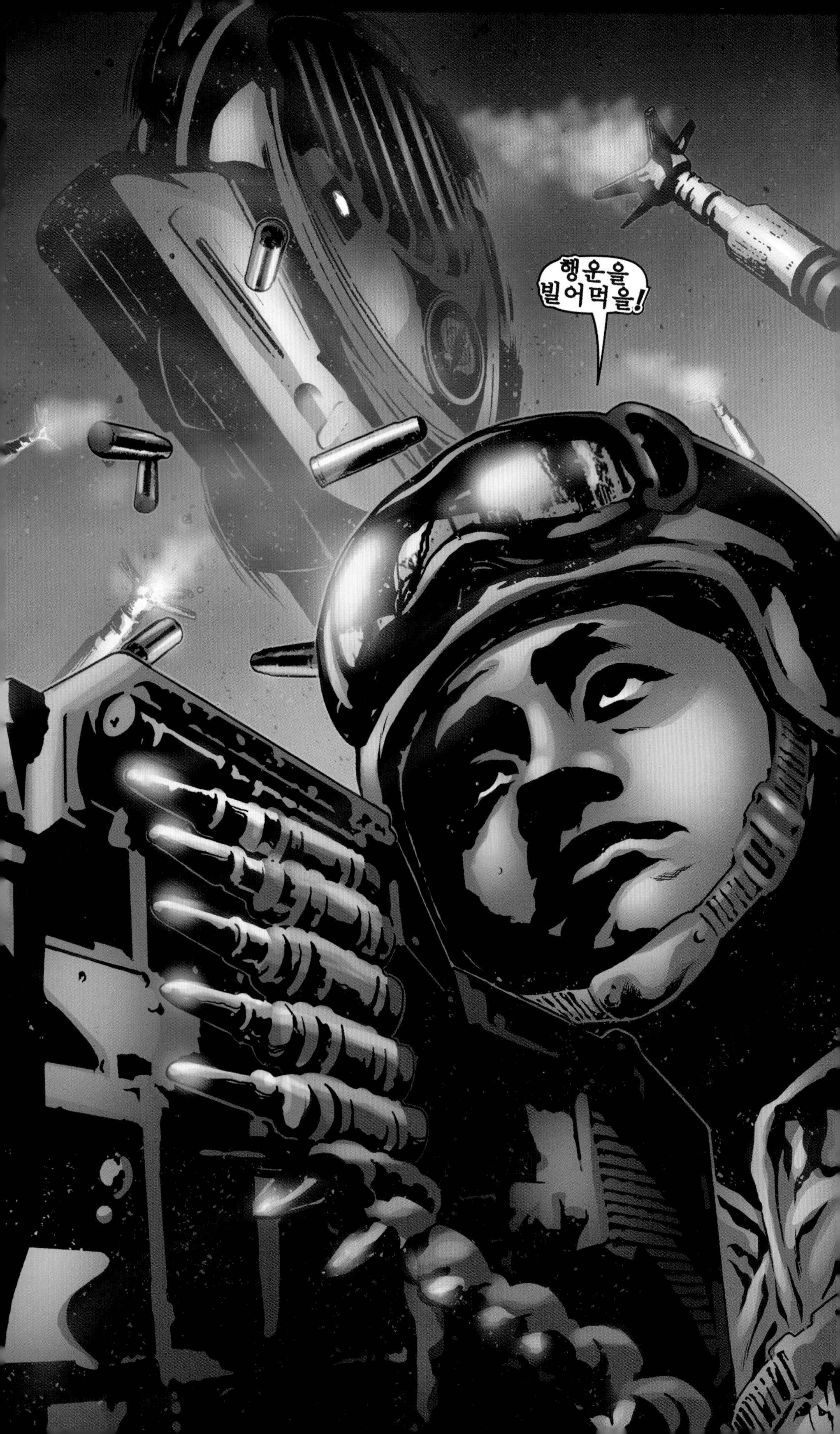
행운을 빌어먹을!

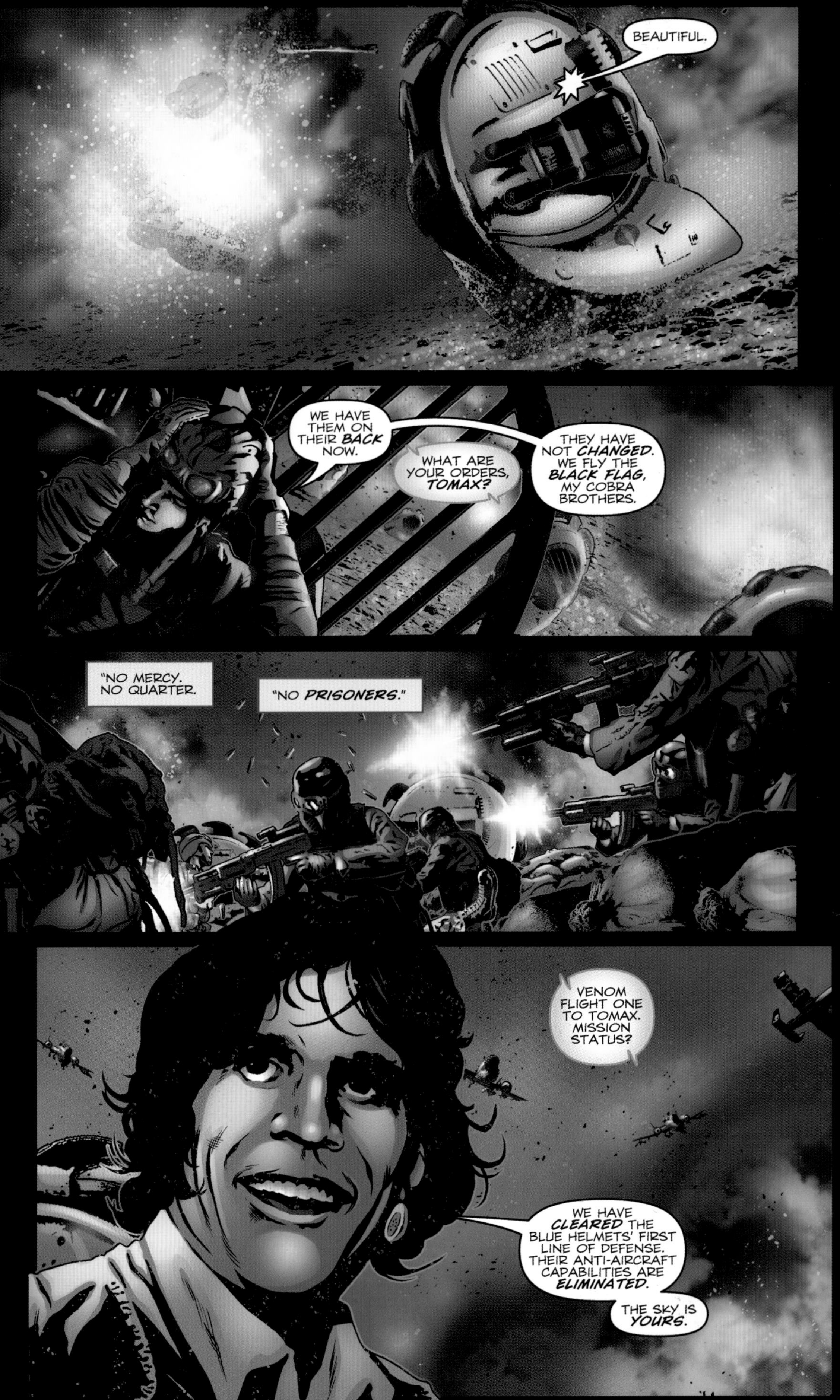
BEAUTIFUL.
WE HAVE THEM ON THEIR BACK NOW.
WHAT ARE YOUR ORDERS, TOMAX?
THEY HAVE NOT CHANGED. WE FLY THE BLACK FLAG, MY COBRA BROTHERS.
"NO MERCY. NO QUARTER.
"NO PRISONERS."
VENOM FLIGHT ONE TO TOMAX. MISSION STATUS?
WE HAVE CLEARED THE BLUE HELMETS' FIRST LINE OF DEFENSE. THEIR ANTI-AIRCRAFT CAPABILITIES ARE ELIMINATED.
THE SKY IS YOURS.

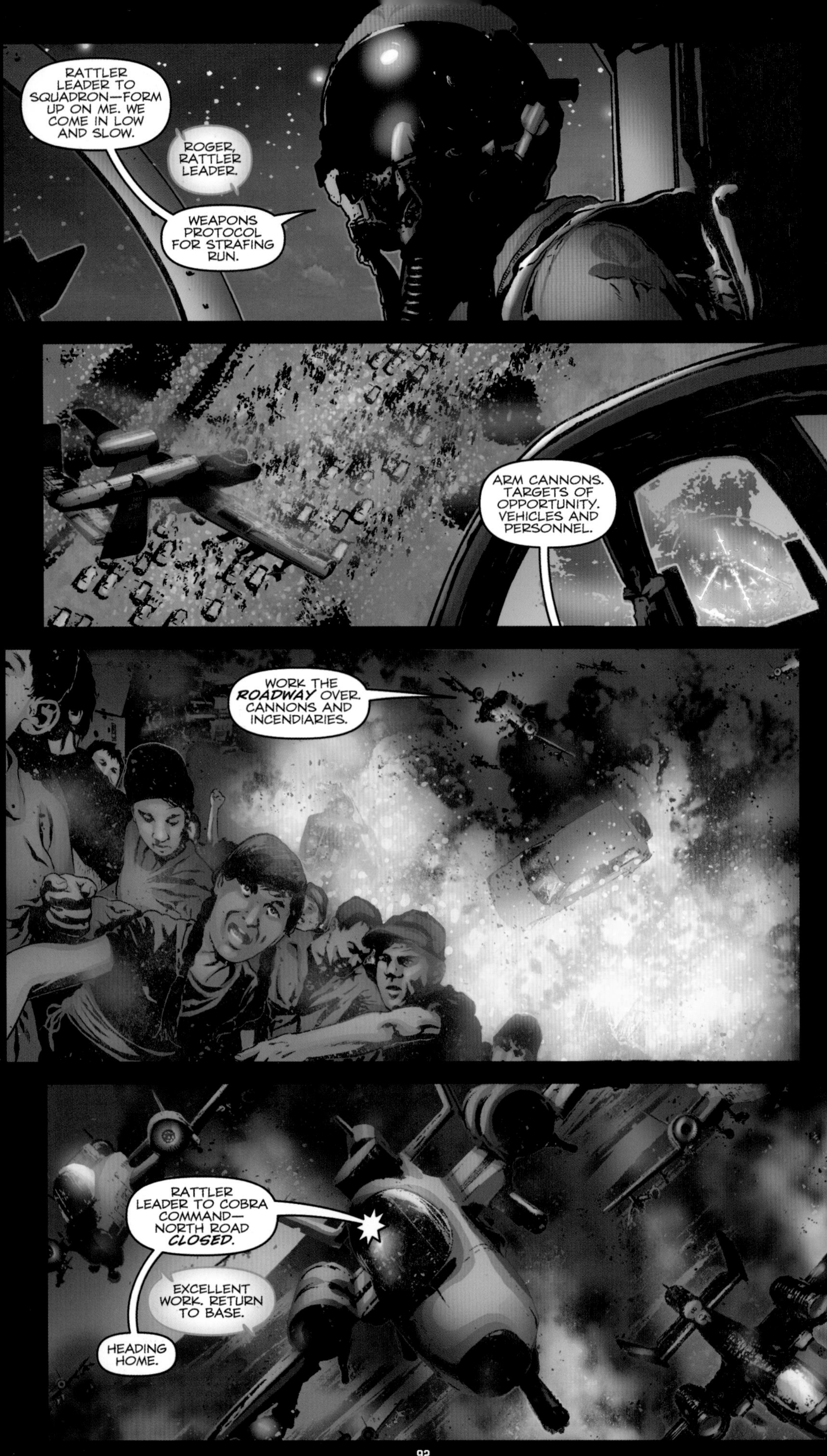
RATTLER LEADER TO SQUADRON—FORM UP ON ME. WE COME IN LOW AND SLOW.
ROGER, RATTLER LEADER.
WEAPONS PROTOCOL FOR STRAFING RUN.
ARM CANNONS. TARGETS OF OPPORTUNITY. VEHICLES AND PERSONNEL.
WORK THE *ROADWAY* OVER. CANNONS AND INCENDIARIES.
RATTLER LEADER TO COBRA COMMAND—NORTH ROAD *CLOSED*.
EXCELLENT WORK. RETURN TO BASE.
HEADING HOME.

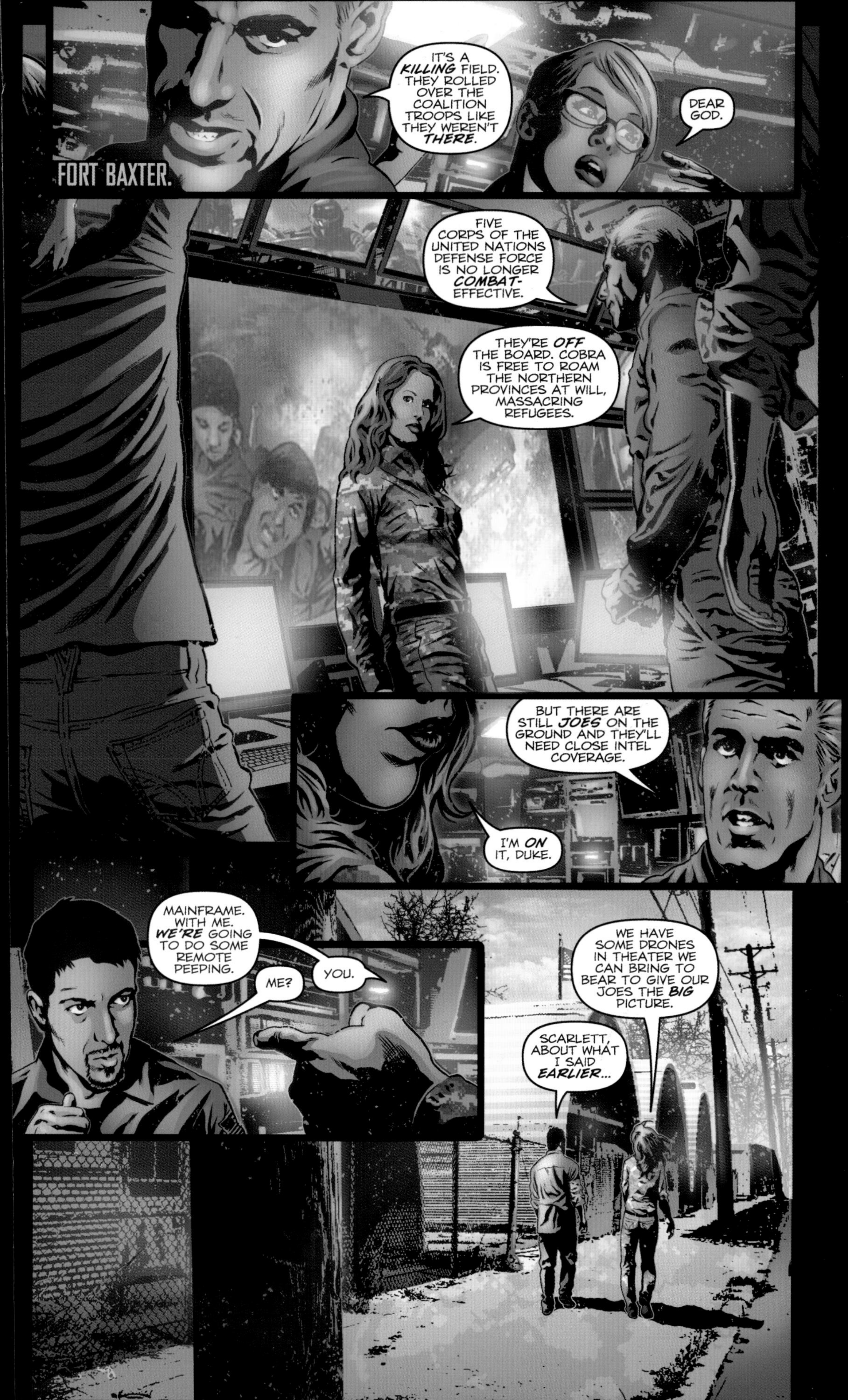
FORT BAXTER.
IT'S A KILLING FIELD. THEY ROLLED OVER THE COALITION TROOPS LIKE THEY WEREN'T THERE.
DEAR GOD.
FIVE CORPS OF THE UNITED NATIONS DEFENSE FORCE IS NO LONGER COMBAT-EFFECTIVE.
THEY'RE OFF THE BOARD. COBRA IS FREE TO ROAM THE NORTHERN PROVINCES AT WILL, MASSACRING REFUGEES.
BUT THERE ARE STILL JOES ON THE GROUND AND THEY'LL NEED CLOSE INTEL COVERAGE.
I'M ON IT, DUKE.
MAINFRAME. WITH ME. WE'RE GOING TO DO SOME REMOTE PEEPING.
ME?
YOU.
WE HAVE SOME DRONES IN THEATER WE CAN BRING TO BEAR TO GIVE OUR JOES THE BIG PICTURE.
SCARLETT, ABOUT WHAT I SAID EARLIER...

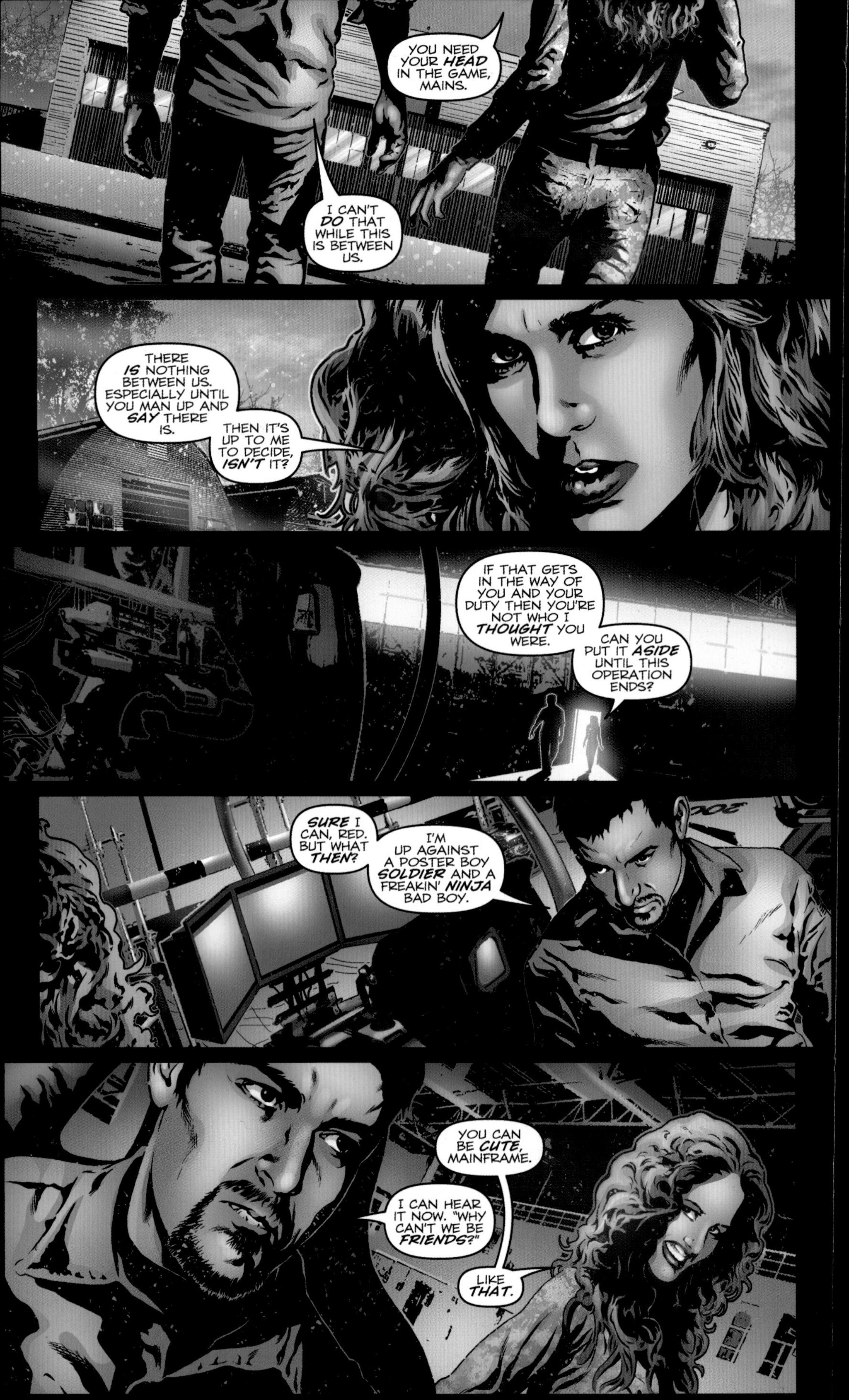
YOU NEED YOUR HEAD IN THE GAME, MAINS.
I CAN'T DO THAT WHILE THIS IS BETWEEN US.
THERE IS NOTHING BETWEEN US. ESPECIALLY UNTIL YOU MAN UP AND SAY THERE IS.
THEN IT'S UP TO ME TO DECIDE, ISN'T IT?
IF THAT GETS IN THE WAY OF YOU AND YOUR DUTY THEN YOU'RE NOT WHO I THOUGHT YOU WERE.
CAN YOU PUT IT ASIDE UNTIL THIS OPERATION ENDS?
SURE I CAN, RED. BUT WHAT THEN?
I'M UP AGAINST A POSTER BOY SOLDIER AND A FREAKIN' NINJA BAD BOY.
YOU CAN BE CUTE, MAINFRAME.
I CAN HEAR IT NOW. "WHY CAN'T WE BE FRIENDS?"
LIKE THAT.

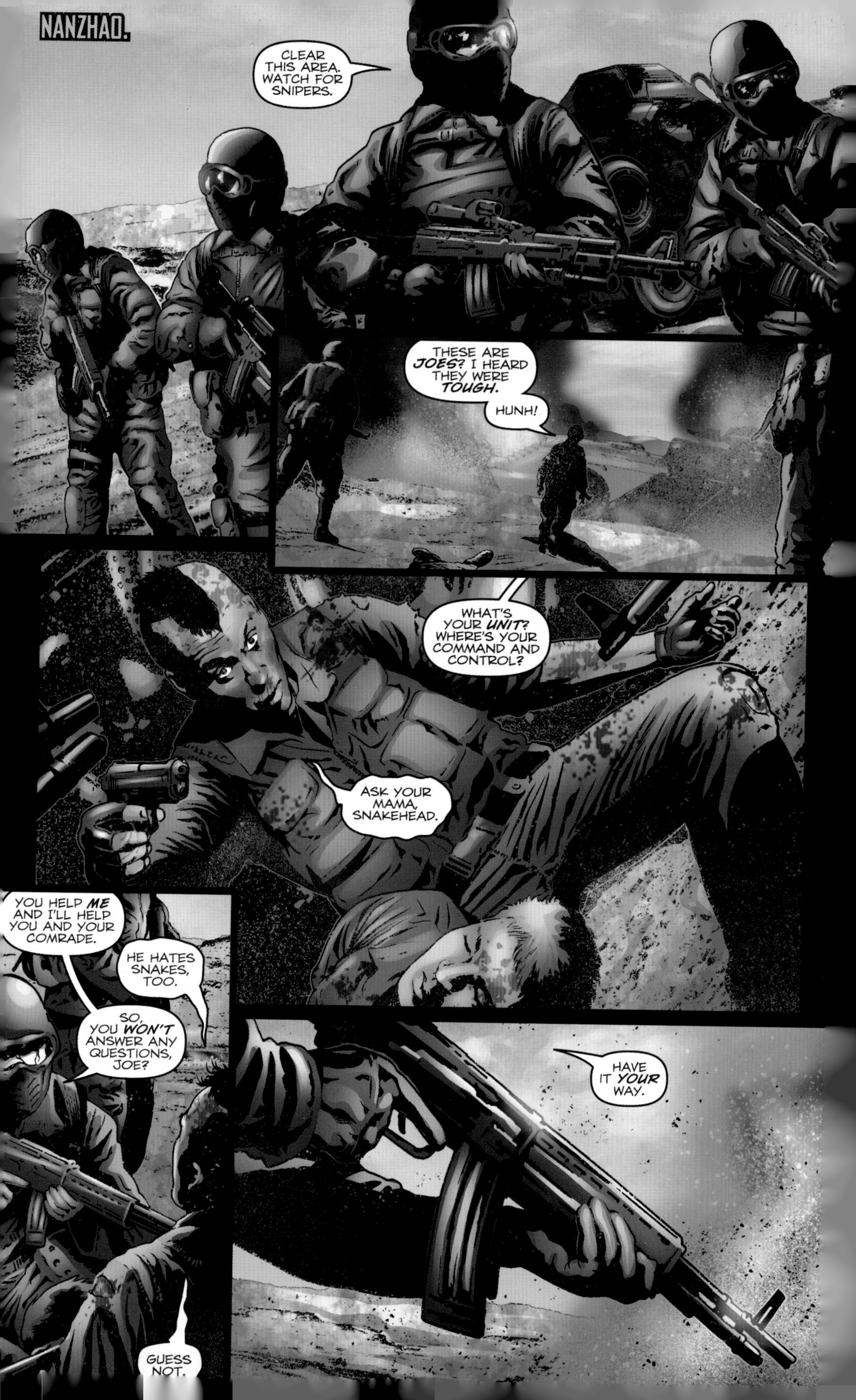
NANZHAO.
CLEAR THIS AREA. WATCH FOR SNIPERS.
THESE ARE JOES? I HEARD THEY WERE TOUGH.
HUNH!
WHAT'S YOUR UNIT? WHERE'S YOUR COMMAND AND CONTROL?
ASK YOUR MAMA, SNAKEHEAD.
YOU HELP ME AND I'LL HELP YOU AND YOUR COMRADE.
HE HATES SNAKES, TOO.
SO, YOU WON'T ANSWER ANY QUESTIONS, JOE?
GUESS NOT.
HAVE IT YOUR WAY.

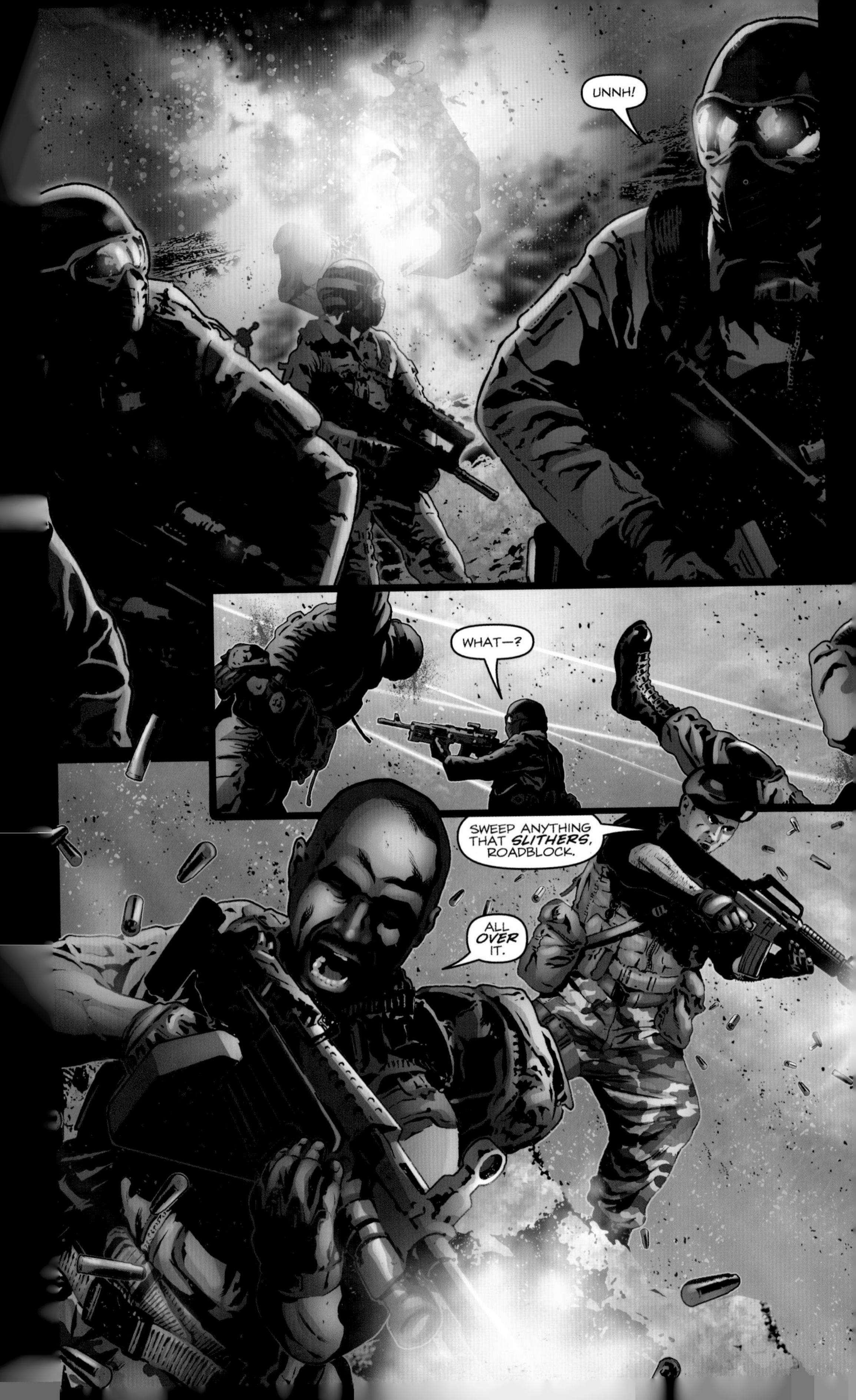
UNNH!
WHAT—?
SWEEP ANYTHING THAT *SLITHERS*, ROADBLOCK.
ALL *OVER* IT.

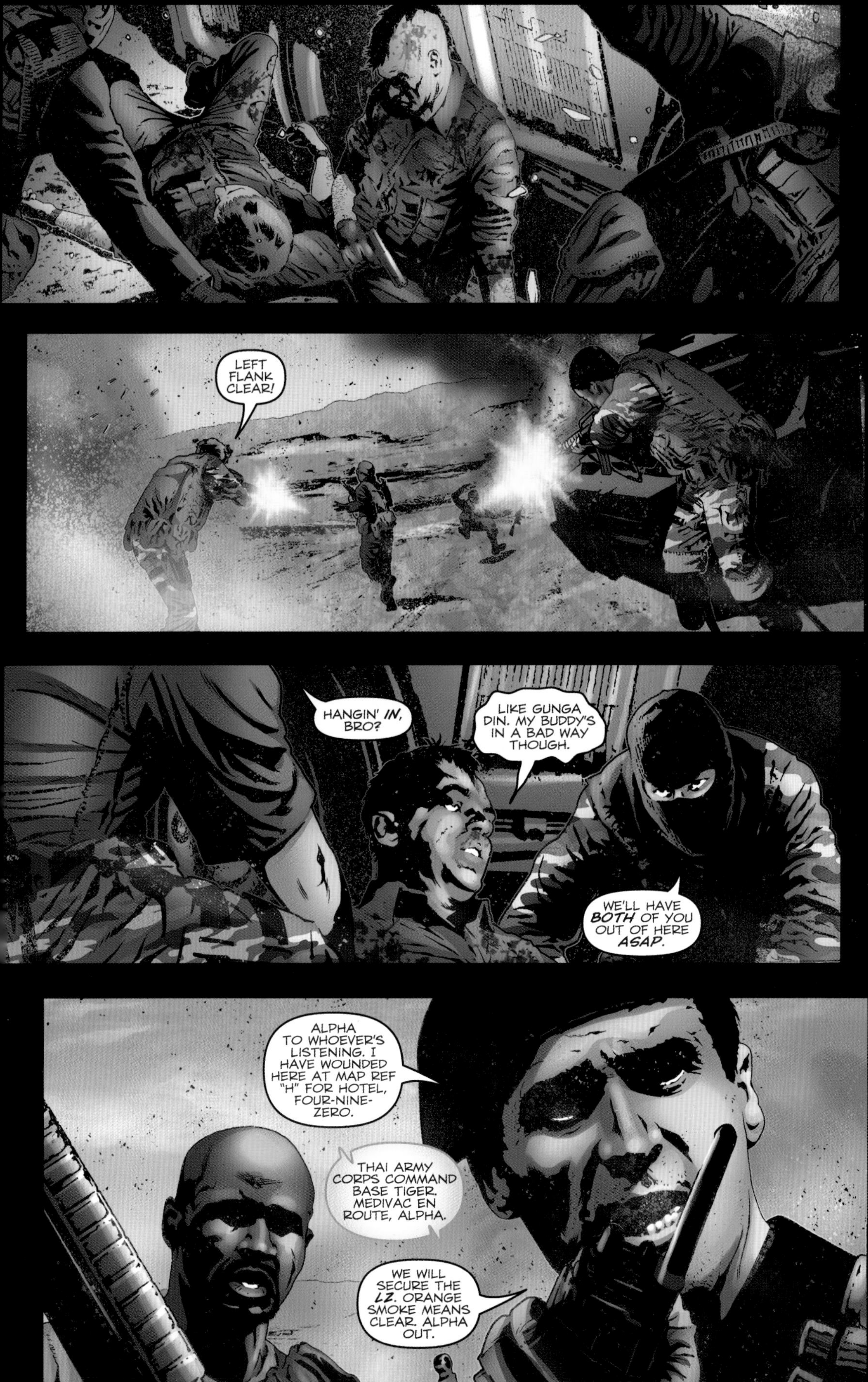
LEFT FLANK CLEAR!
HANGIN' IN, BRO?
LIKE GUNGA DIN. MY BUDDY'S IN A BAD WAY THOUGH.
WE'LL HAVE BOTH OF YOU OUT OF HERE ASAP.
ALPHA TO WHOEVER'S LISTENING. I HAVE WOUNDED HERE AT MAP REF "H" FOR HOTEL, FOUR-NINE-ZERO.
THAI ARMY CORPS COMMAND BASE TIGER. MEDIVAC EN ROUTE, ALPHA.
WE WILL SECURE THE LZ. ORANGE SMOKE MEANS CLEAR. ALPHA OUT.

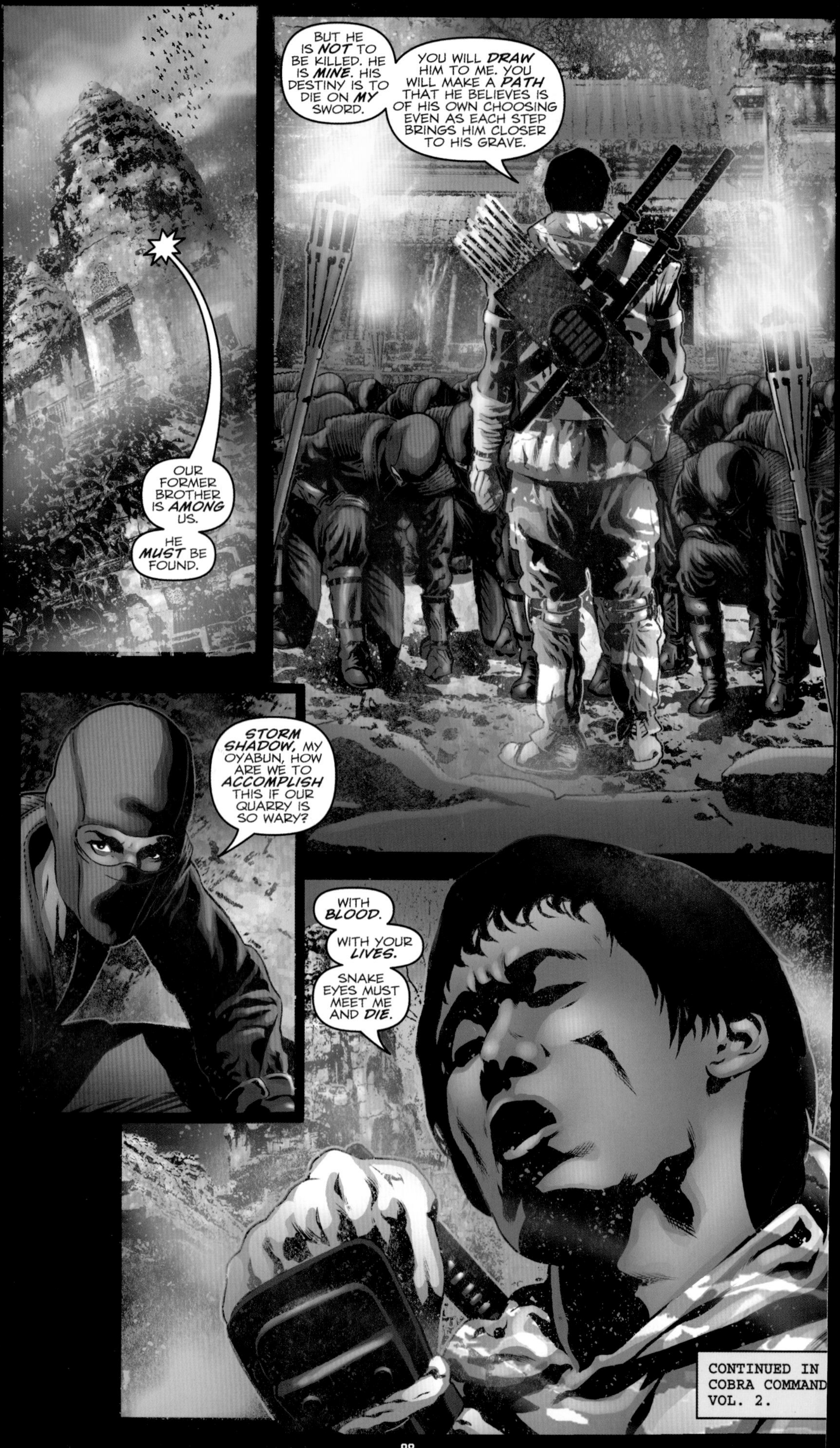
OUR FORMER BROTHER IS AMONG US.
HE MUST BE FOUND.
BUT HE IS NOT TO BE KILLED. HE IS MINE. HIS DESTINY IS TO DIE ON MY SWORD.
YOU WILL DRAW HIM TO ME. YOU WILL MAKE A PATH THAT HE BELIEVES IS OF HIS OWN CHOOSING EVEN AS EACH STEP BRINGS HIM CLOSER TO HIS GRAVE.
STORM SHADOW, MY OYABUN, HOW ARE WE TO ACCOMPLISH THIS IF OUR QUARRY IS SO WARY?
WITH BLOOD.
WITH YOUR LIVES.
SNAKE EYES MUST MEET ME AND DIE.
CONTINUED IN COBRA COMMAND VOL. 2.

COBRA COMMAND

G.I.JOE

Art Gallery

GI JOE #9RI by **Nick Runge**

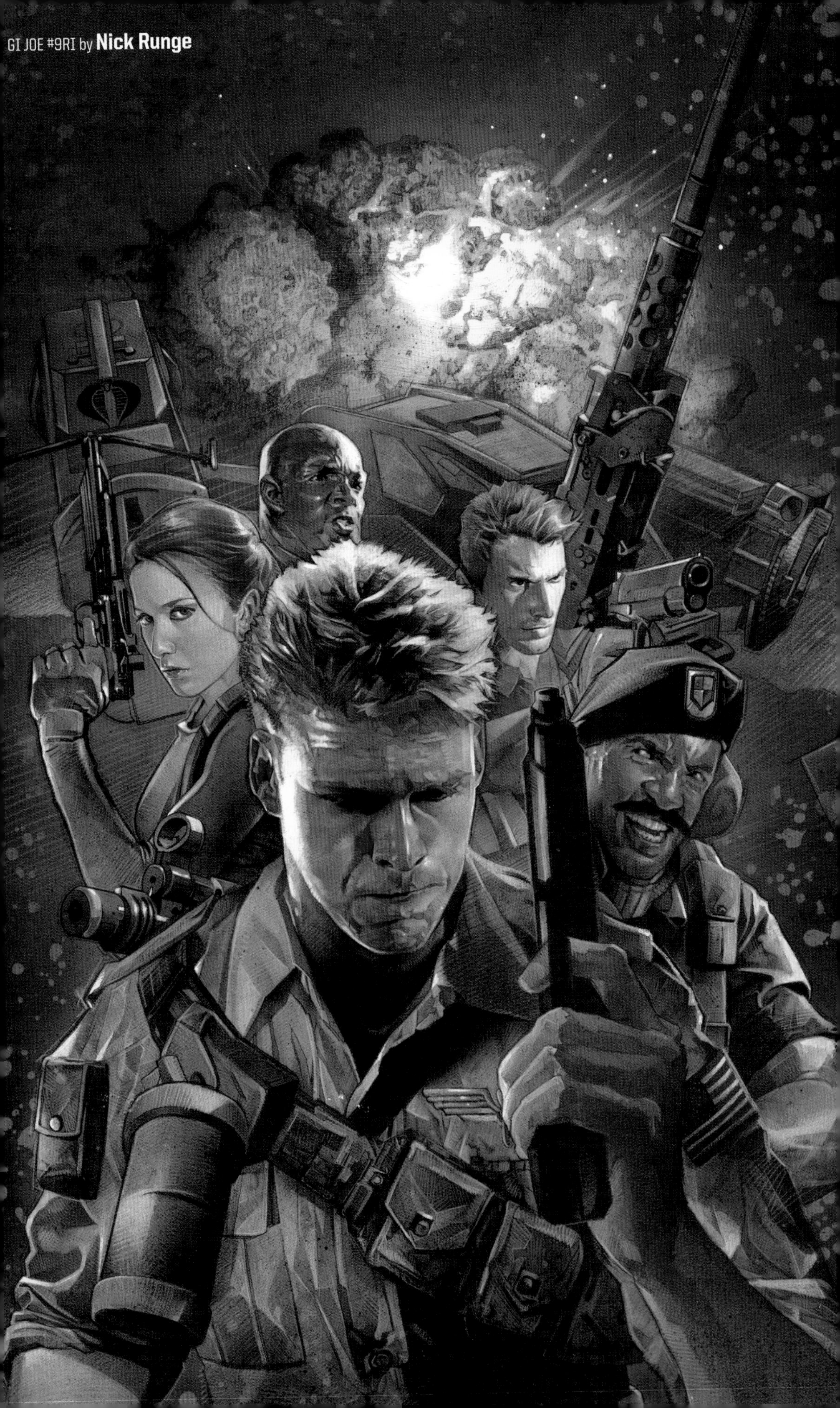

Snake Eyes #9RI by **Nick Runge**

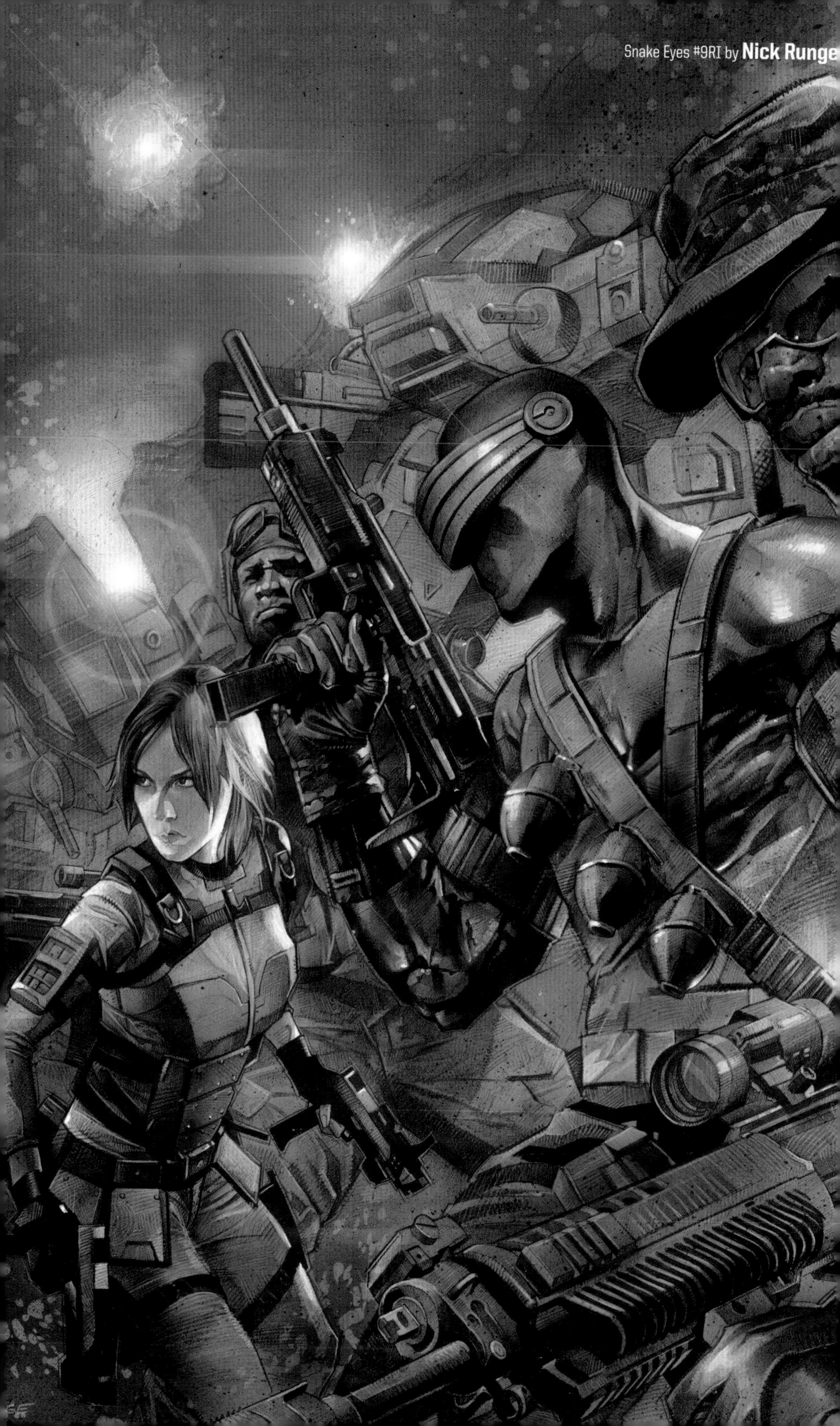

Cobra #9RI by **Nick Runge**

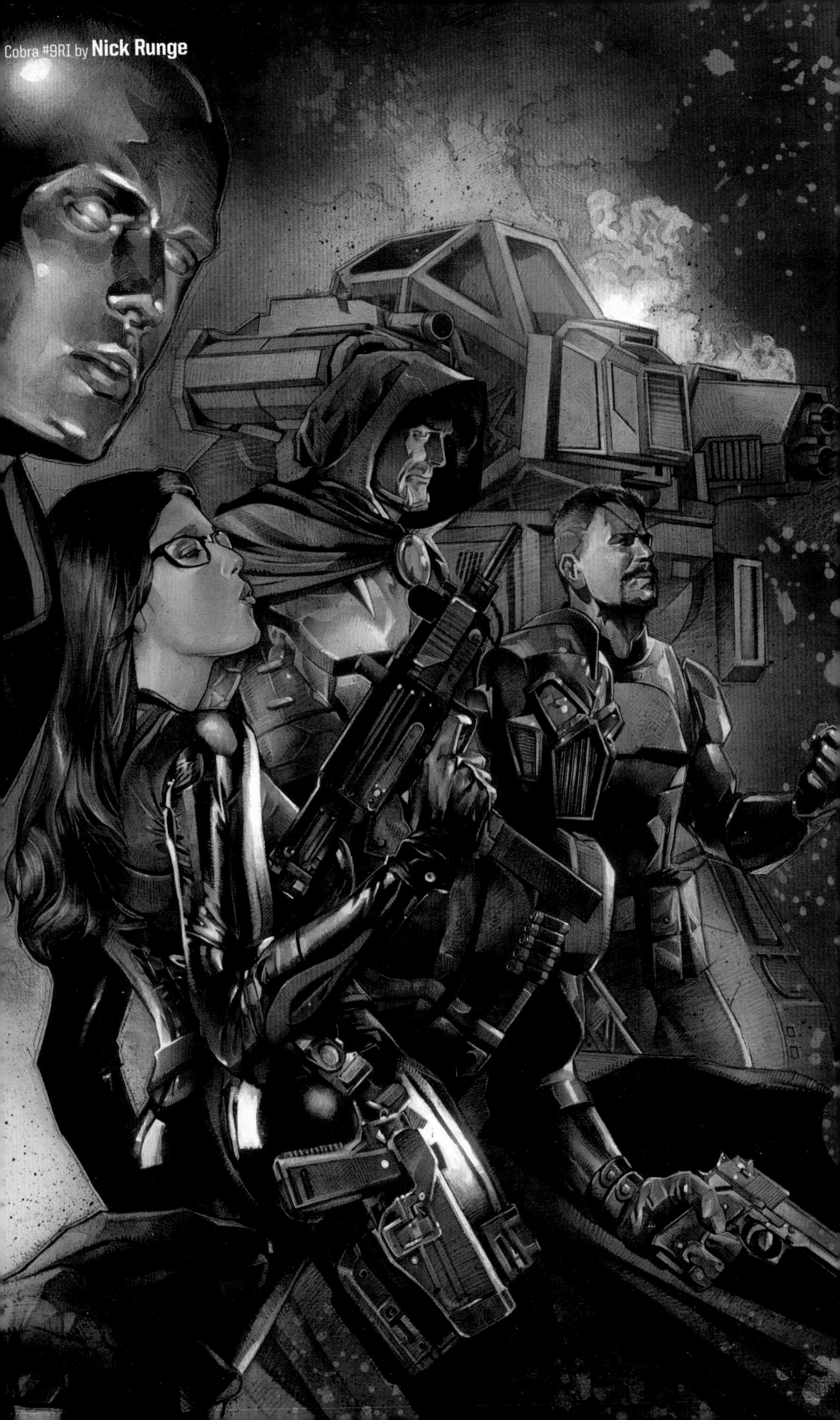